# HR

## The
## New
## Agenda

# Endorsements

This book is a much-needed, cutting-edge, timely and compelling must-read for all current and future HR professionals. It is a comprehensive blueprint and call to action for the Human Resources profession, especially now as we navigate our way through the Covid pandemic, digitisation and new ways of work. It succinctly and convincingly resets the purpose of HR and calls upon HR to step up to the "New Agenda", so that we have HR that is impactful, relevant, responsive and leading business sustainability with a renewed emphasis on humans being at the centre of our organisations. This read is a not-to-be-missed opportunity for every HR professional.

Thanks to the Editor for his extraordinary vision, and the stellar professionals who contributed to this ground-breaking publication on the hottest topics on the New HR Agenda. Thank you for sharing your insights based on deep experience and research, and for helpful guidance and actionable takeaways.

This is a definitive publication that will propel the HR profession forward; it should be compulsory reading for every HR professional and leadership more broadly.

*Dr Shirley Zinn, Chair and Independent Non-Executive Director of Boards*

Paul and his colleagues place humans at the centre and call for a new HR agenda. What I particularly enjoyed was that they are not calling for a complete reinvention; rather they are a reimagining organisations' priorities and adjusting the lens for our future.

The authors, all seasoned HR professionals, consider the ecosystem as opposed to just employees and leaders, as well as the responsibility of business to focus on the greater good. I love the ideas of a fluid talent economy and Black and White fatigue, although we just cannot afford to get tired now. The book closes with outlining the future-fit HR profession. A must read for anyone close to people in the context of work!

*Natasha Winkler-Titus [PhD], Organisational Psychologist (HPCSA) and Past President (SIOPSA), Senior Lecturer/Program Head/Researcher at Stellenbosch University Business School, Founder of SigniFYER*

The pandemic has reaffirmed the centrality of people, especially in our organisations, as the most important asset!

*HR: The New Agenda* stresses the inequality of people in organisations; a company that is inappropriately located can always change its location, but the one that is poor on people, is a dead company.

In *HR: The New Agenda* the authors provide a road map for creating human-centric organisations and therefore ensure the longevity of the organisation.

*Bonang Mohale is the President of Business Unity South Africa (BUSA), Chancellor of the University of the Free State, Professor of Practice in the Johannesburg Business School (JBS) College of Business and Economics, Chairman of both The Bidvest Group Limited and SBV Services. He is the author of the bestselling book, "Lift as You Rise "and "Behold the Turtle"!*

This most timely book offers a comprehensive, challenging and thoughtful travel guide to People Professionals on how to re-imagine and re-invent their future role(s) and contributions in engaging in value-adding ways with the daunting, threatening, but also exciting, new order. Because people will be centre stage in the future success of organisations, communities and society in this new world, People Professionals will have to be at the forefront of the transformation journey into the future. This handy book is a 'must read' for those who want to become 'roadworthy' to undertake this inevitable journey.

*Theo H Veldsman, Work Psychologist, Professor in Work Psychology,*
*Strategic People Effectiveness Consultant*

First published in 2022.

ISBN: 978-1-86922-919-1
eISBN: 978-1-86922-920-7

Published by KR Publishing
Tel: (011) 706-6009
E-mail: orders@knowres.co.za
Website: www.kr.co.za

Printed and bound: HartWood Digital Printing, 243 Alexandra Avenue, Halfway House, Midrand
Typesetting, layout and design: Cia Joubert, cia@knowres.co.za
Cover design: Marlene De Lorme, marlene@knowres.co.za
Editing & proofreading: Jennifer Renton, jenniferrenton@live.co.za
Project management: Cia Joubert, cia@knowres.co.za

# HR

# The
# New
# Agenda

Edited by

## Paul Norman

**kr** publishing

2022

# Acknowledgements

I have spent most of my career at MTN and have been privileged to be part of the growth story of this amazing company. This experience has helped me truly understand the importance of HR, the value it can add to a business, and its critical role in the success of any company. I am grateful to all the MTNers, my Exco colleagues and my HR team for this incredible journey.

To all my fellow authors who made this book possible. Each of you are leaders in your field and are shaping the thinking and practice in your respective areas and companies. I am proud to be associated with all of you and for the privilege you all afforded me of editing this book. Thank you for your confidence in this project. I believe that this book will help raise the bar for HR practice in South Africa.

In November 1997, in a hotel in Cape Town, I first met Dr. Hischam El-Agamy when I attended an IMD conference. Little did I know at the time what an impact he would have on my life. His love and belief in Africa and South Africa are just inspiring. Thank you, Hischam, for kindly agreeing to write the forward for this book.

The team at KR Publishing has been superb in their support, guidance and advice. To Wilhelm Crous and Cia Joubert, a huge thank you for making this book happen.

Finally, to my wife, Tracy. You have shown me what unconditional love is, been my conscience, helped to keep me on my soul's path, and continue to provide me with wise counsel – thank you!

# Table of Contents

# Foreword by Dr Hischam El-Agamy

Covid-19 has disrupted global economies and changed the business landscape, highlighting how poorly prepared businesses and society are to face such an international level of uncertainty.

Recent events have shown that one of the most harmful assumptions organisations make is that the future will be an extension of the past.

Indeed, resulting in the world's crisis, significant shifts in organisation priorities, employee behaviours, and priorities continue to struggle. Organisations will have to adopt new agile cultures to face these challenges, and Human Resources will play a major role in making this happen.

We are seeing changes in business leaders' priorities as they put humanity and the environment at the top of their organisations' priorities. This is the birth of "caring organisations", where organisations put people's safety and well-being at the top of their agenda. This includes adopting sustainable business models to create societal benefit and support the UN's Sustainable Development Goals. As a result, in any organisation, regardless of the sector they operate in, Human Resources activities will significantly transform.

Human Resources are now facing new tasks to support employees' mental health, including building a new structure to allow employees to work remotely or hybrid, and ensuring continuous communications channels to keep employees engaged. These are radical changes that organisations have never faced simultaneously.

The new priorities of Human Resources to support the 'caring organisation' is long and challenging, particularly as employees are demanding a new definition of work-life balance. 'Work-life balance', an expression we have used to explain how to blend work and personal lives successfully, is now being replaced by much more comprehensive definitions of well-being.

The new work environment, remote and/or blended, has introduced new challenges when it comes to strengthening relationships. This environment will require promoting social interactions and installing multiple communications channels. This will be empowered by open dialogue cultures to ensure that all employees are kept informed and engaged. In addition, the Caring Human Resources will extend their role to help workers successfully manage their anxiety levels.

While the relationship between HR and employees is expanding, HR's support of business leaders is also changing.

The Caring Organisation will adopt an agility culture that will deal with ambiguity better and respond quickly to emerging opportunities. It will put humans at the centre of their strategies and help use and amplify the power and impact of rapidly emerging technologies. It will also enable the development of leaders who can detect employees' emotions to develop communication channels that will stimulate collaboration and alignment to achieve the overall organisation's goal.

HR will have a critical role to play in promoting these new cultures and supporting business leaders in their new approach to business and society. The human resources of the Caring Organisation will promote a culture among employees that stimulates their ability to birth new ideas and convert them to add value to employees, business and society. This will involve employees designing their desired future.

HR has been transformed to focus on supporting the new roles of leaders in organisations and defining the new relationships established over the last two years between employees and their organisations.

We are expecting that the "Next to Normal" landscape will be shaped by various trends such as the changing role of the workplace, digital transformation, and new definitions of well-being. It will also bring new topics to the management and board plan, such as inclusion and diversity, climate change, and dealing with uncertainty in the strategy room.

The new Human Resources will have to expand their file of actions, policies and strategies to deal with these changes and support the "Caring organisation".

**Dr Hischam El-Agamy**

*Dr El-Agamy* is charged by IMD Business School for their activities in Africa, Middle East Africa and South & Central Asia. On behalf of IMD he has worked with various companies to help them to align learning to their business strategies. His expertise and teaching experience includes scenario planning, entrepreneurship, family business transformation, private public partnership, and stakeholder engagement.

Hischam has contributed to several advisory assignments for a number of governments in the Gulf region and the government of South Africa in the area of competitiveness and human capital development. He was part of the South African Presidential Council for South Africa competitiveness, working closely with the President Marketing Council, between 2004 and 2009. He also co-directed the IMD MBA programmes in South Africa from 2009 to 2013, working with more than 140 companies to help them on their transformation journey. He is currently teaching on several programmes in IMD for the Abu Dhabi School of Government, Dubai Competitiveness, Absa bank in South Africa, and other companies in Middle East and Africa.

Hischam is the co-founder of Tharawat Family Business Forum, the leading network for family businesses in the MENA region. With his family he built Orbis Terra Media, a global content studio based in Switzerland, which also publishes Tharawat Magazine, an award-winning publication for family businesses and entrepreneurs worldwide.

# About the Editor

## Paul Norman

*Paul Norman* serves as Group Chief Human Resources Officer at MTN Group. He is an experienced Group Executive of Human Resources with a demonstrated history of working in the telecommunications industry at a global level. Paul has been recognised for his HR contribution by the Institute of People Management as HR Practitioner of the year (2003), by the South African Board for People Practices (SABPP) with the Life Time Achievement Award (2012), and CHRO of the year 2019 by CHRO South Africa. He is an experienced Board member, serving on several MTN subsidiary country Boards. He is past Board Member of Advisory Boards of Industrial Psychology at the University of Johannesburg, the Graduate School of Business (GBS) Cape Town and Chartered Medical Aid Fund (CAMAF). Paul holds an M.A. degree from Rhodes University, South Africa and an executive MBA from IMD in Switzerland. Contact information: paul.norman@mtn.com

# About the Contributors

## Prof Kurt April

*Prof. Kurt April* is currently the Allan Gray Chair, an Endowed Professorship, specialising in Leadership, Diversity & Inclusion and the Director of the Allan Gray Centre for Values-Based Leadership at the Graduate School of Business (University of Cape Town), Faculty Member of Duke Corporate Education (Duke University, USA) and Adjunct Faculty of Saïd Business School (University of Oxford, UK). Previously, he was a Research Fellow of Hult-Ashridge Business School (UK), Visiting Professor at London Metropolitan University (UK), Visiting Professor at Rotterdam School of Management (Erasmus University, Netherlands), and Visiting Professor in the Faculty of Economics & Econometrics (University of Amsterdam UvA, Netherlands). Outside of academia, Kurt is the Managing Partner of LICM Consulting (South Africa), Managing Director: Leadership, Diversity & Inclusion Practice at Oxford Acuity (Singapore), Director of Achievement Awards Group (South Africa), and Shareholder of bountiXP (Pty) Ltd (South Africa), as well as an Ambassador of the global movement Unashamedly Ethical. Contact information: kurt.april@gmail.com

## Vanisha Balgobind

*Vanisha Balgobind* is currently the executive Head of Human Resources at Exxaro Resources.

She is a registered Industrial Psychologist with 24 years' experience in the mining industry. Her current role is shaped very much around business strategy and the alignment of the human capital value chain. Her focus is on business transformation, diversity and inclusion and disruption in the world of work, through redesigning organisational principles, employment and reward models, rethinking the workforce of the future and crafting an employee value proposition that is employee centric.

She serves and has served on various forums as a trustee, including the Exxaro Pension Fund, Exxaro Foundation and Chairman's Fund, mainly focusing on social and labour plan projects across the organisation. She is also the Chairperson of Exxaro People Development, which focuses on education programmes and partnerships in the various communities across Exxaro. She is a member of the Ethics Committee and Chairperson of the Exxaro Women in Mining (WIM) Forum, which enables the women across the organisation to have a voice, lead women initiatives, and empower women to enhance their careers within the mining industry. She also leads the Women agenda on behalf of Exxaro through the Minerals Council of SA. She is a prescribed officer of the executive committee and a standing invitee to both the Remuneration and Nomination Committee of the Board (Remco/Nomco), as well as the Social and

Ethics Committee of the Board. She also serves as a member of the Remco of the FSCA in an independent capacity.

Vanisha has completed an MA (Industrial Psychology), Management Development Programme (GIBS) and a Masters in Business Leadership (MBL) from Unisa's School of Business Leadership. Contact information: Vanisha.Balgobind@exxaro.com

## Johan Botes

*Johan Botes* is a practicing attorney and head of the Employment & Compensation practice group in Johannesburg of the global law firm, Baker McKenzie. His team won the Employment Law Team of the Year award at the African Legal Awards in 2019. He holds the degrees of LLB and LLM (Labour Law) and is an accredited change management practitioner. Johan is listed as: an Acritas Star in the Acritas Star Report 2018, 2019, 2020, 2021; a leading lawyer for Labour and Employment Law in Best Lawyers in South Africa 2017, 2018, 2019, 2020; a Lexology Legal Influencer for Employment Law (Africa and Middle East), 2020, 2021; a nominee for Client Choice Award in 2017, 2021; and an "exceptional labour lawyer", according to interviewees in Chambers and Partners, 2020. Johan is a prolific writer who regularly publishes articles and appears in the press commenting on all matters employment law and employee relations. He contributed a minor segment to *When Crisis Strikes* by Francis Herd and Nicola Kleyn (Pan MacMillan, 2020). He is a keen baker and loves weissbier, making it fortuitous that he is also an avid runner and member of Pirates Running Club. He is married to an imminently patient and long-suffering wife, Joandra, and proud father of two daughters, Basia and Luca. Contact information: johan.botes@ bakermckenzie.com

## Dr Mark Bussin

*Mark Bussin* is the Chairperson of 21st Century, a specialist reward and remuneration consultancy. He has HR, reward and remuneration experience across all industry sectors, and is viewed as a thought leader in the HR, reward and remuneration arena. He serves on and advises numerous Boards and Remuneration Committees on Executive Remuneration. Mark holds a Doctorate in Commerce. He has published or presented over 350 articles and papers, and has received awards for his outstanding articles in this field. He has appeared on television and radio, and in the press, giving his expert views on remuneration. Mark is a guest lecturer at several universities and supervises Masters' and Doctoral theses in the Reward area. He is a past President of SARA (South African Reward Association) and a past Commissioner for the remuneration of Public Office-Bearers in the Presidency. Mark tutors reward and finance modules for WorldatWork globally. Contact information: drbussin@mweb.co.za

## Daniela Christos

*Daniela Christos* is a Human Resource (HR) practitioner with over six years of experience in various HR-related domains. She has authored over 50 HR-related textbook chapters, academic, and non-academic articles. Daniela has obtained several degrees, including a General B.A. with English and Psychology majors, a BCom Honours in Industrial and Organisational Psychology (IOP), an MCom in IOP (which she obtained cum laude) and she is currently completing her PhD in IOP with her research focusing on developing a career expatriate performance framework given expatriates' career stage, psychosocial career preoccupations and career commitment. At present, she is working towards becoming a specialised Industrial and Organisational Psychologist. Contact information: danichristos@gmail.com

## Wilhelm Crous

*Wilhelm Crous* has a passion for business knowledge. This passion is realised through Knowledge Resources (which he established in 1991) by publishing business and management books; developing and presenting world-class conferences and training; conducting surveys in the HR/Talent Management field.

Previously, Wilhelm served as the Executive Director of the Institute of Personnel Management (IPM), and is also one of the co-founders of the South African Board for People Practices (SABPP) where he served on the first Board. Throughout his career he has served on various commissions, advisory boards and working groups, all related to professional human resources management specifically, and labour and human capital on a macro-national level. Wilhelm has also been a guest lecturer at various universities and business schools in the areas listed above, and has received numerous special awards, including the Lifetime Achievement Award from the SABPP for his outstanding contribution to the human resources management profession, and the Chancellor's Medal from the University of Pretoria for contributions made to human resources management. In 2017, he received a Lifetime Achievement Award from the University of Johannesburg for his contribution to Entrepreneurship in South Africa. Contact information: wilhelm@knowres.co.za

## Gideon du Plessis

*Gideon du Plessis* is the General Secretary of the trade union Solidarity and the head of the Solidarity Strategy Institute, specialising in strategic labour relations. In 2019 he obtained a Master of Arts degree in Labour Policy and Globalisation from the University of the Witwatersrand. He acts as media spokesperson for Solidarity and regularly participates in radio and television debates on matters relating to labour relations and other topical issues. He frequently writes opinion pieces for newspapers, business magazines and various other media platforms, and he has a labour column in the Sunday paper *Rapport*. He is also a regular participant as a panellist or speaker at conferences and seminars, and participates in submissions to parliamentary portfolio committees. He is a trustee of the Gold Fields Thusano Trust (ESOP) and a board member of the Sentinel Retirement Fund and the State Diamond Trader. He is registered as a Master HR Professional with the SA Board for People Practices (SABPP). Contact information: gideon@solidarity.co.za

## Shelagh Goodwin

*Shelagh Goodwin* is the head of human resources at Media24, South Africa's leading media business and part of the Naspers group. She has worked in the Naspers group in HR, training and organisational development for over 25 years. She was a finalist in the Chief Human Resources Officer of the Year awards in 2019. She holds a Master's degree from Unisa in Organisational Psychology and is a registered Organisational Psychologist. She is currently enrolled at UCT (University of Cape Town) as a doctoral candidate in Organisational Psychology. Her topic deals with the role of psychological safety in the resilience of diverse teams. She has supervised numerous industrial and organisational interns in order to allow them to meet the HPCSA's (Health Professions Council of South Africa) requirements for professional registration. She is also a regular guest lecturer to Master's students at UCT. Contact information: sgoodwin@media24.com

## Selo Govender

*Selo Govender* is the Group Head of Talent and Performance at Discovery Limited. She is a global Human Capital Leader and HR Professional with more than 20 years' experience in different roles within the Education, Business and Corporate HR environments, not including leading the portfolios of Talent and Performance Engagement, Talent Acquisition, Talent Brand, Graduate Development, Learning and Leadership Development, amongst other roles over her career span. She holds a Masters in Business Administration and B. Paed degree. Selo is living her passion and personal purpose of making a difference in others' lives through doing inspirational work in people development. Contact information: SeloG@discovery.co.za

## Akona Makoboka

*Akona Makoboka* is currently the Employee Relations Lead for Accenture, a global professional services company with leading capabilities in digital, cloud and security in over 40 industries. She has Employee Relations and Transformation experience across several industries and geographies, and is viewed as a knowledgeable professional in her field. She has vast experience in addressing audiences on Employee Relations matters at a variety of conferences and seminars across the country and sharing thought leadership in this regard. Akona is a member of SABPP, an internationally certified mediator of commercial and civil disputes, and is currently in the process of obtaining her international MBA in Legal Leadership. Contact information: akona.makoboka@gmail.com

## Andrew Millson

*Andrew Millson* is the Group Executive for Human Capital and Sustainability at Food Lover's Market which he joined six years ago, setting up their sustainability strategy, Earth Lovers, before taking on his current role. He has been in various senior management roles in the corporate, not-for-profit and social enterprise sectors, in the UK, Africa and Europe. During this time Andrew has worked with leaders, individually and collectively, across all sectors to drive sustainability and build leadership cultures that can proactively tackle the major global issues facing humanity.

Andrew has given numerous talks and workshops in several countries on the themes of sustainability, authentic leadership, purpose, values and culture. He has a Bcom Law degree from Nelson Mandela Metropolitan University.

In his current role, Andrew lives out his passion for people and the natural environment. This passion stems from a deep-rooted desire to see all of humanity reach the collective potential in building a more equitable, healthier and greener world for future generations. His approach to this is to facilitate an environment which enables colleagues to express their true selves, to dream their potential and to find congruency between their personal values and their work lives.

Andrew Millson is a father, husband and adventurer. Contact information: amillson@fvc.co.za

## Penny Milner-Smyth

*Penny Milner-Smyth* is Director of Ethical Ways, a niche consultancy focused on the promotion of workplace ethics and integrity. Penny weaves together three strands of her career in her delivery of evidence-based insights with proven practical application. These include an MA (Research Psychology), 30 years' experience as an in-house human resource management leader, and an increasingly prominent role in the global ethics and compliance profession. Registered as a Master Human Resource Practitioner, Penny received an SABPP award for her outstanding contribution to the HR profession in 2021. Today she is an ethics and anti-corruption trends analyst, a speaker, writer and ethics content developer, whose contributions attract a strong following. Her insights from the intersection of employee engagement and workplace ethics have been the subject of numerous interviews, including on the prestigious Great Women in Compliance podcast. She is the author of the Specialist Certificate

Programme in Anti-Corruption offered worldwide by the International Compliance Association. Contact information: penny@ethicalways.co.za

## Jasmin Pillay

*Jasmin Pillay* is the Director, HR Consulting for Microsoft Middle East and Africa, where she leads transformation, scale, empowerment and capability building, as well as people strategy and planning. She holds Industrial Psychology and Business Management qualifications and is currently working on her MBA. Jasmin's broad portfolio over the years has provided direct experience across a variety of international destinations and multi-nationals, including experience with people management and matrixed business environments. Her passion is in creating opportunities for access to learning and empowerment, and she considers herself fortunate to have been a leading member of a skills development initiative in Sudan which included women in a manufacturing environment. Among her professional achievements, Jasmin was identified as a Global Influencer for the PETRONAS Downstream business for Organisational Design and Effectiveness in Performance and Culture Transformation, and been awarded Top Employer for two consecutive years during her tenure at Microsoft South Africa. Contact information: Jasmin.Pillay@microsoft.com

## Dr Thuli Tabudi

*Thuli Tabudi* is the Group Human Resources Executive for the SPAR Group Ltd and is a member of the Executive Committee. She completed a Secretarial Diploma and whilst working as a secretary, enrolled with UNISA and completed BAdmin and BAdmin (Hons) degrees. She completed her Masters and PhD degrees at the University of Johannesburg. She worked for various blue chip organisations before joining the SPAR Group in 1999. She held the positions of HR Manager and Divisional HR Director before being promoted to her current position. She has extensive experience in the Human Resources field in areas such as Organisational Development, Training and Development, Strategy, Employee Benefits and Employee Relations. She served the Commission for Conciliation, Mediation and Arbitration (CCMA) Board representing organised business, and is a qualified Integral Coach. She currently serves as a Trustee on the Durban University of Technology Foundation and the FutureMe Foundation. Contact information: Thuli.Tabudi@spar.co.za

## Ninette van Aarde

*Ninette van Aarde* holds a Master's degree and is an Industrial Psychologist registered with the HPCSA. She specialises in Organisational Design with strong foundational experience as a Human Capital Business Partner. She currently leads the Organisational Design and Performance Excellence practices for Momentum

Metropolitan, a multi-national financial services provider with a footprint in Africa, the United Kingdom and India. She has contributed to four articles and book chapters. Contact information: Ninette.vanaarde@gmail.com

## Dr Dieter Veldsman

*Dieter Veldsman*, who holds a doctoral degree in Industrial-Organisational Psychology, has more than 12 years' experience in organisational development design, HR development and strategic human capital management. His experience spans multiple geographies, with completed assignments in Europe, Asia and Africa, and currently holds the position of HR Thought Leader at the Academy to Innovate HR.

A regular speaker at international conferences and a participant in human capital (HC) podcasts, Dieter has shared his thoughts on employee engagement, organisational development, the future of work, and human capital management at more than 40 conferences. He has contributed to 16 peer-reviewed articles and book chapters, and was recently nominated the Chief Human Resource Officer (CHRO) of the year by the CHRO Association of South Africa in 2021. This complements the SIOPSA award which he received in 2018 as IOP Practitioner of the Year. Contact information: dieterv23@gmail.com

## Prof Edward Webster

*Edward Webster* is the Distinguished Research Professor at the Southern Centre of Inequality Studies and the founder and past director of the Society, Work and Development Institute (SWOP) at the University of the Witwatersrand. His current research interests are the production and reproduction of inequality in the workplace and the use of labour power as a strategy for reducing this inequality. Contact information: eddiewebster99@gmail.com

# Introduction

Since the Second World War, the Human Resource Discipline and Profession has faced many challenges and undergone various stages of development. At the same time, the credibility and status of the HR function had its ups and downs. Today, most organisations acknowledge their Human Resources as their biggest asset, or, at least, it is mentioned as such in their annual reports. In many companies the CHRO serves on the Board, providing input and guidance on people strategy as well as other governance issues.

The impact of Covid-19, the 4th Industrial Revolution, challenges around Diversity and Inclusion, and the socio-economic/poverty/inequality realities on the People Management function calls for a total re-think, re-invent and re-work of HR practices. The Human is now at the centre. It is now time for a New HR Agenda!

## About The Book

The contributors in this book address the most pertinent aspects of the New HR Agenda. New pathways are suggested and case studies where new thinking and ideas have successfully been implemented are also shared. At the same time, new questions are raised and it is clear that the road ahead will be uncertain and challenging, whilst at the same time exciting. The opportunities are legion, however the opportunity to make a lasting positive impact on the people they are stewards of should not be wasted.

You can start reading the book at any chapter, however it is suggested that the first two chapters are read first. These set the scene and provide the background and context for the remainder of the book.

**Chapter 1** describes the impact of the pandemic on organisations and HR in particular. It postulates what the "New Normal" could look like. Eight new HR priorities are analysed. The chapter also highlights that because HR matters, there is a greater expectation from business. That means that HR professionals need to continuously upgrade their skills and capabilities so that they are not found wanting in fulfilling their own mandate.

**Chapter 2** analyses the new world of work, with specific emphasis on the digitisation of everything, the hybrid workplace, automation, robotics and the 4th Industrial Revolution, the gig economy and Generation Z. The HR fraternity needs to grasp that the new World of Work is already here. Against that, HR will have to create an ecosystem where such a world can thrive.

In **Chapter 3**, Andrew Millson describes the importance and power of an organisational purpose. It all starts with: What is the essence of business in a capitalist society? Andrew discusses Food Lovers Market's journey, starting with the book *Conscious Capitalism*, questioning what the business stands for and its impact on people and society, to bring about a more purpose-led organisation.

In **Chapter 4**, Selo Govender proposes a Radical New Talent Management Strategy for a Radical New Workplace. Organisations are now facing a new fluid talent economy, which poses the following two questions:

- What does this do for our traditional recruitment practices for traditional jobs?

- What happens to traditional talent and succession management?

In answering these questions, Selo points out that it means being open to new ways of thinking and working, whether it be deconstruction of work and doing away with traditional jobs and organisation design, or welcoming helpful technologies like the talent market place and continuous performance listening solutions.

The New World of Work calls for accelerating upskilling and reskilling, which is what Vanisha Balgobind covers in **Chapter 5**. She also highlights the importance of creating a culture of lifelong learning and self-learning. The important of leadership in this regard is also discussed. Lastly, Vanisha describes how Exxaro is taking its people into the future. This comprehensive case study will provide organisations with an ideal benchmark to measure themselves against.

The New Ways of Work also call for reinventing remuneration and benefits. In **Chapter 6**, Dr Mark Bussin and Daniela Christos stress that there will be a greater emphasis on: Increasing mandates of remuneration committees; reducing the wage gaps; addressing gender/race/ethnicity diversity and inclusion; the inclusion of ESG measures in STIs and LTIs; evolving performance management for a less contingent and greater virtual workforce; as well as employee wellness and engagement.

**Chapter 7** represents multiple viewpoints on whether it is time for a new HR/ER dispensation in the New World of Work. In the first part (7.1), Prof Edward Webster highlights the plight of the informal sector. This sector has been particularly hard hit by the fall-out of Covid-19. It is also the least organised employment sector. He proposes a number of new opportunities for workers to organise themselves in the informal economy.

In the second perspective (7.2), Gideon du Plessis unpacks the impact of Covid-19 on collective Industrial Relations. He also proposes an Alternative Transition towards a New Bargaining Model which should be considered with the following in mind centralised collective bargaining being under pressure; a movement towards plurism; impact of job security and loss of income of strike action. Gideon also discusses the challenge of organising workers in the digital economy.

In the third part of this chapter 7.3 Johan Botes asks this very relevant question: With the incredibly high degree of personalisation in their regular lives, why would employees then be satisfied with the fruits of a union official, who they are unlikely to see again for a year, and who negotiated a two- or three-page wage agreement wherein everyone is treated exactly the same? He goes on to discuss the implications of that question.

In the fourth section (7.4), Akona Makoboka concludes that companies have always looked to the LRA and BCEA for guidance to determine what rights and benefits employees are legally entitled to. In the current space where South African legislation caught up with developments, companies may need to look across the shores for guidance where jurisprudence has already started to form, and to apply their minds to what is best suited for a business and its employees. The legislation will likely continue to dictate minimum standards, but there is nothing precluding any company from charting its own trajectory and going over and above in a legally compliant, creative manner, in a bid to ensure business success. What is clear is that the general ways of old in employee relations have little to no place in the future of work.

In **Chapter 8**, Prof Kurt April analyses the new diversity equity and inclusion realities and challenges. He also discusses the business case thereof and focusses on Black and White Fatigue and the critical aspect of inclusive leadership. He also proposes a 7-step framework for making progress with regard to diversity, equity and inclusion.

In **Chapter 9**, Thuli Tabudi discusses how social capital can be increased through employee engagement and belonging. She then describes the Spar Group Ltd's journey. The key parts of this are: Organisational Culture, Leadership, Company Values, Staff Empowerment, Communication, Creating Growth Opportunities, Employee Recognition and Fun at Work.

Dr Dieter Veldsman and Ninette van Aarde focus on employee health and well-being in **Chapter 10**. The impact of Covid-19 on on both has been severe, with mental health in the workplace deteriorating substantially. The authors discuss the importance of adapting a holistic approach towards human well-being in describing the Momentum Metropolitan Case. It all starts with "Thinking human first".

In **Chapter 11**, Penny Milner-Smythe focusses on the challenge of HR in terms of governance and ethics for the 2020s and beyond. In the process she explains:

- the global trends shaping the organisational governance agenda;

- the expanded scope of organisational governance in the 2020s;

- new sources of insight for the HR role; and

- the implications for future HR practices and programmes.

For organisations to grow and flourish in the New World of Work they have to become more agile and innovative. That is the Ultimate Organisational Coping Mechanism.

In **Chapter 12**, Shelagh Goodwin describes how Media24 transformed itself from a traditional media company to a digital ready-for-the-future company. She provides a practical framework for team learning, agility and innovation.

A key capability that organisations will need in order to navigate this new world and to stay innovative and grow will be a growth mindset. In **Chapter 13** Jasmin Pillay discusses the Microsoft story in terms of changing the corporate culture to that of a growth mindset. The first port of call was to focus on diversity and inclusion. She also highlights how modern HR can encourage a growth mindset in this new world of work.

For HR to be able to successfully respond to the new HR agenda, it will require continuous upskilling and reskilling. In **Chapter 14**, Wilhelm Crous discusses the challenges for the HR professional, the HR jobs of the future, HR capabilities for a future-fit HR practitioner as well as education and research for the new HR agenda. The point is, as much as HR focuses on getting workforces ready for the new opportunities now and in the future, HR in itself will need to consistently and very intentionally work on upskilling and reskilling its own staff in the HR department.

# Chapter 1

# HR at the Centre

## Paul Norman

We live in a new world. What use to be called "normal", is gone forever. We have been catapulted into a world characterised by chaos, fear, increased discrimination, heightened economic disparity, growing nationalism, and much more. The onset of Covid-19 – the pandemic that hit the world at the end of 2019 and spread globally in 2020 – occasioned this dramatic shift. The world has changed irrevocably, and a new way of life in almost every aspect has been ushered in.

What's more, this change has been accompanied by continuous technological convergence and digital disruption. Yet it is not all doom and gloom. New forms of technology and the impact of the Fourth Industrial Revolution have created opportunities for new players and new skills to emerge.

These forces have changed the very nature of work. How and where work gets done has changed. A premium is being placed on thinking creatively to stimulate innovation, on getting work done faster through agile methods, and on teams and working collaboratively in partnership models for mutual benefit. In this world, the team is the true unit of performance, rather than the individual.

These forces have brought *being human* back to the centre, so to speak. Despite the digitisation of much of the predictive processes and the concomitant automisation of many jobs, it has become clear that specifically human capabilities such as critical thinking, creativity and empathy, to name a few, cannot be outsourced to machines. These capabilities are central to thriving in the new world.

In this context, Human Resources is challenged by a new mandate that puts it centre stage. If businesses want to succeed in the new world, they must have top notch human-centred systems to tap into the true potential of their employees.

To get to grips with the tasks arising from this new HR mandate, we need to understand how forces such as the pandemic and technological disruption are necessitating that companies change how they think, feel about and treat their real source of value – people – and, by extension, how this requires HR to review its priorities and place renewed emphasis on *being human* and on building effective human systems and organisations.

# The Pandemic

The Covid-19 pandemic has dramatically changed how we live. This is not the first pandemic in history; humans have lived through several pandemics before, some of them more severe and virulent such as the Black Death of 1346-1353 (up to 200 million deaths) and the Spanish Flu of 1918-1920 (50 million deaths).

What is different with this, the first pandemic in a time of global connectedness, is that we all seem to be experiencing and coming to terms with the impact of the pandemic simultaneously, while highlighting inequalities across the world and in and between societies, exacerbating divides between "haves and have nots", and in many respects laying bare what had become normal and acceptable in our society. Covid-19 has exposed poor functioning governments; systems that do not serve all people; unequal access to services, information, health care, etc.; and an incapacity or unwillingness to respond to environmental challenges.

The crisis also, however, instilled in us a sense of expectation that the world can change, that things do not have to stay as they are, and that change is necessary if we are to survive as the human species.

Today we are globally and digitally connected, and as much as it holds peril, it also holds promise. What happens in one part of the world is instantaneously visible in other parts of the world. Movements at opposite ends of the political and social spectrum, such as Black Lives Matter, #metoo, vaccine nationalism and the emergence of extremist groups highlight the distances and the deep inequalities between us, and because they are globally visible, they no longer go unchallenged.

In pockets around the world, there seems to be a growing awareness of the world we have created, and a desire to create a better world for all as we emerge from the pandemic.

The pandemic has turned our attention to *being human*, and how we are human together in a sea of death, tragedy, loss and pain. I believe that because *being human* is becoming more valuable to us again, there is a determination to emerge from this pandemic being better at being human, leading possibly to a 'New Normal' where human beings are again at the centre.

Herein lies the opportunity for HR to lead.

# The New Normal

What could this New Normal be?

The pandemic has pushed many companies to experiment with various ways to get work done under unusual circumstances. This has resulted in the development of new systems and processes that will be the foundation for people practices in a New Normal. We witnessed, for instance, the accelerated development and adoption of remote work and digital enablers and solutions. Our adoption of remote practices is growing every day. This will evolve into a hybrid remote work model, which should support human interactions and foster a New Normal of innovation and culture.

As we live through the pandemic, and in our quest for convenience and safety, we are increasingly becoming more reliant on digital tools. This reliance has positive and negative aspects, and will not only bring out what is good, but also amplify the worst in us. The growing consciousness around social justice emphasises that no one should be left behind as the digital footprint expands. The use of technologies like machine learning, virtual reality and artificial intelligence can help people to create environments that feel more connected and inclusive, and, conversely, they could as easily be employed for the purposes of exploitation and exclusion and create increased alienation and loneliness, leading to social fracturing and polarisation.

To feel connected to those around us, our teams and our communities, we need to believe in something greater than ourselves. Being a purpose-driven organisation with a purposeful culture becomes increasingly important. We have seen a rise in social citizenship and a deeper appreciation of diversity and inclusion, and people's well-being is taken much more seriously. Businesses have taken on a much bigger role in society during the pandemic, leading on issues ranging from social equality to the availability of vaccines and driving the D&I agenda. There is renewed emphasis on leadership characterised by deep empathy and an empowering orientation, with traits described in "servant leadership" and similar leadership philosophies. Mental and physical well-being will become a focus to enable strategy and productivity. We will also need to think differently about how we recognise and reward people in this New Normal.

How we engage and keep the loyalty of talent in this world will require new methods to win in a new "war for talent". Virtual talent models are likely to become more ubiquitous.

I believe that our New Normal offers people an opportunity to reinvent how they engage with the environment, make money, learn, work and access services such as health care. We can build more humane systems that could make us all happier and more productive.

3

Companies have an opportunity to prepare themselves for a New Normal by building agile business practices, creating flexible work options, ensuring they are developing the new skills required, making their systems and processes outcomes-driven, and making people's well-being their primary priority. HR has an opportunity to build organisations that are more human and that can make the world a better place for all.

## Disruption and Discontinuous Change

There is a growing realisation that we have entered an age of continuous disruption and discontinuous change. Companies have no choice but to accept this, and it to prepare their companies for dealing with future challenges. By coming to terms with the structural and process disruption and change societies and businesses now face, we can ensure that we rebuild in a more resilient manner.

Some may still believe that the world will return to the way it was when the pandemic is over. Others, like myself, do not believe that this will be the case. Companies will have to become more responsive and adaptive to thrive in the New Normal. Because we can expect more disruption, and because discontinuous change is the "name of the game", building a company based on purpose and a culture that enables agility, collaboration, speed, trust and networked teams within an ecosystem will be the bedrock for delivering superior services and products to our customers. We are challenged to find new ways to structure companies, with new ways of work, new capabilities, new leadership styles, and a fusion of human with technology to create greater value.

Disruption is elevating the value of human beings in companies. As we deal with continuous disruption and discontinuous change, we cannot rely only on intelligent machines that run sophisticated algorithms, but will increasingly need human beings and teams led by human beings to make sense of a world in continual flux.

"Being distinctly human at the core is the essence of what it means to be a social enterprise. To combine revenue growth and profit-making with respect and support for its environment and stakeholder network, an organization needs to ground itself in a set of human principles: purpose and meaning, ethics and fairness, growth and passion, collaboration and relationships, and transparency and openness".

## The New HR Priorities

With this notion of a New Normal as backdrop, and all that it brings with it, it is clear that HR practice cannot remain as it is. As the HR profession we are called upon to make sense of this new context and how best companies can thrive in this new

---

1    Deloitte Insights, 2021.

world. HR must find its voice and new ways to create value. The good news is that we don't have to fight too hard to be relevant in this world. The nature of the change has undoubtedly accelerated digitisation and its concomitant effects on business, while simultaneously impacting our ways of work. The result is that the people agenda has been brought sharply into focus, thereby catapulting HR to centre stage.

This means that the old ways of "doing HR" will no longer be relevant, and it is time for HR to reimagine itself in a post-Covid world. This new role will demand a "new style" of HR professional, as well as CEOs and executive teams who are mature enough to recognise the new value and role that HR must play. Companies will have to make sense of the disruption of the workplace and will need HR functions to guide them through this change. HR must therefore step up and take on the challenge of reinventing its contribution in companies.

As the HR agenda and priorities have changed, HR will need to consider the following:

1. Getting the company ready for hybrid work

    As companies have experienced both the upside and downside of remote working, they will need to take stock and develop hybrid work models that fit their respective businesses. While we are likely to see a surge of hybrid models, they will likely be bespoke to specific companies and industries. HR will need to figure out how they can create a sustainable balance between personal preferences, customer commitments and company priorities. Replanning work with more of an outcomes focus and managing this remotely will be essential. We need to address time and space flexibility and provide guardrails so that employees can manage their time in such a way that they remain productive. Our models need to give substance to the 'Anytime Anywhere' work philosophy and mechanics. For example, we need to clarify which jobs can be done from home permanently, which are to be office-bound, and which could be considered hybrid. As new work structures are created, companies must ensure that fairness and equity are achieved.

    HR must sustain culture and engagement and ensure that productivity does not suffer under these conditions. This means that HR will need to provide direction to companies so that they can make sense of the new normal by providing a workable hybrid work model/framework.

2. Digitising the company

    HR needs to lead the race for internal digitisation; it will need to partner with technology and devise ways to implement and build digital experiences across the business. The heightened focus on personalisation that comes with the

New Normal means that HR needs to build digital solutions that understand the employee base at a segment of one level. Employee experience matters, which means that HR needs to put people before processes and build systems to understand individual preferences. By deploying digital tools, HR can facilitate the growing need for increased collaboration, improved productivity levels, better relationships between line managers and their teams, and better insights into individual behaviours. HR will increasingly be required to drive higher levels of efficiency, requiring a heavy reliance on data analytics for strategic workforce planning, resource allocation, assessing team-based projects and outcomes, employee engagement, etc. This can only be done using vital data insights gleaned through deploying the appropriate digital tools.

3.  Enabling talent and skills evolution

The New Normal brings with it digital acceleration, which means that employees need to be much more tech savvy than before the pandemic. This has been necessitated by the remote working models adopted in almost all companies. Companies have also accelerated how they service their customers – more online, through apps etc. – resulting in the need for new skills sets. HR will need to articulate a clear talent strategy, outlining a strategic workforce plan that is aligned to the new goals of the company and the demand for employees with digital, cognitive, social and empathy skills. To ensure that companies and their talent are resilient and can weather future disruptions, HR must proactively reskill and upskill the existing workforce while simultaneously putting in place mechanisms to access the new talent the company needs. HR must identify and prioritise the skills that are vital and value accretive for their companies in this new world. They must then support their business by ensuring that each employee actively develops one or two of these new skills. These skills could be to learn how to work in agile cross-functional teams across the value chain on a specific outcome, such as a particular customer journey which creates frustration for customers, impacting customer satisfaction levels, and ultimately, customer retention.

Given the major skills focus that is required from companies in the New Normal, HR must step up and be uncompromising in safeguarding their training and development budgets. Given the revenue challenges that many companies experienced during the pandemic, this is easier said than done, yet the last thing that should be sacrificed.

4.  Building an agile, human-centric culture

As the world and companies respond to the pandemic and the resultant norm of remote working, HR must act quickly to develop their companies' agility in building meaningful workplaces. The implications of the new hybrid work model for culture cannot be under-estimated; where employees are dispersed due to 'Anywhere Anytime' working arrangements, how information is shared, leaders lead, performance is measured, and decisions are made will all be impacted.  Given the disparity between working contexts, and when, where and how employees will do their jobs, a deliberate focus on diversity, equity and inclusionary practices cannot be ignored. Organisational structures will have to be flexible enough to respond to the ongoing changes in the external environment. Companies need to incorporate more agile practices, meaning flatter structures, more cross-functional self-directed teams, and faster decision-making to increase efficiency and enable companies to scale more easily and react better to external pressures.

As companies transform their cultures towards this design, it will require reskilling and upskilling their current workforce. People will need to learn to collaborate and work through teams, and deliver outcomes instead of tasks. Leaders need to play the role of agile coaches rather than managers.

All these changes need to be supported by the right culture. Acknowledging this, as well as the impact that constant change and uncertainty will have on people, highlights another new emerging priority – that of mental well-being. Covid-19 has brought with it untold human stress and trauma. Firstly, there is the mortal danger – the threat of the loss of one's own life and the actual loss of family, friends and colleagues. Second, there are the anxieties and pressures of having to adapt to remote working practices, longer hours of work due to the merging of home space and work space and home-schooling and housekeeping, and then the strain on marriages and relationships, the economic hardship due to loss of jobs and furloughs, etc. Companies need to step up and provide greater emotional support, and leaders have to lead with greater empathy.

HR must help the company navigate these challenges. It will need to tap into big data to enable data-driven decision-making on people matters. It must therefore increase its data analytical capabilities. Developing real-time insights into the culture and the well-being of people will be key, which means that becoming much more digital (using bots, AI, VR etc.), will become a necessity and not a luxury.

An intentional culture must be built to provide the proper context for companies to thrive in this environment. Companies will have to build cultures that foster trust, empathy, increased engagement and agility. In essence, a human-centric culture needs a human-centred approach: company decisions will need to be taken from the perspective of the human being, thus, yet again, placing the HR function front and centre.

5.  Nurturing employee well-being

All of us have had to learn to live with more uncertainty, greater complexity and increasing levels of change, which has brought into sharp focus the need for companies to take care of their employees. The pandemic is having an immense impact on our mental health and well-being, and the effects of long Covid are still emerging. Companies have realised that if they want their employees to thrive and function in this world, they need employees who are healthy in a holistic way – physically, psychologically, spiritually and socially. This has become the number one priority across the world and HR must put the necessary frameworks, processes and tools in place to support the employee base. This needs to go beyond the traditional Employee Assistance Programmes. For example, HR could use tools such as a digital well-being app that could cover aspects such as the following:

*   An interactive well-being platform for engagement and a 'CEO Corner' that enables CEOs to post, ask questions and connect with employees.

*   Physical fitness: Multiple web feeds for fitness suites, fitness gamification, leaderboards, one-click surveys, and share and recognise.

*   Mental and nutritional well-being: Supporting employee awareness and providing channels with non-medical source feeds, helpline information and 'reach-out' personal chat channels.

6.  Renewed focus on Diversity, Equity and Inclusion

In many companies, HR has worked on policies to improve and protect the diversity agenda. However, in most instances, companies have fallen far short in building sustainable and meaningful environments. In recent times, movements such as Black Lives Matter and the He4She movements in the US, the riots in the UK, and the recent uprising and looting in Gauteng and KwaZulu Natal in South Africa, highlighted the plight of all those excluded, be it based on the grounds of race, ethnicity, gender, sexual orientation, physical challenge, or others. The pandemic shone its light on practices of exclusion, and companies can no longer look the other way.

It is the mandate of HR to create companies that thrive on being diverse, equitable and inclusive for all. It is time for HR to take the lead and act; HR needs to ensure that processes and policies support this objective, from sourcing strategies and onboarding processes, to creating spaces where these voices are heard in decision-making processes. The introduction of a hybrid work model can accelerate a more inclusive company by enabling gender diversity and increased opportunities for those who are physically challenged, etc., but it will require leaders to be more transparent in their communication, to lead with empathy, and to promote inclusive decision-making.

7.   Launching an EVP that responds to the new normal

As companies struggled through the pandemic, with many not surviving and others barely making it, a key challenge that HR will have to address is to develop capabilities to help their companies thrive in this new world. HR has had to ensure that employees remain engaged, productive and resilient throughout the pandemic, which has helped to chart a pathway towards establishing a new way in which it can add value. One of the key shifts for HR is a fresh look at their employee value proposition (EVP). Taking a proactive approach to talent in the new normal is crucial if companies want to attract and retain key skills.  Any new EVP must offer a framework that is agile and fit for purpose; it must go beyond being a branding exercise and translate into real experiences that touch each employee holistically.

A culture that can adapt to and absorb disruptive external forces is a culture that is agile, collaborative, people-centric, empathetic, and inspires employees to bring their whole selves to work. An EVP must thus focus on engaging employees in a meaningful way and lead to improved engagement levels in the company.

Operationalising an EVP is vital; it must not merely be a branding exercise, but should be embedded in each key process. It is important to implement a series of employee-centred human experiences that bring the EVP to life for all employees. It should further allow a company to pivot its recruitment, onboarding and query resolution processes for the needs of the New Normal. HR could, for example, consider launching a digital hiring platform where potential employees send through a video interview, and AI then picks up specific psychometric cues. Not only would the process be more efficient, but it would allow HR to find better fit candidates based on the intelligence in the system.

Embedding the EVP into the culture is equally important; there needs to be an intentional plan for staff to engage and experience the EVP as it comes to life. This can be done, for example, by leaders sharing their stories of bringing to life certain elements of the EVP. By using real-life examples, this shows staff that the EVP is alive and well in the company.

8.   Transforming HR itself

As mentioned, the pandemic ushered in a New Normal and disrupted the world as we know it. Companies have been forced to respond to survive and thrive, which means that the foundational concepts of organisation need to be rethought and redesigned. As stated in earlier sections of this chapter, HR must lead a new human-centric agile culture, develop new talent models and hybrid work models, drive the company's internal digitisation, reskill and upskill existing talent, shift from task to outcomes, develop flatter structures based on networks of teams rather than hierarchical functional structures, become obsessed with personalised employee experiences, and much more.

In the past, HR generally did not enjoy the confidence of business, despite often having to fulfil a strong and meaningful mandate. This was mainly due to HR not behaving like a business (i.e., understanding the business it serves), not knowing where and how it added value, and not using the tools that the rest of the business used. By being guided by data-driven people insights to improve informed decision-making, HR can win the confidence of business.

CHROs need to consider themselves the CEOs of the people business. Developing this mindset will help CHROs to run HR like a business. They will need to focus on:

- where and how their people strategies create value for the business;

- which priorities (e.g., skills) will increase revenue;

- how they can speed up the business, e.g., by simplifying processes, flattening structures, and empowering employees with faster decision-making;

- how they create the right ecosystem to enable the business to thrive;

- how they can reduce the cost base, e.g., by deploying digital systems and tools, rethinking their talent models, and creating smarter and more agile ways of working;

- how they build the right culture to deliver on the company strategy and increase the employee Net Promotor Score (eNPS), ensuring the best customer (employee) experience, reducing staff churn, and increasing the attraction and retention of new top talent;

- how they use customer value management principles when understanding their employee base through data insights and analytics;

- how they make investment decisions, e.g., which HR technologies to deploy, which skills to invest in, and what organisational capabilities to build; and

- how they create, communicate and implement the people strategy to build a competitive employer brand.

For CHROs to fulfil this new mandate, they will need to transform their own functions. Of course, this cannot be done alone or in isolation. Like the rest of the business,

HR works within an ecosystem, and will need strategic collaborative partnerships to execute its new mandate. The primary partners for HR will be the CEO and the CFO – and, I would argue, the CTO – who need to form a guiding coalition for the HR transformation agenda. The HR operating model must be redesigned to align with the new objectives and ways of work. This also means that the skills required in HR need to transform. HR must be infused with different skills such as data science and analysis, computer science, software engineering, communication, brand management, customer experience, digital marketing, etc. In other words, HR will have to be populated with the skills that will enable it to fulfil its new mandate.

## Conclusion

Few will argue that HR does not hold the centre stage in the New Normal. This time, it behoves HR professionals and particularly CHROs not to squander the opportunity. The HR community needs to accept that this newfound importance brings with it new responsibilities. HR must consciously innovate to stay ahead of the curve and drive outcomes that matter, and they must be ready to be held accountable for the money they spend and the value it creates. HR must be relentless in shaping the organisation's capability to thrive in a world that is constantly disrupted, and step up to play a leading role in transforming the business.

HR matters, and because it does, there is a greater expectation from the business. This means that HR professionals need to upgrade their skills and capabilities so that they are not found wanting in fulfilling their new mandate.

Chapter 2

# The New World of Work

**Paul Norman**

We have lived through unprecedented change over the past two years; no one was left unaffected by the global pandemic. Many lost their jobs as companies downsized or closed completely, and the drastic shift to remote working not only impacted the workforce, but changed the face of the entire world of work.

Traditional work models have come apart during the pandemic. The fixed eight-hour day has been disrupted by remote working practices, resulting in an increase in hours worked and multi-tasking (taking care of kids, home schooling, looking after ill family members, etc.), a blurring between work and home life, a change in patterns of work delivery (less task- and more outcome-driven), a change in organisational structures with functional silos giving way to self-forming agile teams, and an increase in the stress and anxiety related to ensuring that you are noticed and recognised for a job well done by peers and leaders. Remote work has brought into renewed prominence many things we have been speaking about for a long time, such as the importance of being tech savvy, digitising processes, using people data analytics, and building a resilient organisation that can pivot quickly to respond to market and global challenges.

As the world emerges from the Covid-19 pandemic, much of what companies have done in response is likely to evolve into a new way of operating and a shift in the world of work as we know it. The New World of Work will be characterised by the digitisation of everything, hybrid workplaces, new kinds of employment agreements (e.g., virtual talent models), and an integration of automation, artificial intelligence and robotics into the way work gets done. The New World of Work will not be one size fits all: it will vary based on the job you do, where you live, and importantly, what company you work for. Your experience and choices will be framed within these parameters, highlighting an increased drive towards personalisation.

# The Digitisation of Everything

The pandemic precipitated an acceleration of the Digitisation of Everything. For many of us, working remotely and accessing services such as e-commerce, e-learning, etc., has become the norm. Before the onset of the pandemic this was merely a dream for most. What has also become apparent during this time is the big digital divide, especially in developing countries, where access has been limited, or in some cases, non-existent.

Today there are 3.80 billion smartphone users in the world (48.20% of all people), while there are 4.88 billion mobile phone users (61.90% of all people). Current data reveals that there are over 10.37 billion mobile connections worldwide, exceeding the world population of 7.88 billion people.

This level of mobile connectedness spurred the emergence of several forms of digitisation, for example in banking and financial services, e-commerce, online education and healthcare. The pandemic has accelerated our adoption of these online services and in many ways changed our lives, making us much more digital today.

As customers have become more digital, it becomes necessary for organisations to do the same. While technology (and the pandemic) has brought about big shifts in how we work and deliver services to customers, it has also ushered in an age of constant change. Organisations must therefore build capabilities to deal with the digital transformation we are experiencing and transform their entire business, including their leadership and culture. Of course, becoming more digital escalates risks, especially cyber-risks, which will become an increasingly important aspect of the digitisation journey. Companies thus need to rethink their design and processes as they embrace the digitisation journey.

The World Economic Forum holds that digitisation and innovation have the potential to add value to society beyond business, for instance, the environment, public health and biodiversity. It can also drive the empowerment of people through reskilling and upskilling, while enabling greater access to diverse talent and stimulating inclusionary practices. It can further enable improved collaboration and strategic partnerships, leading to "building back better" from the pandemic.

# The Hybrid Workplace

In Chapter 1, the development of the hybrid workplace was introduced as one of the new priorities for HR. I revisit it here because I believe that it is a foundational aspect of the New World of Work, enabling new talent approaches, ways of work, agile practices, and increased employee engagement.

In its simplest form, the hybrid workplace is a model that integrates on-site office work and remote work. This model will vary depending on the company and the industry. There is a growing trend that suggests that employees will resist a full-time return to the office after the pandemic, and many could consider leaving their companies were they forced to do so. This makes consideration of the hybrid workplace model a matter of urgency.

The adoption of a hybrid workplace model offers many benefits for both companies and employees. It is widely known and accepted today (supported by extensive research) that the right culture leads to improved company performance, and vice versa. As we emerge from the pandemic, leaders have a unique opportunity to reshape their organisation's culture as they prepare for hybrid work.

The hybrid workplace could offer employees better work-life balance, less stressful working environments, savings because they are not spending money on transport or food at the office, safety (especially for those who are immune-compromised), and more time, because they do not have to commute to work each day.

For a company, an immediate benefit lies in getting rid of office space it no longer needs. The hybrid workplace also creates new opportunities for talent attraction, since companies are no longer restricted to talent in the immediate city or country within which it operates. Not only is there easier access to talent, but depending on the contract, companies can save by not having to offer the full remuneration suite of benefits. This model may also increase a company's ability to respond to future crises because they can quickly pivot to full remote work if required.

Of course, there is also a downside to adopting this work model, especially in South Africa and many other emerging economies where not everyone has access to high-speed internet. People often also share their homes with several other family members, friends, etc., which can make working from home difficult and complicated. A mix of some employees at the office and others at home will mean that those at the office may get more facetime with their leaders and possibly more exposure to key projects, leading to unequal opportunities. While the hybrid model has advantages for the diversity and inclusion agenda, the pressures on female employees, who may have the added responsibility of taking care of the home and their children, may mean that they become further disadvantaged through such a model.

What is clear is that if companies do not thoroughly plan the implementation of the hybrid workplace model, it could create more problems and lead to lower productivity. Some things to consider when thinking about implementation include the below:

- The hybrid model must be co-created with employees based on what they need and what the company needs.

- Clear guidelines are needed to explain to employees how the model works and how they qualify to participate.

- Employees must have the tools to work remotely.

- Mechanisms must be created to increase time with employees, so that there can be real-time feedback and connection.

- Health and safety took on new significance during Covid (including vaccine policies) and will be a key aspect to address with a return to the office, even in a hybrid approach.

- The implications for the work culture cannot be overemphasised; managing those in the office and those at home will require a steady focus to ensure that the culture of the organisation is not affected negatively. HR needs to guard against the creation of "in" and "out" groups.

- The gains of inclusive practices as the company transitions from a remote environment into a hybrid model must be nurtured. The company should ensure parity between those at the office and those in remote locations as a category of inclusion. An example of this could be using technology wisely to ensure the inclusion of people who work remotely, e.g., by enabling equal access to conversations.

- Leaders need to be intentional about modelling what hybrid work looks like and lead by example. They need to clearly communicate to their teams how and when they will work from home and from the office, thereby helping their teams to know what and how work needs to be executed, and helping them to be more effective in getting the work done. In other words, companies will need to rethink the purpose of the office, and there should be a plan for orchestrated versus less structured interactions.

# Automation, Robotics and the 4th Industrial Revolution (4IR)

The introduction of automation and robotics into the world of work is disrupting normal work practices. It is also creating much anxiety in people who fear that they will be rendered superfluous and redundant. However, as we have seen throughout the pandemic, building human-centric organisations is key for future success, and in making this a priority, many of the 4IR concerns will also be addressed. It is clear that human skills such as creativity, empathy and critical thinking will be essential in this world, thus it is unquestionable that people have a unique role to play in the future world of work.

The term '4IR' often sounds ominous – something that is going to destroy jobs. While this will certainly be true for some job categories, 4IR will also create new jobs. What 4IR is about is automation and analytics; it involves the adoption of cyber-physical systems such as the Internet of Things (IoT) and the internet of systems. The former involves using connected devices to send and receive data, like our smart watches talking to our smartphones today. The latter is the business-owned systems that similarly collect data from IoT systems to drive independent decisions. In today's world, 4IR has become integrated into our everyday environment and way of life so seamlessly that many of us are not even aware of how it has changed the way we live. It might thus not be as scary as we may initially have thought.

Many of us are already living in a world driven by high-speed mobile internet, the use of big data, cloud technology, AI and robotics. We experience many of these technologies and tools when we do our online shopping through platforms like Amazon or Takealot. In time, these technologies will permeate every industry. AI and robotics in particular will change many jobs and the ways in which people work. Many companies have adopted AI into their recruitment processes, where CVs are analysed and shortlists produced, and initial interviews are even conducted by video and then analysed through AI to produce call-back lists. The use of AI in this way is speeding up the recruitment process and often improving the quality of outcomes. It also allows recruiters to save time on transactional tasks and frees them up to add value in new ways by building a deeper, quality experience for candidates, spending more time on on-boarding, etc.

As we live through the pandemic, we have already seen the redefinition of many jobs, such as call centre agents working remotely and companies using technology to assist customer services through chatbots. We saw the widespread acceptance and adoption of digital solutions to respond to the pandemic in education, where schools shifted to e-learning and other online educational platforms, and in health with telemedicine, while even the judiciary has moved online.

The 4IR has also given rise to the so-called "sharing economy". This refers to various platform businesses that have spawned new ventures based on the sharing of resources, systems, etc., such as online ride hailing services like Uber and space-sharing services like Airbnb. This also changes how people work and are employed, as it has driven a need for greater collaboration and strategic partnerships.

The increasing dependence on cloud computing and the IoT, aided by the pandemic pushing companies into accelerated digitisation, has resulted in companies partnering with hyperscalers to help deliver on this growing need. Hyperscalers can simply be described as companies that provide cloud, networking and internet services at scale by offering companies access to infrastructure via an Internet as a Service

(IaaS) model. Such hyperscalers include the likes of Google, Microsoft, Amazon and Facebook. From an HR perspective, these partnerships can also be used to reskill and upskill the existing workforce with, amongst others, digital and cloud skills.

# The Gig Economy

The gig economy refers to short term contract or freelance work. It has its roots in the music industry, where musicians refer to a gig as a job that only lasts for a short period. Wikipedia refers to gig workers as independent contractors, online platform workers, contract firm workers, on-call workers and temporary workers. Gig workers enter into on-demand formal agreements with companies to provide services to the company's clients.

As we emerge from the pandemic, the lessons we learned about working remotely, becoming more digital savvy (using MS Teams, Zoom and other platforms to get work done), and shifting work from tasks to outcomes, have laid a solid foundation for expanding the gig economy, where gig workers are defined as those who work from wherever and whenever they like, and for whomever they want. In many ways, we have all been exposed to some elements of 'gig style' work during the pandemic. We worked from home instead of the office, and our normal work hours were disrupted by being interspersed with other responsibilities such as home schooling and taking care of the vulnerable in our families. We were confronted by the need to discover new meaning in our work and did a lot of soul searching about what got us going each day (purposeful work), and we sought out connections ourselves to avoid isolation. I believe that many of us, having tasted this flexibility and independence, will choose to make this style of work more permanent. More recently, we have heard the term "Great Resignation", which has seen millions of Americans resign from their jobs in response to the Covid-19 pandemic. These resignations appear to be mainly in the Millennial generation talent segment. One of the reasons given for these mass resignations is that employees have experienced work from home environments and a resulting improvement in quality of life, and cannot be attracted back to an office job. Yet others developed new skills during the pandemic and wish to explore these avenues. In some cases, the need to spend more time with family is driving this movement. The pandemic has thus changed humans (employees), the nature of work, and even the perception of time and space. For this reason, companies will have to rethink and redesign their work offerings if they are to stay attractive to the talent market.

These shifts are leading to new ways of contracting workers, giving impetus to the gig economy. Workers and companies have both learned much more during the pandemic about how work can be done. The usual sceptical voices in companies, which ask whether they are getting full value for their money when workers are not in the office, have mostly been silenced, because actual experience has shown that workers are generally working longer hours. In fact, workers have enjoyed more relaxed environments, including not having to waste time in traffic, and have come to see this new way of work as a more acceptable lifestyle. Companies that want to continue to attract great talent and compete in the new war for talent will have to incorporate this new way of contracting more permanently. This is likely to accelerate regulations to bring greater protection to this class of worker, who up until now, it could be argued, did not receive a fair deal from companies.

# Generation Z

The Pew Research Centre defined this generation as those born after 1996, making the oldest among them 24 in 2021. This generation needs to deal with the aftermath of the pandemic and the uncertainty accompanying it. They were also the hardest hit because many of them live in households affected by job losses (parents and siblings), and they themselves (as a generation) are highly represented in service- and hospitality-related industries where job losses were most severe.

The OC Tanner Institute argues that those organisations with healthy cultures are likely to retain their Gen Z employees by a factor of as much as 16 times as companies without healthy cultures. It is therefore essential that companies move fast to integrate their Gen Z employees. These employees bring with them a fresh outlook, and while there is great diversity among them, they also share many key cultural interests and preferences. Integrating them well into the company is critical to improving the employee experience and connections for everyone. The key is having the right leadership that understands how to build a collaborative, team-based ecosystem that is also sensitive to individual differences. This means that while we specifically need to cater for each of the different generations within companies today, personalisation remains at the core.

Gen Z can truly be considered digital natives, since they grew up in a high-tech, hyper-connected world. This means that they will enter the workplace with new behaviours, expectations and preferences.

A study conducted by McKinsey and Box 1824 revealed four core Gen Z behaviours, all of which are founded on their search for truth:

1.  They value individual expression and avoid labels.
2.  They will mobilise for causes.
3.  They believe in dialogue to resolve conflict.
4.  They make decisions and relate to institutions in a pragmatic and analytical way.

Despite the ongoing hype around how different this generation is from the ones before it, research also points out how they are similar in fundamental respects. Despite the fact that they grew up as true digital natives, it does not follow that they prefer communicating via digital tools like tablets and smartphones. In fact, research shows that Gen Z prefer face-to-face communication and have a strong need for belonging. If they connect to a purpose, they will put in the hours to get things done; they have a strong desire to grow themselves and they take their well-being seriously. All these traits, together with their pronounced digital prowess, make them a valuable talent segment for any company today.

Research by the OC Tanner Institute showed that so-called "talent magnets" – factors that influence whether someone will join, engage and stay at a company – are hugely important to the younger generations. Talent magnets include purpose, opportunity, success, appreciation, well-being and leadership. For Gen Z, opportunity, purpose and well-being rated top; they want to make a difference, grow, and have work that challenges them, and they do not want to spend all their time working.

Regarding the actual work that employees do, Gen Z show a greater preference for customer-focused work. Diversity and inclusion is also of great importance to this generation; their drive for inclusion means they are open to diversity in experience and people from different backgrounds, which means they can be good team players. They would like to do impactful work and recognition should come through experiential gifts and symbolic awards.

Gen Z is an important talent segment for any company. They bring both differences from, and similarities to, previous generations. Some of their strengths will help companies to build a more diverse and inclusive culture, while accelerating the new skill sets required for the large-scale digital transformation taking place across industries. Companies should embrace this cohort and engage them to help foster the culture, skills and leadership fit for the challenges of today.

## Conclusion

The world is more digitally connected today than before the pandemic, which brings with it much opportunity, but also associated risks. Fundamentally, the pandemic has accelerated a change in the world of work, which is nowhere more visible than in how companies are adopting the new hybrid model of work. As companies embrace this new model, they will have to pay particular attention to how it is integrated into their culture. This means that HR will have to enable the culture to support this model of work, develop leaders who can lead dispersed teams, work out how to reward and recognise individuals and teams working in this new way, and create tools and ways of work that enhance and encourage diversity and inclusion. This cannot be successfully implemented without a deliberate plan to help the company transition from its current mindset regarding ways of work, decision-making, etc., to those required for the hybrid world.

Companies will have to redesign their current work, workplace and workforce practices for the New World of Work. The merging of technology and human beings to deliver work will lead to companies having to consider a different type of collaboration, i.e., between people and technology. Augmentation is happening quickly in companies today, and both companies and employees will have to ensure that there is a proper interface with technology. Learning how to work with and through technology to achieve an outcome will be a key skill for new employees to master. Companies will also have to clearly define new roles and other skills required from employees to enable them to succeed in this new world.

Building a culture of connection, collaboration and empowerment, with real-time access to employee feedback, will become a critical organisational capability. As companies adopt 'Anytime Anywhere' work, and incorporate gig workers and the unique needs of Millennials and Gen Z (most companies already have 50% plus Millennials in their workforce), the role of leaders needs to adjust from a controlling to an enabling one. Leadership styles also need to change to embrace this new group of digital natives and disruptive thinkers. It will demand that leaders make sense of leading in a multi-generational workplace.

As companies embrace the New World of Work and everything that comes with it, the importance of responding to the human aspect of work cannot be underestimated. These environments will only thrive with an intentional people-focused system that build on commonalities as well as the unique themes in the multi-generational workforce.

The New World of Work is about balance and integration. It is about being human, having fun and playing, while growing in effectiveness and impact. It is about letting everyone find and use their voice and giving them a place to feel at home. It is about celebrating individualism while honouring the collective.

This is the job for HR: to create an ecosystem where such a world can thrive. The HR fraternity needs to grasp that the New World of Work is already here, and we must ACT NOW.

# Chapter 3

# The Power of Purpose[1]

## Andrew Millson

What are we, as individuals, without a wider purpose in our lives? Purpose gives us direction, a reason for being, motivation to be more than we are, inspiration to grow as individuals, and the context for our lives into which our day to day then fills.

The same is true for organisations. Purpose provides a cultural foundation; the reason, beyond profit, for an entity's existence. As John Mackey, CEO and co-founder of Whole Foods Market, says, "Profit is like the oxygen we breathe, absolutely necessary for life, but that does not mean our purpose in life is to breathe".

Purpose provides the wider context in which our organisations operate; it is the intrinsic motivator for our people, a reason to get up in the morning, a force to empower our people, and ultimately, by following this purpose, an opportunity for businesses to genuinely become forces for good in the communities they operate in and society as a whole. Profit follows purpose, and by relentlessly pursuing a 'higher' purpose, businesses will not only be profitable, but as many commentators on this topic note, will benefit from highly motivated, committed colleagues and leaders while fulfilling their obligations to their shareholders.

So why then do we not have more purpose-led organisations, and how do we shift paradigms, from what we would call "business as usual" to having more purposeful organisations? What prevents this shift and how we do build a team of conscious leaders that are fully aligned with this purpose?

Food Lover's Market has been on this journey for a number of years. Are we there yet? The truth is no, but we are committed to the journey, to asking ourselves those hard questions that businesses often hide from, to learning and growing as a collection of individuals, and ultimately helping to build a more sustainable, healthy and equitable society.

---

1   *Please note that this is written from the perspective of the individual, Andrew Millson, using Food Lover's Market as a case study. Therefore, the views and opinions expressed within this chapter are Andrew's in his personal capacity.*

## Where it All Began

Food Lover's Market was founded in 1994 by two entrepreneurial brothers, Brian and Mike Coppin. From humble beginnings with a single 'Fruit and Veg City' in Access Park, Cape Town, the organisation now spans 11 countries, with close to 16,000 colleagues. The business has grown to include 120 Food Lover's Market stores, seven distribution centres, an import-export business (FVC international), 43 liquor outlets (Diamond Discount and Market Liquors), over 300 convenience stores (FreshStop) and 170 coffee houses (Seattle Coffee Co.). What a transformation this has been!

Being founder-led, the organisation has always ensured that its values, growth and culture have been aligned to the founders' principles. Seven years ago, Brian came across the book *Conscious Capitalism* by John Mackay, which is where the acceleration to becoming more purposeful really took hold.

## A Look in the Mirror

The key questions we began to ask ourselves included not just what kind of a business do we want to create, but on top of this we added, "What kind of a world do we want to create?".

This is not an easy question, as it forces the business to take a hard look at the core issues impacting the world globally and locally, and more importantly, the business' role in creating or accentuating these issues. We look at it as a three step process consisting of:

1. **recognising** the social and environmental challenges our world faces;

2. **acknowledging** our role in exacerbating these issues; and

3. **building** a business that proactively tackles these issues.

It involves taking a hard look in the mirror and not seeing what we WANT to see, but seeing things as they truly are. It involves our leadership asking of themselves: "What is our role in this is?" and "What kind of leaders do we need to be in an ever-changing and more complex world?"

According to Einstein, "We cannot solve our problems with the same thinking that created them". The same can be said for leadership: no matter the school of leadership we come from, business needs a new type of leader to build a new type of business, and indeed a new business sector, that can free itself from the perception that business (or rather big business), is simply 'profiteering (greedy?) entities, happy to overlook their negative impacts on society to make a quick buck.

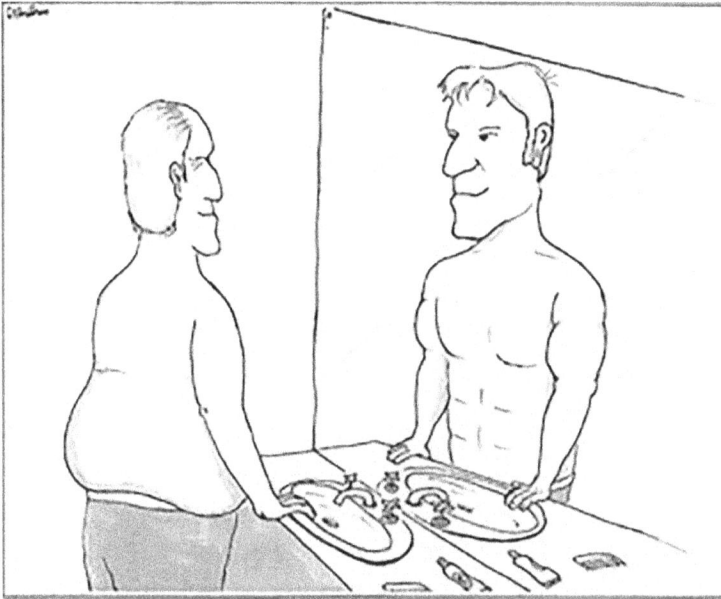

We need a new type of leadership... a new way of leading that is brutally honest with itself and able to acknowledge its role in the "unsustainability" of so many of our operations. Leaders who are sincere about building organisations that have a positive impact in our world.

As we often say at Food Lover's, we need to build a business where every single person – no matter what their job title may say – is truly proud to be the brand.

Again, are we there yet? No, but that is very much the goal.

## Conscious Capitalism

There is no doubt that the book *Conscious Capital* has had a real and profound impact on our business. When Brian first read it, he tasked the entire leadership team with reading it too. What followed was a period of self-evaluation, culminating in the founding of our sustainability strategy in 2016, Earth Lovers. Earth Lovers was, and remains, our vehicle to redress the imbalances in our society, build a healthier population, and address the environmental challenges directly caused by our business and suppliers. This is in large part modelled on some of the learnings that have come out of Whole Foods. In his book, John Mackay talks about the four pillars of conscious capitalism:

- Higher purpose
- Stakeholder orientation

- Conscious leadership

- Conscious culture

My favourite line is when John Mackay defines Higher Purpose as, "Elevating Humanity through business begins with knowing why your business exists".

Profound? Definitely.

Achievable? Only if the organisation is fully committed to asking itself some serious questions.

Necessary considering the current state of the world? Absolutely!

And the great news is that there are now major companies around the world that are already making serous inroads into this. One of my favourite companies, and a true role model for the potential for business to operate as a force for change, is Patagonia. Their mission? "To use Patagonia's resources to do something about our climate crisis." To quote: "We are in business to save our home planet." Wow!

Whole Foods' purpose is equally bold and refreshing: "Our purpose is to nourish people and planet."

Another company pushing the boundaries on the role of business in society is Interface, a global carpet company founded in the same year as Food Lover's Market. It simply states: "We are in the business of creating change."

The list goes on.

Four years ago, we refreshed Food Lover's mission, vision and purpose, along with our values. Our purpose is now to, "Provide our customers with Fresh, Healthy, Affordable Food for Generations to come". The key to this is the phrase "for generations to come". Why? Because one of the major areas where business has sold itself short on becoming a force for good is that it has been hamstrung by short-termism. By shifting the thinking of business from short term to long-term, sustainability automatically becomes ingrained. When thinking long-term about people, they move from becoming commodities to future leaders. By looking at our supply chain over the long-term, we realise we have no choice but to safeguard our natural areas and protect and enhance our natural world (bees in the fruit and veg supply chain suddenly become very important!).

Our purpose and values help to provide the overall context in which the business operates, however the truth is that I am often fairly derogatory about companies' values. Why? Because I have had the privilege of working with a huge variety of companies – in the UK, Europe and here in Africa. All have values, but very few actually live them. To become truly purposeful, we have to move those values off the boardroom wall and ingrain them in our everyday leadership practice. It is these everyday behaviours that underpin the values, and how consistently they are followed, that determine how purposeful an organisation truly is.

This starts with conscious leadership. While this is a phrase that is becoming more common in business these days, it is important to look at what it means. Being conscious is an awareness of your own existence, thoughts and surroundings. Fundamentally, it is an awareness of what you DO.

Unless we are fully aware of our thoughts and of what we are doing, we are not being conscious. Unless we, as leaders, are fully aware of the impact we create in this world, both environmentally and socially, and then act to redress these, we can hardly call ourselves conscious leaders.

## Love and Fear

In the context of consciousness, a common theme we talk about at Food Lover's is Love and Fear. Elizabeth Kubler Ross, a highly acclaimed psychiatrist, is quoted as saying that there are two primary emotions we as humans feel: love and fear. Others, such as joy, happiness, jealousy and anger, stem from these. Too often our actions are simply a manifestation of fear.

"There are only two emotions: love and fear. All positive emotions come from love, all negative emotions from fear. From love flows happiness, contentment, peace, and joy. From fear comes anger, hate, anxiety and guilt. It's true that there are only two primary emotions, love and fear. But it's more accurate to say that there is only love or fear, for we cannot feel these two emotions together, at exactly the same time. They're opposites. If we're in fear, we are not in a place of love. When we're in a place of love, we cannot be in a place of fear."

From a business point of view, it is these two emotions that can ether speed up the journey to being more purposeful, or block it entirely. The diagram below talks to this.

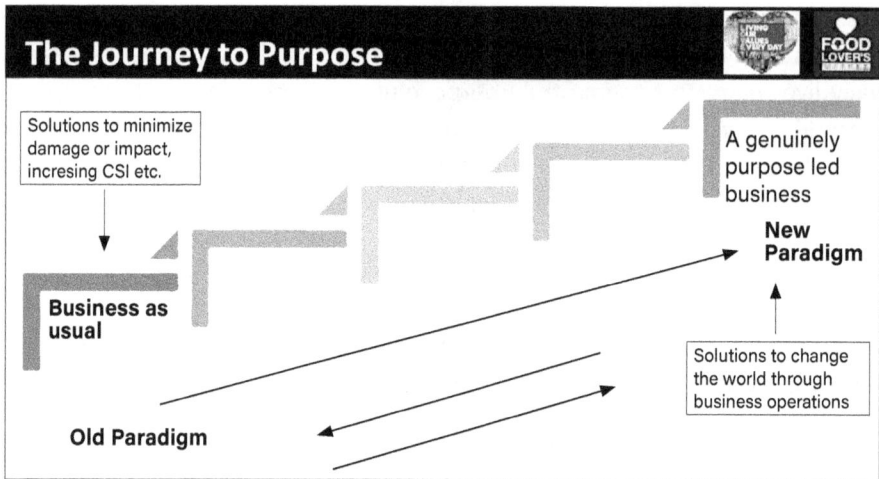

Figure 3.1: The journey to purpose

Fear keeps us stuck in the old paradigm. What are we fearful of?

- Speaking our minds and not belonging.
- Not hitting our short-term targets.
- That others will get our jobs if we develop them and enable them to live to their full potential.
- Losing our jobs.
- Trying something new/stepping into the unknown.
- Admitting to ourselves that our actions cause harm.

Fear keeps us in 'business as usual' mode. Yes, some businesses will bring in carbon reduction measures, CSI etc., but really, if one is honest, without looking at core business operations, these reductionist activities simply make businesses more palatable, not more purposeful. They enable the execs and leadership to carry on with their current business operations while alleviating some of their guilt. They provide a 'feel good factor', but do nothing to shift the business model and truly tackle the social and environmental challenges of our day.

In the eyes of much of society (including our customers!), businesses are something that must be tolerated simply because "they create jobs". However, fear strips businesses of their potential to enact real social and environmental change, or to decouple "business" and "profiteering", as is the perception of so many people.

While fear holds us back, love fast tracks the journey to being more purposeful. It shifts us from the old paradigm of "doing things less badly", to the new paradigm that enables businesses to come up with solutions to change the world, not though CSI, but through their core operations.

People often ask what I mean by 'love' in the workplace, often with a smile or a snigger. Love for me is, firstly and primarily, about loving ourselves, being comfortable in our own skin, and freeing ourselves from judgment of self and others. Whenever I see someone mistreating another human being, I see someone who does not truly love themself. The very best leaders I have come across are those individuals who are totally comfortable in themselves, who love themselves, and who are able to look for the good in others – a key leadership principle our CEO Brian frequently talks about.

The first step in truly loving ourselves is bringing awareness to our thoughts and our actions, without judgement, and then having a hard look at how we want to deal with these. These are, of course, individual reflections, which ultimately will enable us to become better human beings, and therefore better leaders.

The same is true for business and its own self-reflection.

## Acknowledging our Impact on the World

A key milestone in Food Lover's journey was when our CEO convened a full day off-site meeting of the senior leadership of the business to look at exactly this. We asked ourselves the hard questions, and honestly evaluated both our role in this, and what our collective response should be.

We began by looking at some of the major global issues that we felt were most pertinent to the retail sector.

These included, but were certainly not limited to, topics such as:

- carbon emissions;
- climate change;
- the "plastification" of our oceans, beaches and rivers; and
- inequality and poverty.

We looked at it closely and uncomfortably, and worked through our own impact on these issues. The most pressing in the social context of South Africa is inequality. We spoke about the traditional business response, i.e., "We provide jobs, therefore we are addressing this challenge", and looked beyond basic employment (i.e., business employs people and therefore is tackling poverty) into "can someone on minimum wage live a fulfilled life?".

We then took it further... do we feel it fair that children of the leadership team are more likely to get jobs (one day) as managers or in professional services, than as a general assistant working in our stores? The next question was an acknowledgement. If a cashier's or a packer's children are more likely than the leadership's children to one day work as general assistants, while our own children are more likely to be in positions that generate wealth for their family, are we not then contributors to inequality?

From awareness comes action, speaking directly to the heart. "Now that we know this, should we do something about it? If yes, then what? Over what period?"

While these questions led to more questions than answers, it was the first step in truly becoming purpose-led. They are incredibly hard acknowledgments, often with no easy answers. However, as business, it is in our DNA to find answers and solve challenges. While the solutions to these challenges may fall outside the traditional "business as usual" solutions, it is imperative that business does not shy away from taking these first steps. From this we can then set clear actions and goals.

At Food Lover's for example, we are more committed than ever to finding talent that does not look like me, sound like me, or come from the same privileged school as me. We are committed to nurturing and developing talent that maybe doesn't have the same polished edges that my school and university gave me. We are exploring how we can support talented children of long-standing colleagues achieve their dreams.

The same can be said about the other questions. Does anyone want the rainforests, the very lungs of our planet, to be chopped down? Of course not! However, can we be sure that all our products come from sustainable sources and we are not, therefore, unknowingly complicit in this? Another project takes off!

But I should take a step back here, and issue caution. These kinds of meetings and questions come from years of building a more conscious leadership. For example, our commitment to our people has been around since inception. Brian and Mike, to put it simply, have huge hearts. The loyalty they show to their people is paid back by the truckload. I have very rarely seen such a committed group of managers to their leaders. Many of our current managers, whether in stores or DCs, have been in the business for years. They started out as general assistants themselves, have built their careers through Food Lover's Market, and have in turn built Food Lover's Market. The same can be said for many of our suppliers, most notably the farmers who have long-standing relationships with us, built after decades of working in partnership, and an unshakeable trust in the people behind the brand.

# Poverty Spotlight

Five years ago, through internal discussions when we acknowledged that some of our people live in poverty, we committed to seeing what we could do about it. Enter Poverty Stoplight, an NGO that "seeks to activate the potential of families and communities to lift themselves out of poverty".

Poverty Stoplight uses a framework that addresses six core areas of family poverty by asking 50 questions. These are highly personal, not work-related, and include questions related to violence, addiction, family health, finances and housing to name a few.

| Indicator<br>1.  Access to drinking water | Area: Health and Environment | |
|---|---|---|
| Level 3: The home has constant access to drinking water within the house or in the yard. The home has a tap with running water that is clean and drinkable. | Level 2: The home has access to drinking water, but: (a) it is not reliable for part of the day, or (b) it is not always clean, or (c) the source of water is within 100 meters of the home and has to be shared. | Level 1: The water the family drinks is not safe, clean water or they have to walk more than 100 meters from their home to fetch it. |
| | | |

*Figure 3.2: Poverty spotlight*

When we first looked at this, we realised that there was a real risk that by setting off on this particular project, and then not following through fully, we would in fact alienate our colleagues further – the exact opposite of our intended impact. However, doing nothing and continuing as normal was simply not an option.

We began our first sessions over three years ago, and have since done over 800 one-on-one sessions with our colleagues. What do they get? A very clear, visual representation of where they see themselves in those six core areas. This is then turned into action plans for them to work on with their families. We as a business cannot solve all the social issues our people face in South Africa, however we can provide a framework, and corresponding tools, that enable our colleagues and their families to lift themselves out of poverty.

The key intervention we rolled out following this was Me and My Money, in partnership with The Clothing Bank; "M3 workshops create a safe and respected environment where each participant can explore their relationship with money and learn key skills to enable them to become debt free, start saving and develop their life map for financial freedom."

What do we get? We get to fully understand the needs of our colleagues. We now know (not surmise) what the core social issues facing our people are in each region and store.

We have since created two videos about this, the first being for our board with the express purpose of supporting them to become fully aware of the issues facing our colleagues.

## Understanding Reality

The second video followed a colleague's journey to work, from his 4am alarm, through the harrowing experience of walking to the taxi rank in the dark in fear of being mugged, the wait for the taxi and the long walk to his place of work. This was overlaid by him talking about his fears and his hopes for his children.

This is a far cry from how I get to work, how I start my day, and the hopes and dreams I have for my children.

The disparity in our country may seem obvious to many, however for some reason we have the ability to pull a mask over our true selves, cloaked in the way of "how business should be done" or "how business has always been done". This seems to shut down our natural empathy; it enables us to behave towards people in ways that do not take into account their personal situations. It dehumanises people and commoditises them.

By openly acknowledging the issues, we slowly allow people to take their masks off – to look around and see the challenges our world faces. We create a framework, guided by a collective higher purpose, for them to engage in these issues. It goes without saying that this energises people; it makes them feel good and gives them a reason for loving your company, more than just because they're tied to a pay check at the end of the month.

It is important to talk about these big issues not to scare people into action, as this has never worked. It is important to raise them so the business can make a proactive decision about whether it really cares enough to do anything about it.

So, in short, on this topic specifically, a purpose-driven organisation is one that:

- does not hide from these issues;
- actively acknowledges its impact on these; and
- works to firstly minimise, and then proactively increase, its positive impact.

This, however, takes more than just a committed individual or two; it takes a collective commitment from the leadership team to relentlessly follow this path.

## Conscious Leadership

Conversations like the above take bravery. They also take time and the building of trust. Most importantly, they need to be delivered in a way that is free from judgement. I am fortunate enough to work with a leadership team who value out of the box thinking; in fact, this is encouraged and I believe it to be one of the cornerstones of the success of the business.

Crucial in this, then, is allowing the out of the box thinking to be truly out of the box! It should not be limited by how business must be done, or how business has always been done, but through a lens that looks at the opportunity, and responsibility, of business to be a genuine force for good.

At Food Lover's, our CEO has 11 leadership principles which form the basis of much of our leadership work. These clearly define a path for our newer managers as they set out the leadership philosophy and cultural identity of leadership expectations:

- Be bold
- Go big or go home
- Be patient – look, listen and learn
- Believe
- Do it with passion or not at all
- Be consistent and clear
- Relentlessly keep everyone aligned to your vision
- Be yourself
- Have fun
- When you get put in command, take charge
- Look for the good in your people (my favourite!)

*Figure 3.3: Leadership principles*

While the business has been a remarkable success, there is no question we have had our fair share of growing pains. Add to this the complexity of the socio-economic situation in Southern Africa, and we begin to see the challenges facing leadership... it is not for the faint-hearted!

To get back to one of our core philosophies – how we can make Food Lover's Market an amazing place to work for everyone – we have really focused on building a conscious leadership culture. With the speed of growth of the business, it is an area that was maybe overlooked, which is why we have placed an intense focus on building a leadership brand that underpins the overall culture we are trying to create. This is not an overnight process, however, and as Simon Sinek says, you don't create leaders by once-off leadership courses, but through everyday practice.

We also are not looking to simply get rid of any manager who maybe doesn't fit this mould. That would be wrong. We are looking to raise the self-awareness of these managers, give them the space to explore their relative strengths and weaknesses in relation to the expectations, and support their own personal development.

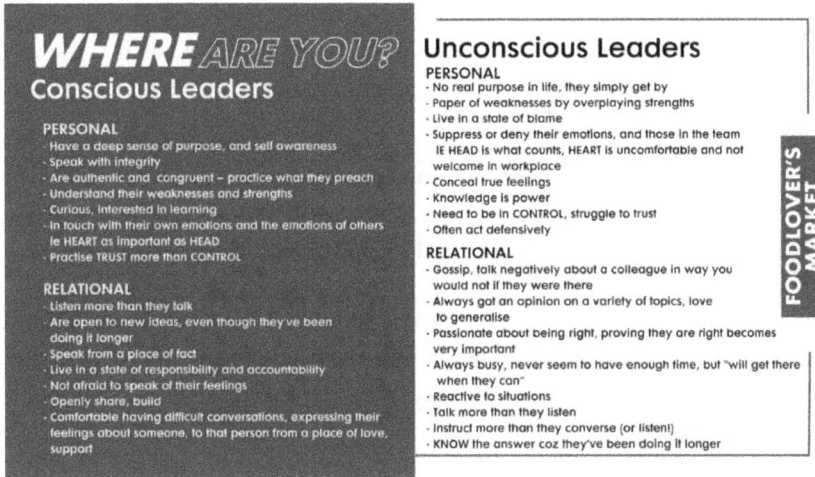

Figure 3.4: Conscious vs. Unconscious leaders

Like many other organisations, we have brought in colleague surveys to give our colleagues a voice, a specific colleague radio show to better communicate, and a WhatsApp line. We are placing more emphasis than ever on the role of the manager to develop more managers from the bottom up.

My personal favourite leadership principle, and one that has become the cornerstone of much of our work in HR, is: "Look for the good in your people." This includes the people who do not look like me, sound like me, or like the same things I do. We all have the ability to change people's lives for the better, but first we all have to look for the good in others.

Each person has a story to tell. We need to listen to their story. They also have a future to be shaped. We need to see how we can help shape it.

# Key Principles in the Journey to Being More Purpose-Led

Some aspects we have found hugely helpful include:

## Context Over Content

Anyone working in change in an organisation, whether the CEO, the HR director or others, needs to agree on the CONTEXT of the change first. Too often we rush into content. This may be what course needs to be delivered, what training is necessary, or which new people are required, however the context of the change needed is not discussed or is glossed over.

Context is essential. Lay out your true feelings, shine the torch of awareness, say what is in your heart, not just what is in your head. Two things may happen:

1.  You find that the organisation has a very different vision from your own, and is perhaps not at all interested in developing a "high purpose". It really is happy just being about profit! It may be disappointing, but you at least know where you stand.

2.  You find that the desire to develop a more purposeful organisation is stronger than you realised, and you can now all commit to developing and following a higher purpose, creating a culture of inclusivity and cementing those values.

I have often found that when talking context, I find many people, including executives, who have been thinking along the same lines – individuals who have been grappling with the same dilemmas in their personal lives, but feeling like they are not able to share this in the workplace.

By agreeing this context, colleagues can take their 'masks' off and express their true feelings. We create a safe space for people to share and to grow, and a foundation for a more purposeful culture to flourish.

## Honestly Evaluate Your Role in Society

The good, the bad and the ugly. I have spoken about this in length above. Don't hide anything. Take everything out the closet. Again, it is critical not to be accusatory or judgemental. All business has an impact on the environmental and society. What is yours?

## Your Values are Not Wall Decorations

Do not compromise! This is hugely challenging; there are always going to be instances, whether we like it or not, where someone makes a decision that you feel goes against the agreed values. Would it be great to say that there should be zero tolerance towards this? Of course it would! But this is not always realistic. It is imperative that the person or people driving the change do not become too distant from the people they are trying to change. While you may retain your moral high ground, you will lose your ability to influence them.

However, that is not to say to just let it go. Anybody can justify just about anything if they try hard enough. It is important to be careful of the stories we tell ourselves, and be alert to stories told to justify a particular decision.

We have had some seriously uncomfortable discussions in the business. Through all these, though, it has been crucial for all parties to honestly agree where our values have been compromised, work through the reasons why, and then put plans and interventions in place to ensure that this doesn't happen in the future.

For example, if you can't get rid of a manager who constantly treats his colleagues badly, but who turns a huge profit, as he (or she) is irreplaceable, then your options would be to provide intensive coaching to this person (short term approach) and/or to invest more heavily in developing managers for the future who can step in when needed (long-term approach).

## Unlearn What You Have Learnt

So many people act the way they do because it is the only way they know how. They are not only reluctant to change, but act aggressively towards it. That is why context is so important. By agreeing the context, change becomes inevitable.

It also takes a great deal of trust, as you are forging a new path and creating a new benchmark. Businesses such as those mentioned at the start of the chapter are pioneers in this. They are changing what is possible and re-writing what it means to be a business. For us in South Africa to genuinely become purpose-led, we need to uncondition ourselves from how business "should be". We are excellent at telling ourselves stories to make ourselves feel better, whether this be that we are "green" because of a few carbon reduction or carbon offset initiatives, or that we are deeply passionate about communities because of annual charitable days or even a charitable foundation. This instead of asking how our core business operations contribute to these trends in the first place, and what we can do to shift the business model to not simply do things "less badly", but ultimately be proactive in building a more wholesome, greener society THROUGH our core business, not in spite of it.

Again, it is not saying what should or should not be done. It is shining a light on the reality of the situation, making sure we let go of the stories we tell ourselves to make ourselves sleep better at night. It about being honest with ourselves and more authentic in the way we do business.

## Build a Strategy That Links to Your Purpose

It would be a complete waste of time to have a strategy that does not link to purpose. If purpose is about building a long-term sustainable business that benefits communities and societies for generations to come, then your strategy needs to reflect that. Short termism needs to be avoided.

While I understand that short term targets need to be met (this is inevitable), there must always be an eye on the long-term goal, or purpose. The conflicts that arise between short term targets and long-term goals need to be addressed and challenged. It is in addressing these conflicts that the organisation's culture will really establish itself.

## Build an Army of Activists

At the end of the day, while the CEO may be influential, there is only so much he or she can do. There may be hundreds (if not thousands) of individuals who are only too happy to take a lead in developing a more purposeful culture, no matter what their formal role, if you provide them with a platform for doing so.

The more conscious, trusting and committed the leadership, the more powerful the army. In effect, you need an army of lovers to create a culture in every department in every store, where the people on the shop floor become the guardians of the values.

An army of activists is fun. People are people – most do something in their spare time to support those in need, the sick, or the environment. Tap into this and let them build a tidal wave of positivity that sweeps through the business and makes it hard to go back to business as usual.

# Conclusion

While much of what I have spoken about are personal reflections, I am fortunate enough to work for a family business with a leadership that is committed to making change. As I have said before, we are not there yet; there is a long way to travel on this journey, with many more difficult discussions to be had, I am sure!

However, there is no doubting the need for this journey. For those who question the capacity, willingness, or even the role of business in creating change, I ask two questions: Do you think the world is in a healthy state? The answer is inevitably "No". The second question is, if you could, would you change it? Would you like a healthier, happier society? The answer is inevitably "Yes".

At the end of the day, a business is simply a collection of individuals. Nothing more, nothing less. If those individuals who comprise "the business" are brave enough to ask themselves hard questions, and committed enough to act on the answers, then change is inevitable.

If we can tap into the personal values of our people, help them to love themselves fully, shine their light, and be true to who they REALLY are, not who they think they should be or what their business card says they are, we can tap into a collective consciousness that can change the world.

Business has the potential to be a genuine force for good. It has a chance to be a catalyst to make this world a more equitable, just, greener and healthier place for all. Perhaps this is more of a responsibility than an opportunity.

This is not about judging other people or other businesses. It is not about competing to see who is the "best". For us at Food Lover's Market, it is about starting to take our own steps on this journey, unsure to be honest of where it will end, but confident that it will lead to us developing and fulfilling our own higher purpose. I have no doubt that we will make mistakes along the way, but I am also confident that by starting this journey, ideally alongside other businesses in South Africa, we will be able to contribute to a creating a future that we all want to be a part of.

In this beautiful, complex country, by developing and promoting a new way of doing business – a new contract, if you like, between business and employees and between business and our planet – we can start to repair some of the damage our past has caused and give meaning back to people. We can restore dignity, pride and a sense of belonging, and we can really help our country grow and develop into its true potential.

# Chapter 4

# Radical New Talent Management Strategies for a Radical New Workplace

**Selo Govender**

## The Age of the Open, Fluid Talent Economy

The dynamic new world of work sees a different type of agile employee emerge – one who is immune to the dynamic forces of change, willing to collaborate with diverse individuals, and able to apply judgment in increasingly complex situations. World Economic Forum data indicates that 54% of the global workforce will require significant upskilling and reskilling as technology continues to disrupt work.[1] These changes in the profile of the employee and workforce requires organisations to re-imagine their traditional talent and people practices.

Indeed, the most radical change to our talent strategies is described by Ravin Jesuthasan and John Boudreau in *Work without Jobs*, where they suggest that the way we have traditionally organised work and workers is now "obsolete".[2] A new work operating system is emerging, challenging our traditional talent strategies and mindsets. This new system deconstructs work into tasks and projects that may be assigned to employees, machines, robots and contingent workers in an open, fluid talent economy called a "talent marketplace". In this new talent economy, skills are the new currency and workers will no longer be identified or required to hold a specific job but rather to apply their skills and talents wherever the organisation may need them.

These shifts challenge the very foundations of traditional organisational development. Mindsets and behaviours of leaders and HR professionals are changing from jobs and organisational structure hierarchies to an agile, flexible task and project-orientated approach focusing on skills utilising different types of resources – human, machine, full-time or part-time employees or contractors.

---

1   World Economic Forum, 2020.
2   Jesuthasan & Boudreau, 2021.

41

Within this new paradigm the talent has more choice in terms of the types of work and projects they undertake, resulting in less hierarchical relationships and structures in organisations and more internal talent mobility. Organisations like PepsiCo, Unilever and Schneider Electric have adopted internal mobility and open talent marketplaces to enable employees to seamlessly trade their skills for the best matched opportunities. This is all being enabled by sophisticated AI technology that has taken the talent development world by storm.

A few questions regarding the new fluid talent economy are:

- What does this do to our traditional recruitment practices for traditional jobs?
- What happens to traditional talent and succession management?

With the right solutions and technology partnerships, AI can strengthen your recruiting, employer branding, hiring, performance and development and enable you to target and tailor outreach better and faster, making it more relevant and fruitful for both your candidates and your HR team.[3] Deeper insights into your audience help promote your company's culture and values in authentic, engaging ways, no matter who you're trying to reach.

With the advent of intelligent technology that is able to find and match people with the right skills to the appropriate opportunities, you will not need to follow traditional recruitment practices. Traditional talent acquisition (TA) processes have been challenged and changed by technology innovations that create digital candidate journeys and are changing candidate behaviours. Additionally, the audience for these solutions has expanded beyond external applicants to passive prospects, internal employees and flexi/gig workers. Talent technology and evolving organisational operating models require leaders to rethink how talent interacts with their organisation and how they design workflows.

Today's AI capabilities increase efficiency and can assess an applicant's fit based on potential instead of just past performance. The same is true for employee development and career pathing. Analytics can evaluate an employee's prior work experience and performance, then suggest optimal development opportunities and potential advancement paths.

## Traditional Talent and Succession Management is being "Turned on its Head"

According to the Bersin report, *The New World of Talent Mobility: Flexibility Rules*, "The pandemic has only increased the need to move the right people in the right role

---

3    Boudreau & Donner, 2021.

quickly and effectively. Data shows that organizations that quickly hire and redeploy needed talent are 4.4 times more likely to meet or exceed financial targets and 5.3 times more likely to provide meaningful work to the workforce". A focus on capabilities will help create deeper skills, bring people together, create mentoring, and leverage the expertise within organisations. In 2021 and beyond, capability development becomes a strategic business strategy for the future.[4]

Succession management, one of the core practices in talent management, is being challenged. Strategic and facilitated internal mobility is now seen as a core development strategy to build future capabilities. It is not so much to just identify talent in a hierarchy and about "replacement planning" anymore, but more so about providing meaningful, impactful development experiences through deliberate, planned movements. Most companies use succession models based on replacement planning. Nine-box grids and succession models used by many organisations in this century go back to World War I, when the army used replacement charts to show leaders who could take a soldier's place if they were shot in the trenches.[5]

The Covid pandemic in 2020/2021 and move to a new world of work has seen some interesting talent management developments emerge, with some organisations adopting a hybrid approach of traditional succession and talent management vs. agile. Traditional succession planning was "resuscitated" in the last year to de-risk organisations so that senior executives know exactly who is ready to take over if critical roles are impacted due to unforeseen circumstances like the pandemic, normal attrition, or retirement.

A succession management benchmarking report in 2021 revealed that succession planning is still a senior management imperative, focusing on executive roles, typically C-suite executives, and senior leaders one level below, however the talent leaders surveyed also indicated the intention to expand to other roles and skills.[6] The focus is also no longer on just roles, but critical skills and critical people or talent.

Executives often use organisational hierarchies and relationships to determine critical roles and when conducting succession planning. This tends to be based on proximity bias rather than an objective evaluation, however. In 2017, McKinsey shared that executives "assume incorrectly that the most critical roles are always within the 'top team' rather than three, or even four, layers below". Critical positions and people can be found throughout an organisation as opposed to just at the top. This has become evident during the pandemic and the move to remote and/or hybrid work models. Some positions demand a higher degree of responsibility, complexity and specific

---

4    Boudreau & Donner, 2021.
5    Bersin, 2021.
6    Barriere, Owens & Pobereskin, 2018.

skills based on the value the roles generate in the organisation, thus it has become critical to ensure that the best talent is allocated to these roles. Reallocating talent to the highest value initiatives in the organisation is seen as being as important as reallocating capital, thus CEOs and executives have to apply careful consideration when undertaking this exercise.[7]

While making sure that your best talent is allocated to the most critical roles, another key succession and talent management priority for executives and CEOs for the next five to 10 years is diversifying the leadership bench and achieving diversity goals. Women and people of minority groups are less likely to be represented among senior leaders at most organisations. A survey conducted by Gartner in 2017 revealed that only 19% of positions in the C-suite were held by women, despite the fact that women comprise almost 60% of the workforce. Racially and ethnically diverse employees also struggle to gain representation among senior leadership, accounting for only 13% of all senior leadership positions. Advancements with automation and technology are thus not the only priorities that have been accelerated due to the pandemic and new world of work. Having the best and most diverse pipeline of critical skills and leaders who are representative of the regions in which the business operates will set organisations up for success, not just from an equity perspective, but also from a diversity of thinking, innovation and value generation perspective.

A lack of visible diversity across leadership teams is a top challenge at many organisations across the world, where the demographics of the leadership team are not reflective of the broader employees, customers or populations as a whole. This gap is partly driven by unconscious bias within succession management practices. Many leaders have taken steps to address this problem through unconscious bias training, however insights from training often fail to be embedded and sustain behaviour change. To effectively combat bias in succession, executives and HR leaders should implement tactical interventions in key areas of the succession planning process to increase visibility of diverse talent and enable objective decision-making.[8]

Over half of the heads of diversity and inclusion (D&I) identified influencing succession planning efforts as a top priority in 2021 and beyond. To effectively mitigate bias and create more diverse leadership pipelines, HR and D&I leaders should help their talent management partners embed bias mitigation efforts across the talent life cycle. Implementing small nudges in existing succession management processes is a scalable and less resource-intensive solution to mitigate bias.

Organisational barriers such as unsupportive cultures, biased talent and business processes, and non-inclusive stakeholders are also more pernicious to the

---

7    Gartner, 2021.
8    Gartner, 2021.

advancement of underrepresented talent than "individual" barriers such as missing skills and behaviours among the underrepresented talent. Executive leaders must prioritise resources for identifying and addressing organisational barriers to advancement, such as unclear career paths and steps to advancement, a lack of sponsorship, limited exposure to senior leaders and a lack of mentors.[9]

To advance underrepresented talent, executive leaders must deliberately coach and guide leaders and managers to understand and alleviate the barriers and challenges experienced by underrepresented talent in the workplace. There must be a focused approach to build and enable growth-focused networks for underrepresented talent to help them with their performance, development and advancement. Specific collaboration efforts must be implemented with HR to redesign specific talent processes that create the most "opportunity for bias". Executives and HR should promote diversity by personalising targets for leaders/managers and their teams, and empower them to meet those targets. Inclusion must be constantly evaluated through employee surveys and ensure employee confidentiality to produce high-quality data. Organisation-wide equity can be improved by looking at the outcomes of diversity and inclusion initiatives throughout every stage of the employee life cycle, especially promotions, recruiting and performance management.[10]

## Democratising Talent Management in the New World of Work... The Need for Social Connection

Intelligent learner experience platform and talent marketplace technologies are supporting the development of the breadth and diversity of talent required in organisations, not only the top layers. These platforms help to *democratise talent management*, facilitating career development, unlocking skills and helping to future-proof workforces. This is done by utilising powerful AI engines, enabling enterprises to harness the hidden potential of talent throughout the organisation by matching people to internal career opportunities that are right for them, and provide mission-critical organisational agility, visibility and insights.[11]

A talent marketplace facilitates the internal gig economy and can transform how work gets done, but deploying it requires doing away with traditional organisational structures and ways of working. Talent marketplace platforms can also integrate Human Resources Information Systems (HRIS) and other enterprise system data. The platforms "learn" from participants, project- or workflow-owners, team managers and sometimes peer feedback, before, during and after the work engagement. This

---

9    Gartner, 2020.
10   Gartner, 2021.
11   Gloat, 2020.

learning then refines the participant and work assignment profiles, providing data to infer employee capabilities.[12]

Talent marketplaces also present opportunities in times of market turmoil or sudden organisational change by enabling companies to increase their number of projects and the speed with which they are deployed, thereby reducing the load on the talent acquisition process.

Organisations can use the internal talent marketplace to create or expand their internal gig economy as an alternative to layoffs, for example, organisations can give affected employees the option to join a project pool. Once in the project pool, employees work on temporary assignments where needed until they can either transition to a new full-time role in the organisation or leave it for another one. This model avoids the worst effects of sudden and widespread layoffs – poor publicity as large numbers of employees leave all at once, as well as lower productivity and disengagement amongst the remaining employees.

Whilst these advances with sophisticated technologies and Artificial Intelligence will help build agile organisations, the need for humanity and human connection has become more pronounced. In today's rapidly changing work environment, 'connector leaders' or managers are critical to helping organisations achieve long-term success.[13] Experts explain that the organisations that are most successful at developing their employees have focused on cultivating intentional connections where leaders connect employees to the right people and resources at the right time. Leaders who focus on enabling deliberate connections and networks are key to driving sustainable performance in today's new hybrid work environment and fluid talent economy. Some thought-provoking insights shared regarding the need for overall human connection indicate the following:

- *"Employees want to be seen as people, not just workers, where work is a subset of their lives, and not separate from it."*

- *"The connector manager boosts employee performance and more than increases the likelihood that an employee will be a high performer."*

- *"It's not about micromanaging employees' work, but rather building deeper connections and understanding what employees need to perform more sustainably in their work."*[14]

---

12    Gartner, 2020.
13    Roca & Wilde, 2019.
14    Roca & Wilde, 2019.

The Covid-19 pandemic and the age of continuous disruption has also shown us that organisations need to reimagine their performance management approaches. With the advent of the fluid talent economy, traditional performance management needs to be adapted to the new world of work of "tasks and projects" and the new profile of workers. Many organisations have adopted a continuous performance engagement approach which entails a culture of regular, honest and open discussions rather than the traditional review sessions held episodically once or twice a year. Employees are also encouraged to adopt a self-directed approach, taking accountability for their performance and development.

With agile teams working in a hybrid model, comprising a combination of face-to-face and remote work, they can connect more frequently on specific deliverables and projects that require focus. What is critical is that every individual understands their goals, their links to the business priorities, and delivers on the expectations in a purposeful, values-driven way. The pandemic and new world of work has demonstrated that continuous performance engagement is ultimately about mutual care, trust and respect through personal connection:

- As a leader I care and my team can trust me to ensure goal clarity, provide the right environment, resources and support.

- As an individual I care about my leader, my team and I can be trusted and empowered to deliver on expectations.

- As team members we care about each other and support the team and organisation to achieve our goals and ultimately our purpose.

- As an organisation we care about our people. We trust, respect and empower them to deliver on our ambition and purpose.

There is visible, shared accountability amongst all stakeholders in ensuring that the work outputs and expectations are clearly defined, understood and executed on. Leading organisations are also adopting cross-functional team performance approaches to support organisation-wide projects. These projects require cross functional skills, capabilities and resources to achieve success. To improve performance management for employees and make it truly employee-owned, these organisations are employing three key strategies:

- Place employees at the centre of performance management's design and prioritise components that provide utility for employees.

- Make employees the designers of performance management – leverage employee perspectives throughout the design process and engage employees as designers, not just consumers of performance management.

- Help employees direct their performance management through structured and adaptable guidance and tools – ensure that employees can tailor their performance management to deliver both what they want and what they need.[15]

Success for the new world of work is thus about increasing the utility of performance management by making it more seamless, business-driven, employee-owned and human-centred through deliberate human connection and collaboration. We need work cultures that embrace continuous performance engagement and feedback, which foster a forward-looking growth mindset through feedback that is in-the-moment, informal and frequent. This enables organisations to create a trusted environment in which employees feel empowered to take control of their own growth and development.

## Conclusion

Whilst we make these significant shifts to evolve our HR function using sophisticated talent technology solutions and artificial intelligence, now is the ideal time for forward-thinking HR leaders to develop innovative people practices and tools to strengthen relationships and improve connections between employees, leaders and teams. We need to integrate the best of both people and technology during this unprecedented period of disruption to support organisations with the necessary insights to build growth strategies in alignment with company goals by getting the right talent with the right skills in the right roles. That means being open to new ways of thinking and working, whether it be the deconstruction of work and doing away with traditional jobs and organisation design, or welcoming helpful technologies like the talent marketplace and continuous performance listening solutions. Our HR teams will thus also require reskilling. It will need more expertise in IT support, data analytics and deeper knowledge about teams and hands-on supervision. We did not have to go through massive changes in the past, however the pressure is now on, and it is coming from the operating level, which makes it much harder to cling to old talent practices.

---

15   Gartner, 2021.

Chapter 5

# People Development for the New World of Work

**Vanisha Balgobind**

*"I never teach my pupils; I only attempt to provide the conditions in which they can learn."* Albert Einstein

# Introduction

The new way of working has created the environment for new ways of learning to the shift from employer driven to employee driven, for employees to take ownership for their own development, anytime, anywhere. With the impact of Covid-19 on industries and workforces, the very nature of the new way of working and learning is disrupted, from remote working to virtually embracing working and training or development.[1] The opportunity to disrupt the world of work presents itself through digital enablement, innovation and growth that can transition the workforce to the benefit of businesses.[2]

In recent research by Schwartz, Hatfield, Jones and Anderson[3], the future of work can be defined as many forces of change affecting three connected dimensions within an organisation. This includes work (the 'what'), the workforce (the 'who') and the workplace (the 'where'). Work will be significantly augmented through analytics-based decision-making, human and robot interface as colleagues, as well as gamification to enhance the fun in employee engagement. The workforce provides the context in terms of skilling people through various talent networks, and talent development will extend beyond organisations to include the whole ecosystem. Finally, the workplace refers to the ability to create a place that fosters collaboration both locally and virtually to create seamless resources on demand.

---

1   Baker, 2021.
2   World Economic Forum, 2020.
3   Schwartz, Hatfield, Jones & Anderson, 2019.

The fast pace of technology adoption is expected to continue, and may accelerate in some areas. The adoption of cloud computing, big data and e-commerce remain high priorities for business leaders, following a trend established in previous years, however there has also been a significant rise in interest in robots and artificial intelligence.[4]

According to the *Future of Jobs Report* released by the World Economic Forum in 2020, automation, together with the Covid-19 recession, continue to create further disruption for workers. In addition to the current disruption from the pandemic-induced lockdowns and economic contraction, technological adoption by organisations will transform tasks, jobs and skills by 2025. Almost half (43%) of the businesses surveyed indicated that they are set to reduce their workforce due to technology integration, while 41% plan to expand their use of contractors for task-specialised work, and 34% plan to expand their workforce due to technology integration.

As we enter the post-pandemic era, the emergence of remote working and digital dexterity is becoming a key factor in the performance of employees. Apart from the focus shifting to developing the skills needed to work remotely, a virtual learning platform to increase opportunities for learning is vital for both organisations' people strategy and employees' learning opportunities.[5]

# Embracing the Future of Work

The future of work has already arrived for several organisations. Most (84%) employers are set to rapidly digitalise working processes, including a significant expansion of remote work, with the potential to move 44% of their workforce to operate remotely. To address concerns about productivity and well-being, about one-third of all employers expect to take steps to create a sense of community, connection and belonging among employees through digital tools, and to tackle the well-being challenges posed by the shift to remote work. Online learning and training are on the rise but look different for those in employment and those who are unemployed.[6]

There has been a four-fold increase in the number of individuals seeking out opportunities for learning online through their own initiatives, a five-fold increase in employer provision of online learning opportunities to their workers, and a nine-fold enrolment increase in learners accessing online learning through government programmes. Those in employment are placing a larger emphasis on personal development courses, which have seen an 88% growth rate, while those who are unemployed have placed greater emphasis on learning digital skills such as data analysis, computer science and information technology.

---

4    World Economic Forum, 2020.
5    Baker, 2021 & Gartner, 2019.
6    World Economic Forum, 2020.

Organisations, and more specifically HR executives, should focus on future of work strategies using a three-pronged approach, i.e., hiring new people with critical skills; retraining or upskilling current employees; and the ability to use technology to enhance business performance.[7]

Skills gaps will continue to be high as in-demand skills across jobs change in the next five years. The top skills and skill groups which employers see as rising in prominence include critical thinking, analysis and problem-solving, and skills in self-management such as active learning, resilience, stress tolerance and flexibility. On average, companies estimate that around 40% of workers will require reskilling of six months or less, and 94% of business leaders report that they expect employees to pick up new skills on the job, a sharp uptake from 65% in 2018.[8] According to Schwartz, Hatfield, Jones and Anderson[9], the jobs of the future that are already being seen in the working environment are becoming more machine-oriented and data-driven, which also provides context for the human interface and the changing work requirements that organisations continue to embrace in redefining these roles in terms of new capabilities, skills and practices.

Developing and enhancing human skills and capabilities through education, learning and meaningful work are key drivers of economic success, individual well-being and societal cohesion. As organisations continue to evolve and embrace the future model of work which encompasses technological, social and economic factors in shaping how individuals are developed to create not only job preservation but also economic and social growth.[10]

# The Learning Organisation

The future of organisations is not a fixed destination, but one that is evolving and adapting at the pace of both the maturity of employees and the business landscape. In ensuring that people are enabled to support the business strategy, leaders must embrace not only changes to jobs or roles, but also harness the ability of people to become agile, adaptable and reskilled. The ability to create a learning organisation that will reduce time to implementation and increase speed to competency for the benefit of the organisations. According to Senge[11], "learning organisations are those where people continually expand their capacity to create the results they truly desire, where new and expansive patterns of thinking are nurtured, where collective aspirations are set free, and where people are continually learning to see the whole

7    Gartner, 2019.
8    World Economic Forum, 2020.
9    Schwartz, Hatfield, Jones & Anderson, 2019.
10   Pawar, 2016.
11   Senge, 1990.

together". This will create the momentum to ensure that people have the capacity to learn at all levels of the organisation. Real learning at the heart of what is human and the ability to re-create ourselves, both as individuals and organisations will continue to evolve. Innovative learning organisations identify with five key components: systems thinking, personal mastery, mental models, building a shared vision, and team learning.

## The Employee Value Proposition as a Key Differentiator

In redefining the future of work and the multi-generational factors of the workforce, an organisation's holistic employee value proposition is a key enabler to ensure that the human capital strategy and its implementation is focused on the needs of the workforce in a differentiated way.

Minchington, in an article by Browne[12], defined an Employee Value Proposition (EVP) as a set of associations and offerings provided by an organisation in return for the skills, capabilities and experiences an employee brings to the organisation. It is an employee-centred approach that is aligned to existing, integrated workforce planning strategies as it has been informed by existing employees and the external target audience, in support of the employer brand. According to Pawar[13], the EVP is the equalisation of the rewards and benefits that are received by employees for their execution of their role and performance in the working environment.[14]

The value proposition should identify the unique and differentiated people policies, processes, practices and programs that demonstrate the organisation's commitment to employee growth, management development, ongoing employee recognition, community service, etc. It should ensure the key reasons that people will choose to commit themselves to an organisation, and is a methodology used by organisations to develop an EVP that ensures that present and future employees find the organisation to be brand attractive, engaging and a phenomenal place to work. Employee value propositions are imparted through an organisation's activities and practices, and bring out emotive benefits for present and future employees. These EVPs duplicate an image of organisations to its intended interest group and becoming These EVPs duplicate an image of organisations to its intended interest group and becoming a brand ambassador for the organisation".[15]

---

12    Browne, 2012.
13    Pawar, 2016.
14    Manyika, 2017.
15    Pawar, 2016.

## Smart Workforce

An article by Manyika[16] highlighted that organisations face gaps in skills they need in a more technology-enabled workplace, and can thus benefit from playing a more active role in education and training, including providing better information about needs to learners and the education and training ecosystem, and providing better learning opportunities.

Workers of the future will spend more time on activities that machines are less capable of, such as managing people, applying expertise, and communicating with others. They will spend less time on predictable physical activities and on collecting and processing data, where the automation of machines already exceeds human performance. The skills and capabilities needed will also shift, requiring more social and emotional skills and more advanced cognitive capabilities, such as logical reasoning and creativity.

Scaling and reimagining job retraining and workforce skills development that enables individuals to learn marketable new skills throughout their lifetimes will be a critical challenge. Midcareer retraining will become increasingly important as the skill mix needed for successful careers changes. Businesses can take a lead in some areas, including with on-the-job training and providing opportunities to workers to upgrade their skills.[17]

# Defining Capabilities

While different emerging skills are not necessarily new skills, they are increasingly in demand. New research[18] that explored 'employability skills' in internet job postings for the last four years shows that employers request communication skills above all others. It also found that the top ten employability skills, in order of employer emphasis, are communication skills, organisational skills, writing, planning, detail orientation, team work and/or collaboration, problem-solving, time management, research and computer/digital skills. For technicians and trade workers, employers still place emphasis on the specific technical skills required.

According to Torii[19], capabilities are the set of skills, behaviours and dispositions that allow an individual to convert their knowledge into meaningful action in a range of different settings.

---

16  Manyika, 2017.
17  Arora, 2020.
18  Torii & O'Connell, 2017.
19  Torii & O'Connell, 2017.

It cannot be emphasised enough that people can no longer rely only on technical skills and trade skills such as carpentry, mechanics, bricklaying, etc., i.e., they also need a set of transferable skills such as digital literacy, critical thinking and creativity.

## Accelerating Reskilling and Upskilling

The ecosystem of skilling comprises both learning and training programmes from a workforce development perspective to support the transition at speed and scale towards future competencies required in the workplace.

Organisations focus on the job placement of first-time entrants into the workplace or training for immediate needs, while the emphasis should also be on training for the future of work. According to research conducted by Accenture in 2018, new skills to be included in the digital environment include digital, technical and human skills, together with a growth mindset. This will encourage relationship building, self-awareness, problem solving and creativity, cultivating a growth mindset supported by understanding innovative technologies to build the future skills and workforce.[20]

In adapting workforce interventions that will move organisations towards transitioning the workforce and to empower employees to learn and to reskill, this provides opportunities for organisations to create new, innovative career paths and expand access to learning through lifelong learning, mentorship and peer learning in shaping the future of workforces.

According to research conducted by Price Waterhouse Coopers[21], the benefits of upskilling include:

- employee retention by investing in employees' learning and development;
- succession planning that provides employees with development and exposure in support of career progression;
- increased productivity; employee satisfaction which creates internal satisfaction and increased commitment;
- talent attraction; and
- creating a culture of learning.

---

20   International Labour Organisation, 2020.
21   Price Waterhouse Coopers, 2018.

# Lifelong Learning and Self-learning

Continuous learning has become the norm of today's rapidly changing work and life dynamics. Lifelong learning should be the cornerstone principle for education policies and the creation of learning societies should become an essential strategy for facilitating learning throughout life for individuals and societies.[22]

Lifelong learning is defined as an all-purposeful learning activity undertaken throughout life to improve knowledge, skills and competencies from a personal, social and employment-related perspective.

According to Arora[23], learning can take place in various forms:

- *Formal learning:* consists of learning that occurs within an organised and structured context such as formal education or internal company training. These may lead to formal recognition or certification based on assessments.

- *Non-formal learning:* learning that is embedded in planned activities that are not explicitly designated as learning, yet contain important learning elements such as vocational skills acquired at the workplace or on-the-job learning and exposure.

- *Informal learning:* learning that results from daily activities related to family, work or leisure. This is often referred to as experiential learning.

For learning to be impactful and value adding for employees or learners, it must be supported by:

- The personal development of empowering individuals:

- a thorough, extensive and continuous learning path creates well-groomed and nurtured individuals who are armed with the skill sets and capabilities to handle difficult scenarios and/or circumstances in their professional and personal arenas. The risk of uninformed decision-making is minimal, and the ability to bounce back in case of mistakes/faults is higher than usual. Empowering individuals with knowledge goes a long way to enhancing their living standards and lifestyles.

- Higher employability and growth:

- an increase in the knowledge levels due to any form of learning (formal or informal) is known to have raised the employability quotient and productivity levels of individuals. They are better equipped to manage and prioritise tasks due to enhanced exposure to various areas of expertise.

---

22  Arora, 2020.
23  Arora, 2020.

# The Role of Leadership and Mindsets

As Warren Bennis notably said:

> "...the process of becoming a leader is much the same as the process of becoming an integrated human being."[24]

Leaders wanting to transform their organisations must begin by transforming themselves, starting with their mindsets and the agility and adaption to lead transitioning organisations.[25]

To build and lead agile organisations, leaders must develop three critical sets of capabilities: firstly, they should adopt new personal mindsets and behaviours; secondly, they should learn to help teams work in new ways; and thirdly, they should learn how to build enterprise agility into the design and culture of the whole organisation.

Fundamental reactive-to-creative mindset shifts are critical to foster a culture of innovation, collaboration and value creation at the heart of agile organisations.

*Certainty to discovery* focuses on a mindset that underlies the way traditional organisations replicate the past and known best practices. This way of leading works best in a predictable environment in which leaders can foresee the future with high degrees of precision. Leaders are required to shift to a creative mindset of discovery, which is about playing to win, seeking diversity of thought, embracing risk, and fostering creative collision. Leaders must encourage innovation through continual experimentation, testing and learning. This does not mean innovation as one small activity within the business, while the rest focuses on execution, but rather building innovation into the core way of working and executing for leaders everywhere.

*Authority to partnership* speaks to a mindset where organisations are traditionally designed as siloed hierarchies based on a reactive mindset of authority. The relationship between leaders and teams is one of superior to subordinate.

As organisations design for collaboration, they employ networks of autonomous teams. This requires an underlying creative mindset of partnerships, of managing by agreement, and psychological trust and safety. Such organisations strive to tap into ideas, skills and strengths through freedom, trust and accountability, which requires peer-to-peer relationships based on mutual acceptance and respect. Leaders should develop relational expertise, create conditions for effective teamwork, build networks

---

24  Bennis, 1993.
25  De Smet, Lurie & St George, 2018.

and burst silos. Partnership requires not only trusting, listening, and collaborating, but also being prepared to own and influence less.

## Challenges Affecting People Development Post the Pandemic

Considering the impact of the pandemic, connectivity is becoming a new human right. Access to medical services, education, training and work opportunities increasingly depends on connectivity in the current world of work. A new type of inequality in the form of access to connectivity is widening the gap between those that have, and those that have not.

The pandemic has shown that it is disruptive, accelerating some trends that impact both short-term and long-term transformations, which puts pressure on adapting "traditional" employment contracts.

The International Labour Organisation[26] advocates for a human-centred approach to these transformations. As the world is moving towards a digital society, countries are urged to look at their skills needs and anticipate future skills and labour demand to create appropriate job opportunities though adequate infrastructure. Strengthening the link between digital skills and digital jobs is critical; many jobs are being fully or partially transformed into digital jobs, which enables the digital economy.[27]

The Covid pandemic continues to accelerate the pace of digital priorities in organisations from a people perspective, by optimising digital processes and using digital technology capabilities for recruiting, onboarding, workforce planning, reskilling of employees, people analytics, workplace well-being within a virtual environment, and the process of protecting and access to HR data.

---

26   The International Labour Organisation, 2020.
27   Torii & O'Connell, 2017.

# The Exxaro Story

## Our People, Our Heartbeat! Taking our People into the Future

**Our purpose is to "power better lives in Africa and beyond..."**

Exxaro aspires to be a multi-core business beyond coal, looking to renewable energy and other minerals. The forces that continue to shape its strategy include the impact of climate change within its communities and operations, energy transition with growth in disruptive technology within the energy sector, and the transition towards a low carbon economy with significant socio-economic implications for the business.[28]

Exxaro is one of the largest black-empowered diversified mining companies in South Africa. Exxaro's asset portfolio includes coal operations and investments in iron ore, residual pigment manufacturing and renewable (wind) energy (Cennergi). The organisation prides itself on being more than just a mining business, and strongly believes that empowering the local communities in which it operates and making a positive impact are central to its purpose.

---

28   Exxaro Resources, 2020.

The company's Sustainable Growth and Impact Strategy and it's five strategic objectives are to:

- transition at speed and scale;
- make its minerals and energy businesses thrive;
- empower people to create impact;
- become carbon neutral by 2050; and
- become a catalyst for economic development and environmental stewardship.

The company assumes and actively practices a balanced approach for sustainable growth and impact to ensure that a future is secured for every one of its stakeholders. Exxaro's purpose to 'Power Better Lives in Africa and Beyond' will be achieved by responsibly investing in resources that will improve and sustain life on the continent. In the last decade, Exxaro has established itself as an organisation that is respected by its peers for its innovation, ethics and integrity, and has been recognised as a leading performer in the FTSE Russel ESG Index. It employs approximately 7,000 permanent employees and 16,000 contractors across its mining operations.

The resources industry is regulated with a social context and impact, including environmental responsibilities; the safety and development of employees; and a focus on diversity, inclusivity, human rights and fairness, which goes beyond the financials of the business.

The company believes that its values have stood the test of time and remain relevant to support the implementation of the Sustainable Growth and Impact Strategy. They help the business to understand the difference between right and wrong, and ensure that its actions live up to its purpose to 'Power Better Lives in Africa and Beyond.'

Exxaro's values are:

- empowered to grow and contribute;
- teamwork
- honest responsibility; and
- committed to excellence.

Meaningful communication and transitioning of the organisation relating to strategic issues are driven through the connext2NEXT platform, which supports positive employee engagement within Exxaro. Through the connect2NEXT journey the organisation continues to enable a culture of being adaptable, empowered to take ownership and accountability, being open and connected through teamwork and collaboration, being responsible, and embracing the diversity of its strengths and abilities to enhance personal growth and performance.

The company's diversity and inclusion approach is a key strategic enabler and aims to create value from employees' diverse talent and mindsets. Diversity and inclusion is a key component in ensuring that Exxaro achieves its Sustainable Growth and Impact strategic objectives by enabling an inclusive culture that empowers its people, irrespective of gender, race and background, to successfully contribute to delivering on the organisation's purpose. The implementation of the Diversity and Inclusion Strategy is managed through the diversity and inclusion framework, which adopts a phased approach aimed at increasing alignment and promoting a diverse and inclusive culture that delivers business and stakeholder value. The key objectives of the diversity and inclusion framework are:

- promoting an aspirational vision for the Exxaro brand on both national and international platforms through strategic partnerships in terms of the promotion of diversity and inclusion to stakeholders;

- promoting a diverse and inclusive workforce through actions, practices, leadership and culture by enhancing employees' experiences through a compelling EVP to become the "employer of choice";

- achieving regulatory compliance targets by 2022 and 50% of women on management levels by 2025; and

- being a catalyst in accelerating the company's focus to enhance its business purpose and stakeholder value creation.

The Diversity and Inclusion Strategy seeks to support Exxaro's employee value proposition, which is based on the co-creation of an innovative and agile work environment, which offers value-adding people solutions while affording employees a fulfilling work experience with growth and development.

Exxaro's human capital aspirations continue to reinvent the workforce in achieving sustainable agility, capabilities, people practices and resiliency to enable its growth strategy. The world of work continues to create disruptions and enables changes for the future of work to be revisited more often, to ensure that the human capital strategic direction is aligned with the ever-changing context of the business.

The key aspirations that shape the people strategy are focused on creating an employee experience that speaks to the human-centric brand of Exxaro's employees, communities and societies at large. The quality and competence of the company's people is key to the strategy, and the dependency on robust talent management and people development practices is key to the success of the brand, performance and employee offering.

# Exxaro's People Strategy

Exxaro's people strategy is a journey that has evolved over many years with the establishment of the organisation in 2006. As it continues to evolve its strategy to remain relevant to its shareholders, employees and communities, the alignment of the people strategy continues to transition over time. With the focus in the last few years being on the Fourth Industrial Revolution and how this impacts the organisation from a people perspective, this has created not only momentum, but also enabled the organisation to become innovative in solving problems using digital solutions and rethinking the workforce skills and capabilities mix, speed and agility, in a predominately mining environment where there are very inherent cultures and behaviours that have been in place for decades.

Human resources is therefore more than a function; it is a distinctive capability that is embedded in every part of the organisation. It shapes the transitioning and aspirations of the organisation over the years. With the Covid pandemic amongst us as a nation and globally, the acceleration of the digital priorities within the people space has become more relevant and pressing; it has forced Exxaro to embrace the employee experience with many renewed or new lenses such as:

- the continuation of automating the recruitment and onboarding experience;

- personalising the HR offering and at the same time managing the protection of employee data;

- increasing the focus on employee well-being enhanced by a virtual work environment; and accelerating the reskilling and upskilling the current workforce.

With the focus of this chapter being on people development, it necessitates a conversation on the impact and offering of people development that creates an environment that is built on the premise of people being enabled, developed and empowered to manage their careers, and the ability to add value to reach their business' outcomes and ultimately financial performance. As part of the people development framework, the organisation continues to address capability gaps, poor learner engagement, loss of production hours, as well as the improvement of the employee value proposition.

To capture the essence of the people strategy and its alignment to the business strategy, the holistic framework of Exxaro's aspirations are indicated in the diagram below. It is all encompassing and not only drives the organisation's strategic intent, but it also ensures that the shift in culture, behaviours, people analytics and the ability to skill and reskill the workforce with relevant capabilities are top of mind.

Our aspiration continues to be to:

*"Co-create an innovative and agile environment, offering value-added solutions and an exciting employee xxperience through growth and enablement."*

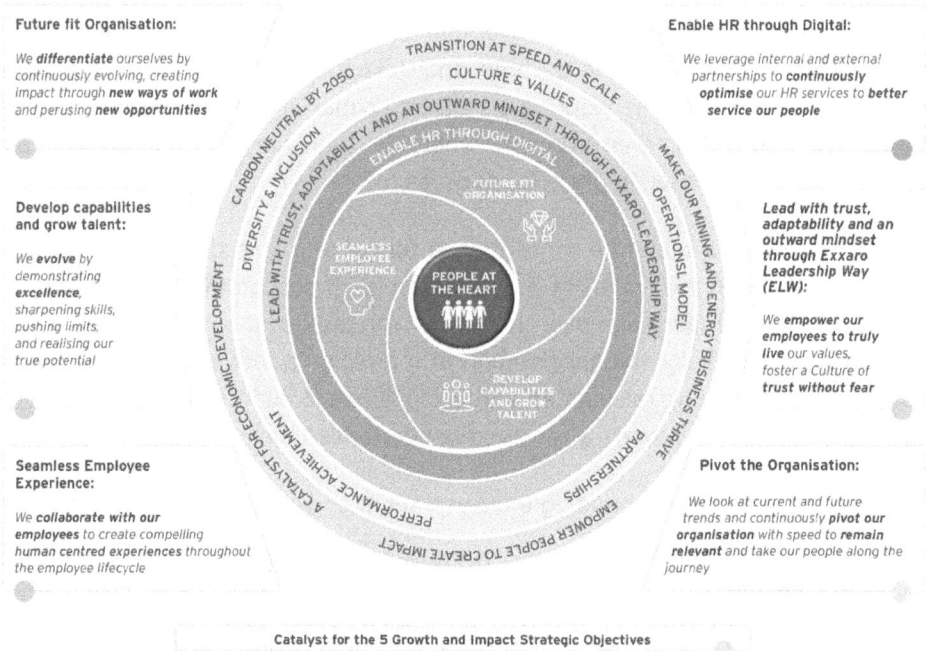

Catalyst for the 5 Growth and Impact Strategic Objectives

**Figure 7.1: Exxaro's people strategy**[29]

Exxaro's priorities will be fundamentally underlined by governance, compliance and processes to enable a robust and ongoing change readiness.

The contributing areas to the success of the company's people strategy as depicted above lies in the following:

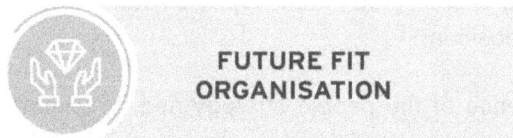

## FUTURE FIT ORGANISATION

Boost flexibility to cater for the multi-generational workforce by introducing new ways of work, fluid roles, multiple employment models, and remuneration and benefits to

---

29   Copyright: Exxaro 2021.

recognise and reward employees in line with the company's future of work thinking. This is enabled and supported by Objectives and Key Results (OKRs), Exxaro's new measurement approach against set objectives to ensure progress and impact on the business strategy.

This also enabled Exxaro to revise the current competencies and redefine the new competencies required for the organisation, which positions it to deliver towards the new strategy and capabilities required.

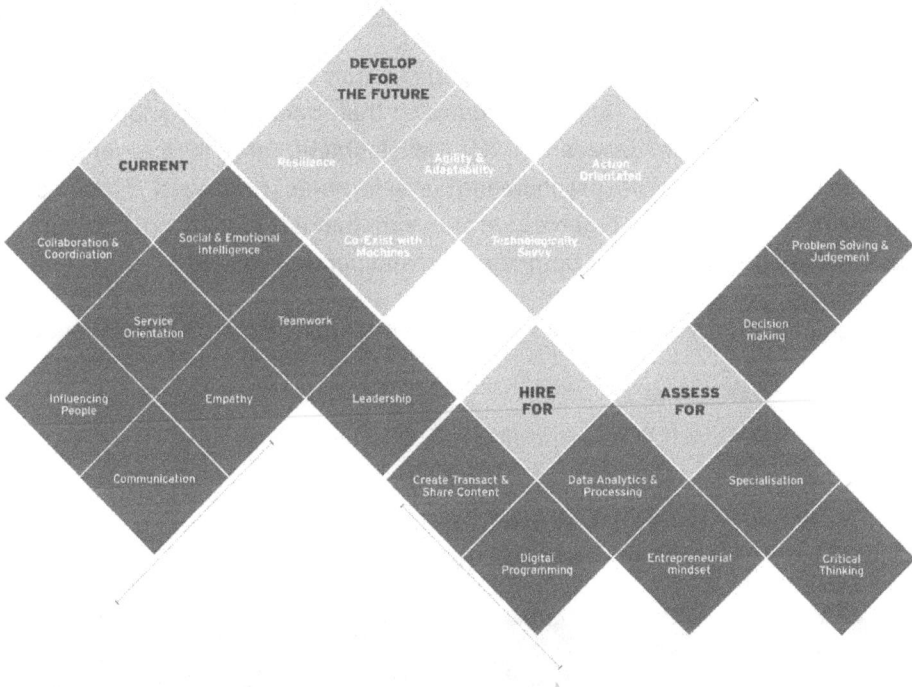

*Figure 7.2: Exxaro's organisational competencies matrix*

**ENABLE HR THROUGH DIGITAL**

Through the digital journey and a fit-for-purpose Hr operating model, the enhancement of HR services and access to data by utilising digital analytics, automation, or applied intelligence solutions, allows the HR function to shift their attention to strategic tasks and decision-making rather than wastage of time and effort on transactional accuracy.

To enhance Exxaro's HR efficiency and employee experience smart workforce offerings of digital interview tools, onboarding, sourcing solutions, a virtual learning platform for employees and their communities were introduced.

**DEVELOP
CAPABILITIES AND
GROW TRUST**

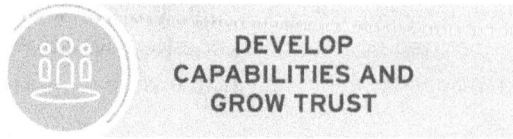

Exxaro also continues to partner and collaborate with its ecosystem to provide an internal blueprint of capabilities that clearly defines what work should be done and by whom. This will inform how the organisation is structured, how its people collaborate, and what roles and skills are needed in the current and future business.

Exxaro's talent aspiration is built on the fundamentals of ensuring that the company co-creates an innovative, agile environment that offers value-added solutions and exciting employee experiences for development, growth and enablement opportunities. The use of psychometric assessments (Industrial Psychological Services (IPS)) enables the organisation to ensure that it is identifying strengths and gaps to develop employees for both retention and personal growth.

The diagram below depicts the focus areas that underpins Exxaro's talent framework.

**Ensures the
right skills at the right time
at the right place**

| Strategic Workforce Planning | Talent Acquisition | IPS | Learning | Talent Pipeline | Talent Planning |

| COMPLIANCE | PROCESSES | SKILL & CAPABILITY | DIGITISATION |

LIVING OUR VALUES

*Figure 7.3: Exxaro's talent framework*

In ensuring Exxaro becomes future ready to deliver towards its strategy, the development of the business competencies model and enabling its journey towards the smart workforce speaks to enabling employees to ensure that their development is focused and intentional to create the right skills and capabilities.

The learning vision is to provide engaging learning opportunities that create ownership of employee development and enhance knowledge retention.

As shown in the diagram below, Exxaro's learning landscape focuses and continues to focus on:

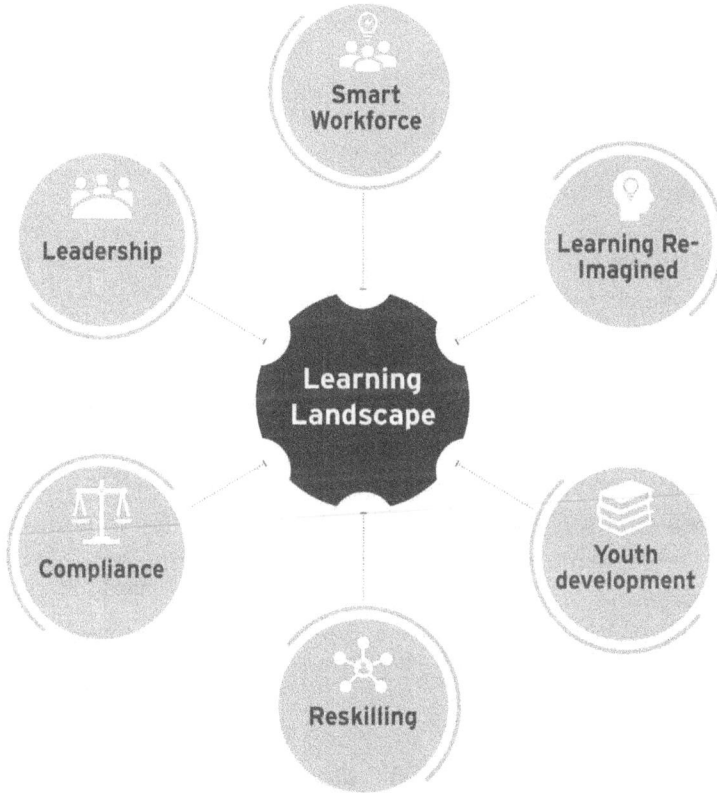

Figure 7.4: Exxaro's learning landscape

Exxaro continues to upskill its internal employees' capabilities and talent by introducing artisan programmes, adult education training, compliance inductions, and smart workforce enabled catalogues such as design thinking and biomimicry that are effective and efficient to ensure the minimal number of production hours are lost. The company's fully equipped and accredited training centres provide training, while the virtual learning platform, MyNexxt, provides employees with an array of learning and development opportunities

As a mining organisation, the communities around the mines are a key stakeholder; the company knows that the local socio-economic factors are vital to the success of all employees and their families.

Exxaro has therefore introduced, in partnership with its communities, enterprise and supplier development programmes, as well as a virtual platform for e-learning and mentoring. This will enable the communities to become employable by growing their skills and becoming equipped to secure jobs. There can be no denying that if small, medium and micro enterprises (SMMEs) grow and sustain themselves, they have massive potential to contribute positively to economic growth and reduce the triple crisis of unemployment, poverty and inequality.

## LEAD WITH TRUST, ADAPTABILITY AND AN OUTWARD MINDSET THROUGH EXXARO LEADERSHIP WAY

Best practice shows that leadership is crucial in shaping the future of Exxaro, thus the Exxaro Leadership Way (ELW) initiative, which brings the company's leadership culture and values together to achieve its purpose, forms the basis of the new leadership way for the success of the strategy. The ELW has three key pillars which enables leadership development, namely leadership philosophy and enabling leadership mindsets and behaviours. To ensure that Exxaro's leaders are enabled to lead during ongoing transitioning, focused programmes enable continuous leadership development and mentorship at various levels in the organisation. Leadership development, which is done in a phased approach, is initiated by leadership assessments to identify the gaps for development, purpose-driven leadership conversations, mentor and mentee relationships, and ongoing coaching and feedback.

Exxaro's Leadership Way (ELW) continues to be implemented, driving the connect2NEXT (C2N) journey through the organisation's values, culture and behaviours with support from the leadership. Exhibiting ethical and inclusive behaviours is required to lead and support teams as the organisation transitions to the new way of work and responds to the Diversity and Inclusion Strategy.

## SEAMLESS EMPLOYEE EXPERIENCE

Exxaro continues to exceed employees' expectations by continuously providing an improved employee value proposition across employees' lifecycles in the short- and long-term. A great employee experience is bolstered by access to meaningful information and engagement throughout the talent lifecycle. This also positions the employer brand from an internal as well as an external perspective to become the

Employer of Choice in the mining industry.

**PEOPLE
AT THE HEART**

Exxaro's employees will always remain central to the business; its motto is: "Our employees are our heartbeat." The company continuously reviews and transforms the employee brand to achieve differentiation in the market by being open and connected and leveraging partnerships to realise the strategy. Exxaro continues developing an inspirational legacy through pivoting the organisation with speed and agility to remain relevant in the new world of work. A transformed organisation represents diversity, equity and inclusion; celebrating differences; and recognising strengths.

# Conclusion

By no means is this how, what and where people development for the future of work will end up. The times are moving with such speed and if organisations do not adapt, they certainly will need to rethink their business models. Yet again, as we move towards the new world of work, our focus as HR professionals is, and will continue to be, to define our employee offerings to cater for individualised offerings for multiple generations that will exist within the workforce at any given time. In addition, we are required to charter our way through the pandemic towards the new normal, consistently reshaping the workforce through resilience and adaptability. This creates both challenges and opportunities, but most of all, it requires CEOs and HR executives to revise their people strategies to create sustainable multi-generational workforces for the future that are robust enough to transition during the good and the tough times. The dynamics of remote working or a hybrid workforce will also force us to review our people development strategic intent and the implementation thereof. The focus for people development will potentially move from not only technical capabilities, but it should also include space to ensure that employees are emotionally and mentally equipped to face the challenges of the new world of work.

# Chapter 6

# Reinventing Remuneration, Benefits and Recognition for the New Reality

**Dr Mark Bussin & Daniela Christos**

## Introduction

We knew that one day we would be working in a virtual reality. We did not know, however, that "one day" would actually be the next day.

Before the Covid-19 pandemic struck, organisations were focused on their people. Certain remuneration trends cropped up continuously, which mostly related to building employee trust so that they would remain loyal to the organisation. Retention methods stole a large portion of the organisational budget as did building security for employees. However, subsequent to the emergence of the "new" workplace, have we actually regressed? To answer this question, we will look at trends from 100 years ago to determine what the basic remuneration practices were all about. We will progress to more modern remuneration practices and discuss the almost overnight change that Covid-19 forced upon remuneration, including the after-effects of Covid-19 leading to a workplace that is no longer a "place". Further trends emerging from the pandemic will be addressed. Finally, we consider what the future holds for Total Reward, which is broader than just remuneration and includes benefits, performance management, succession, talent management and recognition, to assess whether the past has any bearing on where we are now and whether we can use it to inform our future remuneration decisions.

## 100 Year Old Remuneration Trends

What did remuneration look like 100 years ago? Is it possible that we have come full circle? Can past remuneration practices offer any advice to the future of remuneration? After doing some research, the following topics popped up as trends from century old remuneration practices:

- Piece work
- Day work
- Week work
- Sales incentives
- Bonuses for quantity of production
- Bonuses for quality of production
- Bonuses for reliable attendance
- Profit sharing
- Stock participation plans
- Pension plans
- Mutual benefit associations
- Remuneration for salespeople
- Remuneration for office workers
- Executive and foreman incentives[1]

The abovementioned key words have little emphasis on topics such as job security, fairness, employee well-being, work-life balance and all the key topics of pre-Covid-19 organisations, although admittedly, 100 years ago there was less empathy and we have moved to a more human-centric approach. Instead, the focus tended to be on forms of gig assignments, paying over short-term periods rather than focusing on the long-term, incentivising for quality and quantity, and ignoring values such as loyalty to, and tenure in, the organisation. This is in strong contrast to the pre-Covid-19 organisation that focused on developing and nurturing long-standing relationships with employees in the organisation.

However, the "modern organisation" with its people-focused principles and practices changed drastically as Covid-19 hit the world in early 2020 and paralysed most countries and organisations. Organisations were completely redesigned, despite all the research, training and interventions they had invested in.

# Organisational Changes Resulting from Covid-19

Physical distance is one of the largest implications for organisational design.[2] With lockdowns, employees have been forced to work from their own premises. A vast number of organisations have chosen to remain virtual or have opted for more flexible

---

1    Bloomfield, 1923.
2    Foss, 2020.

work, such as a half week office attendance schedule. Not only have employees had to move to a virtual workspace, but those who cannot work virtually (such as waitrons in restaurants and service-related workers) have had to search for jobs inside the virtual workspace. This means that there is less of a demand for physical labour and more of a demand for cognitive labour.

The psychological contract has also been adapted as the shift from a physical to a virtual workplace means that leadership has been forced to place trust in employees. Employees are now less likely to be micro-managed as they need to prove their input in terms of the final product they produce. The final product thus acts as proof of their work, rather than the time spent in the office. This has resulted in performance-dependent remuneration.

As a result of the focus on outcome rather than input, combined with the increasing number of retrenchments and salary cuts, it is no wonder that organisations are beginning to shift toward using contractual workers who are paid per project or outcome. Does this ring a bell at all? We refer here to the remuneration trends of the prior century when organisations valued an outcomes-based approach over retention.

The largest implication of Covid-19 is that it brought about a 'work from anywhere' mentality, highlighting that 'work is no longer a place.'

# Work from Anywhere

Prior to the pandemic, people rarely questioned why they had to be at work a certain time and were required to stay until a certain time. It was a common occurrence to expect trouble if one arrived at work late or left early, but much less common to get into trouble for staying late. That begs the question: why is it necessary to wake up, say, an hour earlier to spend that hour in traffic to get to work, and then spend another hour in traffic getting home? Surely we would be more productive if we didn't lose two hours of our day to traffic? Why go sit at a desk that's too low for you and a chair that is uncomfortable for eight hours or more of your day? Why not work where you receive the most comfort or where you feel your productivity will be heightened? What about those colleagues who scream across the workplace to each other or talk overly loudly on the phone all day long, interfering with your concentration?

Now that people have experienced the benefits of working from home, it's not surprising that many are reluctant to go back to the office. It is also not surprising that organisations are increasingly adopting a flexible approach. Essentially, prior to Covid-19, we all worked according to one work structure, but this structure did not work for all of us. Although Covid-19 caused a lot of devastation, the one positive outcome is that it showed organisations how to gain the most productivity from their employees. In fact, Gallup has consistently found that remote work and flexible work schedules largely influence an employee's decision to accept or refuse a job offer.[3] Employees are now beginning to oppose the traditional work structure and policies that have ruled their working lives for so many decades.

Not only does a physical workplace work against employees' energy and motivation, but it also limits their access to a healthy lifestyle and imposes on their work-life balance and their ability to provide the utmost care for their loved ones. Thus, according to the unanimous voice of the public and summed up by Satya Nadella, CEO of Microsoft, "Work is no longer a place you go. Work is about making things happen where you are and having the experience you need to get things done available on every device, wherever".[4]

# Further Covid-19 Trends

Over and above the shift to a virtual workplace with more flexible work schedules, the following trends have been exposed:

1.  For most organisations, 2020 was about staying in business, preventing job losses, taking pay cuts, and benchmarking with institutional investors as to their views on STI (short-term incentive) and LTI (long-term incentive) targets. The general theme was "no in-flight changes" to any variable pay metrics.

2.  2021 has ushered in a feeling of "more of the same" and "2020 take 2". It has led to employee anxiety and the onus is on leadership to show compassion. Retrenchments and job losses continue, pay cuts have stopped, and the government has had a slight shift towards livelihoods on par with lives (there was previously a very strong leaning towards lives ahead of livelihoods). World Federation of Advertisers (WFA) policies and procedures are now in place and STI and LTI targets have been recalibrated for the "new normal".

3.  The total remuneration philosophy has remained mostly intact with no sweeping changes. 21st Century advises that there should be an update of policies for relevance in today's environment. The most common updates required are mostly on the variable pay, flatter structures, broader bands, wider pay scales and a revamp of performance management. Performance management revamps include –nuking inputs and activities and replacing them with outputs, outcomes and impact.

---

3   Uerbach, 2018.

4   Goss, P. (2015). Microsoft CEO: Work is no longer a place you go to. Retrieved from: https://www. techradar.com/news/world-of-tech/microsoft-ceo-work-is-no-longer-a-place-you-go-to-1308609

4.   While base pay cuts happen in cases of alleviating retrenchment, a minority of organisations are giving employees a once-off allowance to cover the additional cost of using their own data when working from home. For the most part, these have remained as is.

5.   Most organisations have revisited their STIs, metrics, quanta and scheme rules. For example, organisations have the right to revisit targets if the assumptions that were made differ by more than 20%.

6.   Share incentives has been an area of overhaul, especially for shares that are under water. Where organisations have had say 10 years of stellar results, and now through no fault of their own the top executives are not "in the money", retention arrangements are being made.

7.   Other trends on variable pay relate to banking of STIs and LTIs or conversion to share-based payments with longer vesting periods for past performance before Covid-19; revision of target setting to adjust to new strategies during Covid-19; increased usage of environment, social and governance (ESG) targets in light of a re-setting of business priorities; and a deliberate focus away from shareholderism to stakeholderism.

8.   In a recent Just Capital survey, the top 100 American companies surveyed had increased their Executive median pay by 18%. This was way ahead of lower level worker increases, which was more closely aligned with inflation at 4.2%. The wage gap, which we refer to as the vertical pay gap, is increasing globally, with no sign of it being arrested. Studies such as those conducted by Green and Zhou in 2019 have found that pay inequality is associated with decreased employee morale and productivity, and ultimately, organisational performance.[5] The concept of fairness determines employees' effort to assist organisations in reaching their goals. If remuneration is not perceived as fair among employees, they are less likely to support or remain at an organisation, and will direct their efforts toward assisting organisational goal achievement at an organisation where they feel they are treated fairly. For this reason, organisations have received increasing pressure to reconsider their remuneration policies. Focus has been placed on closing the wage inequality gap, but with such a large gap, companies need to rethink their remuneration strategies on a large scale. Organisations are increasingly disclosing their wage gap in their integrated reports, which demonstrates a commitment to track it and try to close it.

---

5    Green & Zhou, 2019.

The horizontal pay gap – the pay gap between jobs on the same level doing similar work, is of equal concern. That gap in South Africa is around 15%, and only by constant transparency and reporting will we stand a chance of closing it.

9. Remuneration committees are being compelled to address diversity and inclusion – not only at executive level, but also at management level. Companies are routinely setting diversity targets and conducting gender/race pay equity audits. They are also moving from meeting the JSE listing requirement of diversity statistics at Board level to actively targeting Board representation through inclusion. This speaks to the previous motivation of organisations to accommodate their employees' feelings of fair treatment. The topic of diversity in the workforce is also applicable to generational diversity, where different generations have different reward preferences. Generation Z employees, who comprise about 36% of the workforce globally, have introduced a requirement for individualised rewards, and expect to be rewarded according to their preferences. This has caused organisations to rethink their rewards strategies in the face of diversity challenges.

10. The inclusion of ESG measures in corporate scorecards, STIs and LTIs is a growing trend that has been accelerated by the move to stakeholderism and the effects of the Covid-19 pandemic.

11. In a recent worldwide study by GECN (Global Governance and Executive Compensation Group) of ESG measures in incentives, Social Metrics are the most common measure. Around 61% of the companies surveyed were implementing Social Metrics, followed by Customer (37%), Governance (32%), Environmental and Climate (25%) and Community (10%). In the Social category, employee engagement, diversity, equity and inclusion (DEI), and health and safety are the most widely implemented. Within the customer category, customer satisfaction is the most common.[6]

12. The new way of working is an important trend that is causing a major change amongst companies and their workforces. Many directors view virtual Board meetings as just as effective as in-person meetings. The lack of non-verbal communication is stated as the highest-ranked challenge of virtual meetings, but even in this less optimal environment, most directors believe that they have been able to perform their work effectively.

13. Virtual Board meetings are here to stay. Based on their experiences over the last year, large majorities of directors expect to see virtual Board and committee meetings in the future. They also view virtual Board engagement as a useful tool

---

6    21st Century, 2021.

to enhance Board effectiveness. Companies are allowing employees (who can) to work remotely and are realising that the contingent workforce can be replaced by virtual full-time equivalents who are more integrated and aligned to the company culture and vision. This is having an interesting impact on salary benchmarking globally. Multinationals are taking the cost of living and purchasing power parity of various countries into account when setting global pay.

14. Performance management has to be adapted for remote working conditions and is moving from inputs and outputs to outputs and outcomes. Employees are being empowered to act as leaders and are given more autonomy and purpose. The methods and speed of communication are being adapted for the virtual environment.

15. Agile work teams are quickly established to capitalise on opportunities and then disbanded just as quickly once the project is complete. New opportunities and career paths need to be developed to adapt to the changing environment of work, so re-training and re-skilling of employees has become part of the new employee value proposition as companies transform into learning and development centres. Organisations face challenges rewarding individuals without causing internal conflict and feelings of unfairness as some are awarded more than others. Agile team rewards bring about challenges such as these, and may rather demotivate employees and negatively affect their performance. Thus, agile team remuneration trends point to challenges in the reward system. We have learnt that to overcome this, team rewards must be paid on top of fair base pay. You can expect to see a growth of team-based pay.

16. Another major trend is employee wellness and engagement. Approximately one quarter of South African employees are taking antidepressants and report anxiety and financial insecurity as being part of their lives. Most organisations are reviewing their employee value proposition – with a huge emphasis on employee wellness – whether it is an outsourced tailor-made programme or an in-house designed programme. Companies are including employee wellness measures in their ESG implementations, prioritising employee engagement, employee retention and employee health.

17. The new social contract and the business purpose of preserving human life and livelihoods are significant challenges, but if executives step up by walking the talk with employees and stakeholders, it will go a long way to addressing the current social and environmental problems that arise during times of crisis.

18. With the workplace moving to a virtual space, organisations now have the opportunity to access talent anywhere in the world, without imposing relocation

challenges on these individuals. This means that talent has the opportunity to work in any country they wish, without needing to acquire a work visa, having to undergo the experience of culture shock (feelings of disorientation that expatriates or foreigners undergo when having to live or work in another country with an alien culture and way of living), or undergoing familial challenges arising from the need to work elsewhere. Yet with the elimination of the obstacles that prevent talent from being able to work internationally, organisations now not only have to compete nationally, but internationally, too. In this instance, organisations are re-examining their remuneration practices to compete internationally.

19. The World Economic Forum predicted that by 2030, over one billion people would need to be reskilled to keep up with the demands of technological advances. The Covid-19 pandemic has accelerated this need insurmountably, meaning that organisations have had to cultivate an agile workforce that is prepared for this drastic change. This has resulted in the need for upskilling and reskilling, however these come with remuneration implications. Skill-based pay systems will increase as organisations will hone in much more carefully on what skills they are prepared to pay for.

As we can see, the remuneration world has faced many challenges and changes as a result of Covid-19. All these changes imply that we need to adapt and change in accordance. So, what does the future have in store?

## Changing with Change

In this section, we emphasise changing with change. Organisations need to build a home for reward; remuneration committees and remunerating executives needs to be discussed; and employees now need to take accountability for their jobs. These are discussed below and depict what the future has in store for the world of remuneration.

# Remuneration Committees and Remunerating Executives

As the business world feels the effects of the Covid-19 pandemic and takes steps to adapt, remuneration committees are asking how they should approach their executives' remuneration during the evolving landscape. Why is it so important for Boards and remuneration committees to address this issue?

Firstly, South Africa is one of the most unequal societies in the world, with the world's largest Gini co-efficient – a measure of inequality between the "haves and have-nots". Secondly, business purpose is moving quickly from "making profits for shareholders" towards a "new social contract – a commitment to collaboration that addresses shared social and environmental problems". This involves the move from 'shareholderism' to 'stakeholderism', in other words, a move from capitalism towards prioritising the protection and quality of life. Thirdly, governance has been catapulted into the limelight under the banner of ESG, with a fresh look at ESG measures that address the 'reset' that society is demanding. These themes have resulted in the following top seven remuneration committee and executive remuneration occurrences around the world, both in developed and developing economies:

- Increasing mandates of remuneration committees.
- Reducing the wage gap or increasing the median pay of workers.
- Addressing gender/race/ethnicity diversity and inclusion.
- Inclusion of ESG measures in STIs and LTIs.
- Evolving performance management for a less contingent and greater virtual workforce.
- Employee wellness and engagement.
- The design of new pay systems for new profile leaders.

Remuneration committees' mandates have been challenged by the wider stakeholder (for example institutional investors, regulators, shareholders), and internally, to become more inclusive and farther reaching in their oversight. Remuneration committee charters are extending their original mandates from all aspects of executive compensation, disclosure and shareholder engagement to include broad-based human capital strategies; human capital management (e.g. retention, talent management, diversity, pay equity, gender and ethnic gap, recruiting practices, performance management, workforce management, employee engagement and employment value proposition); talent management policies, programmes and processes, including training and development, promotions, termination provisions, and others; succession planning; and internal disclosures.

The wage gap or pay ratio (measures of pay between the CEO or top earners and the bottom earners or median of all employee salaries) has become a growing issue worldwide. The alternative remedies that are being considered around the world include some of the following: legislated compensation caps; governance structures; percentage of wage bill spent on executives; executive pay limits as a portion of net income; five year moving average pay gap targets; executive pay freezes or variable pay deferments (largely driven by Covid-19); and profit sharing across all staff. Remuneration committees are responding to this by adopting strategies that address the growing wage gap, not only to arrest it, but also to try to reduce it over time. The wage gap in South Africa is currently worst in the extractive industry, where the CEOs earn 41.3 times the median of all other staff at the 50th percentile, as shown below:

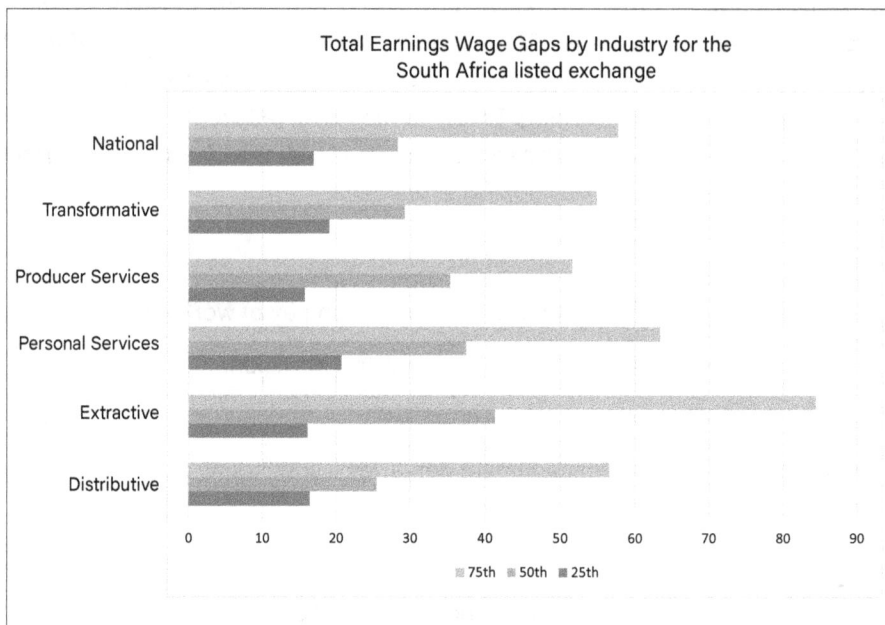

*Figure 1: South African Total Earnings Wage Gaps*
Source: 21st Century RewardOnline[7]

Remuneration committees are being compelled to address diversity and inclusion – not only at the executive level, but also at the management level. Companies are routinely setting diversity targets and conducting gender/race pay equity audits, and are moving from meeting the JSE listing requirement of diversity statistics at Board level to actively targeting Board representation through inclusion. Currently, non-executive Boards are made up of approximately 50% White, 40% Black, 5% Coloured and 5% Indian members. Gender diversity is split into approximately 67% male and 33% female, but this is worse in the extractive industry with only 28% female members.

The inclusion of ESG measures (the shift to non-financial measures) in corporate scorecards has become a growing trend that has been accelerated by the move to stakeholderism and the effects of the Covid-19 pandemic. Typical measures include the following:

- Social: fatalities, injuries, illnesses, exposure to harmful substances, workplace policies, gender balance, diversity and inclusion, employee engagement, employee voluntary turnover, training and development, behaviours, ethics, values and culture.

---

7    21st Century, 2021.

- Environment: greenhouse gas (GHG) emissions (South Africa is the 14th largest emitter in the world), non-renewable energy, renewable energy, environmental incidents, air quality, land management, water and wastewater management, waste and hazardous materials management and sustainability measures.

- Customer: customer satisfaction, customer net promoter score (CNPS), customer complaints, customer resolutions, product quality and product safety.

- Community: community incidents, community complaints and community investments.

- Governance: governance at the Board level, governance at the executive level, risk management, compliance, behaviours, ethics, values and culture.

There is a worldwide move to increase the inclusion of intangible assets in a company valuation. For this reason, ESG measures are becoming a growing part of executive incentive key performance indicators (KPIs). In South Africa, ESG measures make up between 10% and 30% of short-term incentive measures and 10% to 20% of long-term incentive measures. If ESG measures in incentives are warranted, then management and the compensation committee will want to consider emerging best practices in design:

- Select one to three goals that are consistent with the company's purpose, reflect business priorities and culture, and resonate with plan participants; in other words, don't overcomplicate or dilute the focus of the plan.

- Weight measures in a meaningful way (most companies currently weight such measures at approximately 20%).

- Set clear goals for each measure.

- Determine whether to incorporate measures in short- and/ or long-term incentives, considering the time horizon of the journey as well as the challenge in setting goals.

- Craft the narrative for communication materials to investors, employees and other constituencies to test the consistency and credibility of the message before decisions are made.

Leaders require new leadership profiles for the new way of work. These include dealing with constant change and uncertainty; evaluating and taking prudent risks; embracing a decentralised environment with remote working; creating a learning and development environment (as opposed to traditional management); empowering employees and creating a culture of trust; and embracing company purpose and a vision of long-term value creation and sustainability.

The pay system needs to be customised so that it meets the needs of the changing environment and executive profile. Crucial elements of the new pay system design need to include an emphasis on the risk reward ratio (variable pay mix and pay/performance link); finding the leading indicators in the business; a renewed focus on recognition; increased use of team-based incentives; increased use of discretion in incentives within governance guidelines; lengthening and increasing long-term incentive components; and increasing employee choice of benefits and customisation.

The collaboration between a new social contract and the business purpose of preserving human life and livelihoods is a challenge. If executives step up to this challenge by walking the talk with employees and stakeholders, it will go a long way to addressing shared social and environmental problems that arise during times of crisis.

The above-mentioned points allow for insight into to the world of remuneration committees and executive committees. Now it is important to consider the role of the employee in the new world of remuneration.

# Owning your Space

Now that work has become far more contractual in nature, employees are expected to make themselves look attractive so they are hired by organisations. This means that the greater their knowledge, experience and 'hard' skills, the more enticing it will be for an organisation to use their services. There are other such factors that determine whether an employee owns their own job. These are expounded upon below, with the expectations of how organisations should assist employees in the process.

# Organisational Imperatives

Actively seek out recognition opportunities: Let your high potentials know they are being noticed. I would wager that the leading reason for employees getting stuck is that they do not recognise their own potential. Many of these employees, although they possibly don't have a proven track record, may be exhibiting the appropriate competencies to you. These competencies need to be encouraged and resulting actions celebrated by letting them know the strengths that you see in them.

Empower employees: There is little doubt that employees looking for success emulate their superiors to some extent, so ensure that you live the values that you would like to see embraced. That said, it is imperative to empower employees to build their own successes. Set the bar at a reasonable height, allow employees to achieve some wins before inching the bar up, and realise that making mistakes is part of any growth journey.

Have career conversations: For many years we have been running culture surveys, and "career pathing" always features as a top driver of employee engagement. In our experience, the number one lever in getting employees to full advocacy and company alignment is co-designing a career path aligned to their competencies.

Embrace feedback: Allowing ideas to formulate in employees' minds and encouraging avenues for them to be expressed means that organisations need to be able to embrace diverse thinking. This is challenging with a top down "my way or the highway" approach to managing a business. By being receptive to feedback that may be different to your own perspective, you are encouraging employees to think like an owner and challenge the status quo. If you are brave enough to do this, you will be surprised at how much "richer" an outcome can be.

Have agile decision-making methods: Agility in decision-making is one of the greatest differentiators in an owner-run business. In my view, one of the finest value propositions of working in our organisation is that *everyone* has direct access to the leadership team. There is no greater reward than seeing one of your ideas get rolled out with the full support of the executive team. The more layers there are between idea and execution, the more unlikely it is that the environment will be primed for the owner mindset.

Build a performance-based reward model: The benefit of linking remuneration to performance outcomes is that to a certain extent it allows ambitious employees to be the masters of their own financial destiny. Even those employees not driven by money will recognise the importance of this differentiation. We have found that when an organisation doesn't link pay with performance, the effect is an organisation-wide decrease in performance levels and an increased risk of talent looking elsewhere for opportunities.

Address fair pay for gig workers: Gig workers are not covered by company benefits such as medical aid or retirement plans. This means that their pay has to be fair in order for them to live life on a par with their peers and afford them the financial access to the health, safety, food needs and educational needs of their children so they may be able to live a quality life. We should not forget that they are also responsible for additional costs such as training. All gig workers should receive equal pay for equal work, equivalent to the going market rate for that particular trade, but should also be compensated according to the external factors that they do not receive from full-time employment at an organisation. These individuals must be financially recognised for their risk taken and their outcomes produced, and should also be respected as professionals.

Build trust among employees: With the largescale downsizing that came with Covid-19, employees who have remained at the organisation may be left with trust issues as they have seen what the organisation is capable of doing and feel that their jobs are no longer secure. In such cases, it is important to be entirely transparent. When employees are taken by surprise, the after-effects are amplified. Communicating with facts is an effective way to help employees understand what is going on and why. Allow them to air their questions and provide them with psychological support. This demonstrates that you are truly concerned about their welfare and are committed to concretising the relationship.

## Conclusion

In this chapter, we focused on remuneration, benefits and recognition of the new reality. Beginning with a discussion on remuneration 100 years ago, before moving to a discussion on a more modern approach that focuses on the employee as an individual being, the chapter went on to focus on the new way of work brought upon by Covid-19. The chapter highlighted the effects of a workplace that is no longer a place, and considered what the future of remuneration holds in store. Thus, it is evident that we have almost come full circle. The remuneration practices that were previously used, such as a focus on "piece work" or "week work", replicates the current situation. The focus on "outcome" rather than input is a century old practice that seems to be returning to the remuneration world. It seems that the psychological contract has changed so much that employees no longer rely on employers for job security, but rely on themselves to make themselves employable.

# Chapter 7

# Multiple Perspectives on a Possible New IR/ER Dispensation for the Post Covid-19 World of Work

## 7.1 Informal Workers and Flexible Organisation Seizing the Covid Moment*

**Prof Edward Webster**

## Introduction

The picture of unions in Africa is bleak; they are weak, fragmented and largely in the formal economy. Only about 5% of employees are unionised, and where unions do exist, they are mainly in the public sector, although there have been some innovative responses in various sectors in recent times. Often these responses are the result of support from global unions such as UNI-Global, the International Transport Federation (ITF), and Building Workers International.

The situation worsened with the surprise arrival of Covid-19, which has been devastating for the livelihoods of working people. The high number of informal workers in sub-Saharan Africa, about 80%, has made the impact of Covid-19 especially harsh. A street trader, for instance, could no longer make an income. Covid-19 has revealed the weaknesses, and in some cases non-existence, of social protection systems in Africa.

So what has been the impact of Covid-19 on workers organising in Africa? Does the pandemic and responses to it present further weakening or an opportunity for the revival of labour organising?

---

* This article was first published in the South African Labour Bulletin on March 8, 2021.

Many people answer this question in a pessimistic way, arguing that Covid-19 and new technology is replacing labour, i.e. workers will be displaced by machines.

Constant technological innovation has always driven capitalism, beginning with the introduction of the steam engine two centuries ago, through to the current digitisation of the economy.

I want to approach this topic differently. Africa needs to advance technologically, but it does not necessarily have to go through the same stages as the advanced industrial world did. For example, Nigeria has 150 million smart phone users and only 200000 fixed line phones. Instead of first having fixed lines then going digital, it has leap-frogged into the digital age. Access to the internet is uneven in Africa and development has been irregular. Side by side with the introduction of advanced digital technology, there is also the use of pre-colonial tools such as the zamazama in the mining sector.

We need to look at the changing world of work from an African perspective. This article makes three points. Firstly, it outlines the nature of the labour market in Africa; secondly, it suggests that workers are organising but not always into traditional trade unions; and finally, it suggests five ways in which Covid-19 has opened new opportunities for worker organising.

# The African Labour Market

In Africa, the industrial working class is the minority of wage earners. The labour market is divided into 'classes of labour', in other words, there are people who sell their labour either directly in a wage labour market, or indirectly through a product market. In this way they support themselves and their families. Categories like workers, peasants, employed and self-employed merge. Working people earn a living through wage labour and make a living through various livelihood activities. They combine employment and unemployment. In shantytowns, people are sometimes unemployed and sometimes work in wage labour in small workshops or doing service work.

It is possible to identify five urban 'classes of labour', as the diagram and explanation below show.

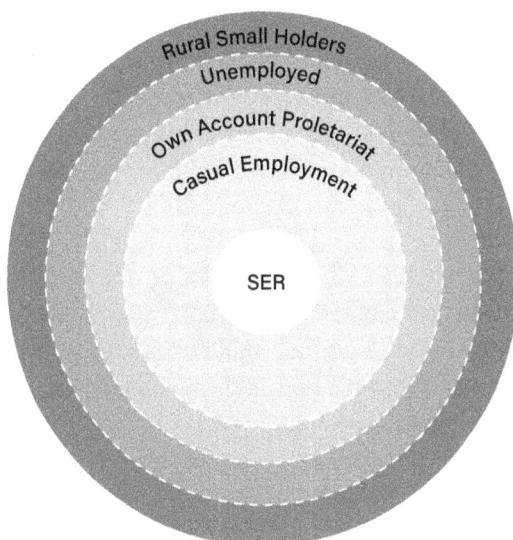

*Figure 8.1.1: Fluid Classes of Labour*

With the exception of South Africa, in Africa a minority of workers are in formal wage employment or in Standard Employment Relationships (SER), often in the public sector. These jobs have some security through an employment contract, a regular wage, social protection in the form of benefits, and some form of workplace representation. The ILO calls this "decent work".

The majority in the cities do casual paid wage work, either temporary or part-time, sometimes paid in kind, and often employed by a third party such as an employment agency or labour broker. This includes dependent contractors – people like Uber drivers and other gig economy workers.

Gig workers are so-called independent contractors who do short-term work and often depend on one organisation for work. This is not traditional wage employment but has some features of wage employment because they depend on the owners of, for example, Uber.

There are also 'own account' or self-employed workers. These workers are involved in informal survival activities such as street traders, waste pickers, and small businesses making clothes or selling goods and services, often employing family members. These 'self-employed proletarians' engage in complex employment relationships, for example, workers

at bus terminals in Dar es Salaam cover many occupations such as callers, supervisors, agents, loaders, sweepers, vendors and money-changers (often women who sell small change to the conductor for a fee). There is also the 'pigga setti' or seat-warmers (the bus will not leave until it's full), and side-mirror menders.

Then there are the unemployed with few or no unemployment benefits. They survive in households where they share economic resources or engage in various survivalist activities. They are part of an informal security regime. Finally, there are peasants or smallholders based in agriculture, using mostly family labour. They are often dependent on remittances from household members who move between towns and the countryside.

This uncertainty about what class these workers belong to raises difficult questions for union organisers. Who is a worker? Is a person who owns one minibus and drives it themselves a worker? If they own two minibuses and hire a person to drive the second one, what are they? If they own 200 minibuses, what are they? Is a street trader a worker or an entrepreneur?

Let's look at the responses of working people to this unclear nature of work in Africa.

# Informal Workers and Hybrid Organisation

The lack of clarity on who is a worker leads to hybrid (a combination) forms of organisation. Organisation combines the function of a trade union using collective bargaining with a cooperative or jointly owned, democratically run enterprise.

The diagram below shows this.

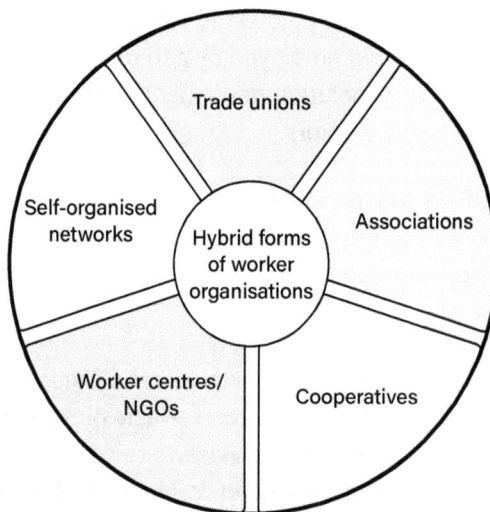

*Figure 8.1.2: Hybrid forms of worker organisations[1]*

---

1    Ludwig, Webster, Spooner & Masikane, 2021.

At the top of the diagram is the traditional trade union, but side by side are associations of workers such as the Kampala Operational Taxi Stages Association and the Kampala Metropolitan Boda-Boda Entrepreneurs. These associations represent casual wage workers and self-employed operators who want to become successful entrepreneurs.

There are also NGOs and labour support organisations such as the Casual Workers Advice Office in Johannesburg, which provides legal, educational and organisational support for precarious (insecure) workers attempting to organise. The new workers in the gig economy also organise themselves into WhatsApp groups that act like union support groups, sharing information on work, working conditions and also operating as stokvels (informal credit groups). Informal workers are thus developing hybrid organisations to address far wider needs than those of formally employed wage workers.

Traditional unions remain important as they provide support and access to institutions that have resources (institutional power) that can assist emerging organisations. This shows that the traditional form of a trade union can be organisationally flexible. For example, the Amalgamated Transport & General Workers Union (ATGWU) and the ITF give support to informal associations in Kampala, but in Johannesburg, unions and informal workers do not have an alliance. This makes it difficult for gig workers to build sustainable organisation.

Current trade union organisation cannot meet all the needs of informal workers and new workers in the digital economy, thus unions will need to transform and rediscover their power.

# New Opportunities for Worker Organising

Covid has brought opportunities to revitalise worker organising.

Firstly, new technology opens up the opportunity for digital organising. This does not replace face to face organising, however on-line organising can reach a larger number of people and hugely reduce costs. Yet the use of the internet is uneven in Africa. In South Africa, for example, only 56% of the population and 11% of households have access to the internet, but this is higher internet coverage than most countries in Africa. The graph below compares access to digital technologies in some countries in Africa.

Access to digital technologies

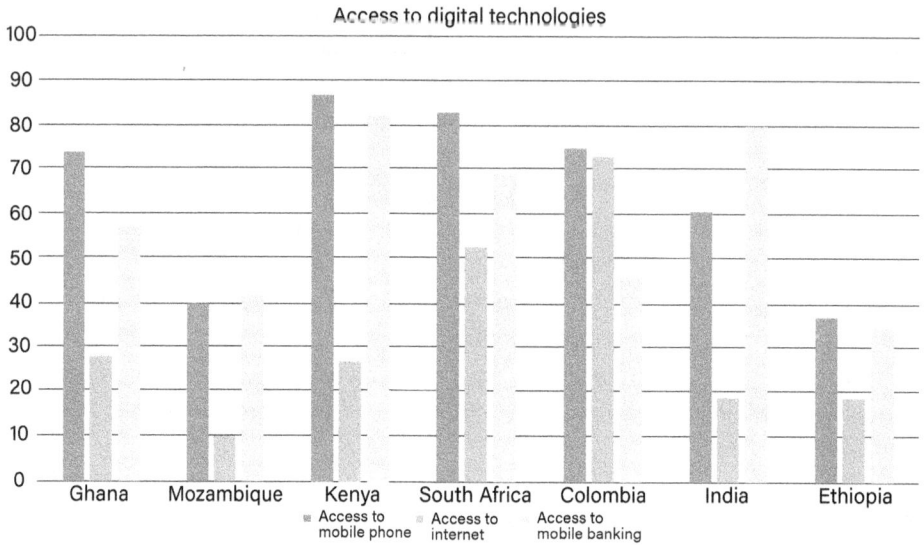

*Figure 8.1.3: Access to digital technologies[2]*

Secondly, Covid-19 has broadened workers' demands, highlighted the key role of the state in providing support, and shown that workers need to focus their demands on the state. Already the South African Government is discussing the possibility of a Universal Basic Income Grant, which until recently was dismissed as unrealistic

Thirdly, Covid has widened the definition of what we think of as labour. There has been a major shift in the recognition of the informal economy, for example in food production and distribution, in services, and in paid and unpaid care work. These 'essential workers' are often women, who need a strong voice and are ready to be organised.

Fourthly, the growth of working from home during Covid-19 opens up an opportunity for worker organising. Home workers are still workers and should be recognised as such, as the ILO did in 1996 in its Home-Work Convention. Trade unions must recruit them as members, and employers need to recognise home workers in their value chains and ensure they get a fair income. Governments should include home workers in national statistics on the labour force and give them a voice in decision-making.

Fifthly, the pandemic has provided an opportunity to increase worker participation and ownership of the workplace. One of South Africa's largest unions has developed a counter strategy to retrenchment, which consists of four pillars:

---

2    Castel-Branco, Mapukata & Webster, 2020.

- The establishment of Workplace Recovery Committees that must include managers, workers, unions, staff and non-union members.

- Work-sharing instead of retrenchment for up to 12 months.

- Reskilling of workers through training programmes.

- Wage concessions and debt to equity swap, i.e. what the company owes can be turned into worker shareholding through a debt equity swop (Employee Share Ownership Schemes).

## Conclusion

The future will be fought over and hotly debated.

On the one hand, labour displacement may increase rapidly and unemployment and inequality will deepen. On the other hand, a situation may unfold similar to post-war Europe, where there was a push for equality which led to important advances for workers and the unemployed in education, health and transport through the welfare state. The period also saw advances in human rights, beginning with the UN Declaration of Human Rights in 1948, and major changes in the rights of women.

But Africa is different in important ways from Europe and the global North, as it has higher levels of informal work, serious public debt, and under capacity of the state. This means that responses to Covid-19 will be different. In particular, the ability of the state to implement redistributive projects will be a challenge.

In spite of these difficulties, the current moment offers some important opportunities.

Already, some policy responses have been implemented. For example, the South African government agreed to a grant for workers in the informal economy and to the unemployed. The rollout was disappointing, but the idea only arose because of the Covid environment.

If we want to achieve a more equal society, labour must take advantage of this moment to introduce new ways of organising, and to rebuild the labour movement from below.

# 7.2 A new IR Dispensation in the New World of Work

## Prof Gideon du Plessis

~~~~~~~~~~~~~~~~~~~~~~~~~~~~~~~~~~~~~~~~~~~~~~~~~~~~~~~~~~

# Introduction

Industrial relations worldwide finds itself in a 'humpty dumpty-scenario' owing to the disruption caused by the Covid-19 pandemic. This discipline now needs to be put back together and the result may not look the same.[1]

Despite its negative consequences, the pandemic caused a much-needed reset to the adversarial industrial relations environment in South Africa. The pre-Covid-19 conflict in industrial relations was driven not only by union-employer actions, but also by tension and rivalry between trade unions.

When the disruption came, the positive impact the pandemic had on industrial relations was first experienced during the first half of 2020 in the National Economic Development and Labour Council (Nedlac). It was seen especially in the way in which labour, business, community and government representatives had to reach agreement on various measures to mitigate the impact of the pandemic on the lives and livelihoods of workers.[2]

## The Effect Covid-19 had on Collective Industrial Relations

Various aspects of industrial relations were impacted by Covid-19, but the most notable impact was on the dynamics around collective bargaining. The causes and effects of this disruption laid the foundation for a much-needed new IR dispensation.

## The Effect of Unemployment on a New Union-Employer Bargaining Model

*Cause*

The legacy of the pandemic for workplaces worldwide will undoubtedly be millions of jobs destroyed and radical changes in employment practices.

---

1    Kochan, 2021
2    Crous, 2021

When the pandemic struck, trade unions along with employers had to find creative solutions to make up for production and remuneration losses, as well as minimise job losses. To achieve this, employees and employers needed to make concessions, with employees either having to work more hours, which meant weekend and public holiday work, or fewer hours, resulting in a reduction in remuneration. Likewise, many senior managers and executives consented to a salary reductions or bonus freezes.

Strike action also dropped in 2020, giving momentum to the collective industrial relations reset, just when the so-called 'non-consensus-seeking wage negotiation style', which developed alongside the positional bargaining model, was the order of the day. The post-consensus negotiating style could be described as a poker-faced, positional style of bargaining that gives minimal leeway for consensus, and a win-lose compromise is the goal.[3]

The post-consensus style became prevalent in the industrial relations environment because entry-level workers who were part of the labour force before 1994 had become extremely frustrated by the fact that after more than two decades, their living conditions had not improved significantly. In parliament, politicians were also setting an example of being intolerant and inflexible in their demands; violent student and community protest actions were being justified; and – importantly – successes were being achieved in this way.

Negotiators and mediators battled to master the new style as it was developing in the mining sector post-Marikana, resulting in two five-month strikes by mining union Amcu in the platinum sector (2014) and at the mining house Sibanye-Stillwater (2018).

Although some elements are still present, the pandemic disrupted the non-consensus style. Major wage negotiations were deferred in 2020, for example, the three-year wage agreement signed by unions and the Steel and Engineering Industries Federation of Southern Africa (Seifsa) at the Metals and Engineering Industries Bargaining Council (MEIBC) in 2017, expired on June 30, 2020. The parties, which included the forceful metal workers union Numsa, agreed to extend it until June 30, 2021. Seifsa said the conclusion of the historic 'standstill agreement' was the first of its kind in traditional industry collective bargaining arrangements. According to Seifsa, "It marked a watershed moment when business and labour together recognised the devastating impact that the Covid-19 pandemic has had on companies and employees alike across the sector".[4]

---

3    Kahn, 2021
4    Mkentane, 2021

## *Effect*

The give-and-take approach that the pandemic forced upon the role-players in 2020 started to create the basis for a move towards the implementation of the win-win, interest-based employer-trade union bargaining model, away from the non-consensus and positional bargaining models.

The positional model, which had become the norm since the 1980s, means that unions submit an endless list of unrealistically high wage demands, and employers kick off with unrealistically low wage increase offers. This is followed by drawn-out power games.

The interest-based model is being used successfully in the USA and in northern European and Scandinavian countries, where the focus is on shared interests and finding mutual benefits.[5]

Here, an interest refers to a basic need – such as employees needing job security and employers needing to be sustainable – that is addressed, and objective measures are used to find collaborative solutions in the absence of enforcing a self-centred interest.

Progressive employers and unions have an important role to play in embracing this win-win model to stabilise industrial relations to rebuild the economy.

# Alternative Transition Towards a New Bargaining Model

Where the outdated positional model will live on, it should take a different form, because during the pandemic, employers and trade unions have not only experienced the pressure of the economic legacy of the pandemic, but have also been subjected to time pressures to conclude deferred negotiations as soon as possible. First, trade unions and employers learnt to deal with preliminary wage negotiation issues and the motivation and responses to demands in writing or by means of virtual meetings, which has become established practice in certain bargaining forums. The continuation of this practice will speed up negotiations and alleviate the logistical challenges associated with physical meetings.

Second, given the catastrophic effects of the pandemic, the list of union demands have become shorter, and the emphasis in many negotiations has shifted from above inflation increases to 'social wages', such as medical care, vaccination, occupational health and safety, skills development and retirement benefits. Third, employers

---

5    Fisher & Ury, 2011

started to link increases to a change in conditions of employment, or production output. Fourth, wage agreements are typically multi-year in nature and most have a three-year duration to increase long-term workplace stability and allow sufficient time to reach agreed production targets.

Progressive unions also started to shift their focus when consulting on retrenchment packages, and more emphasis has been placed on upskilling for 4IR and green jobs as part of severance packages, to ensure that retrenched workers are marketable in the new world of work.

All of this reflects a clear shift away from the pre-Covid-19 bargaining approach.

# Centralised Collective Bargaining under Pressure

Regardless of the bargaining model applied, centralised collective bargaining in various economic sectors will, over the next few years, shift increasingly to the workplace as individual employers want to take charge of the impact wage increases have on their sustainability, or where a bargaining council becomes dysfunctional.

As an example of employer preference to negotiate their own tailor-made agreement, employers in the coal and gold sectors withdrew the mandate of the Minerals Council South Africa (previously Chamber of Mines) to negotiate wage-related matters on their behalf at a centralised forum. This brought a nearly four-decade practice to an end.

This development poses a challenge to the capacity of trade unions, as negotiations would increasingly start to take place at various workplaces rather than at one central bargaining forum.

This development is not unique to South Africa; centralised collective bargaining has been under pressure in many countries since the 2008 financial crisis, with digitalisation indicating that the further informalisation of employment relations will lead to the marginalisation of collective bargaining in general.[6]

# Movement towards Pluralism

## Cause

Prior to the pandemic, inter-union rivalry was the order of the day. Behind it was membership growth, historic battles, self-interest and leadership egos. The result of this rivalry was that the majority union at a workplace would negotiate a threshold for

---

6    ILO, 2017

union recognition with the employer, and other unions would then either be excluded from the workplace or only enjoy limited organisational rights.

This so-called 'majoritarian principle' led to an escalation in inter-union conflict, and elements of this were part of the reason for the conflict at Lonmin Platinum Mine in 2012 that eventually resulted in the tragedy at Marikana.

A common response to the application of the majoritarian principle is the formation of coalitions between unions. The intention is to either form an opposition bloc against the majority trade union and to jointly reach the threshold for sufficient representation, or to establish majoritarian status of representivity to prevent another union from gaining any form of recognition. Underlying this is the 'winner takes all' principle, according to which a trade union or unions that have more than 50% support enjoy most of the power and benefits.

In practice, unions in a coalition retain their individual status while combining membership numbers for recognition and collective bargaining purposes.

Where a minority union fails to meet the threshold for workplace recognition and a coalition is not possible, the legal route is through Section 21 of the Labour Relations Act (LRA), which has been amended in such a way as to give a minority union, or minority unions acting jointly, an opportunity to show via an arbitration process that it/they has/have a meaningful interest in a workplace and should therefore enjoy recognition. This legal remedy is arduous and expensive to follow, and the process also creates tension between the minority and majority trade unions involved.

## *Effect*

The severe impact of the pandemic on job security will result in workers being less conscious of the colour of the union T-shirt they are wearing and reducing their support for union threshold initiatives, and rather unite them in their goal to retain employment.

Cooperation between rival unions also got a boost as leaders of the four major union federations showed signs of cooperation in their jointvCovid-19 campaigns to protect the lives and livelihoods of workers. On 7 October 2020, coinciding with World Day for Decent Work, a national one-day "strike" was called by Cosatu with support from its rival, the Federation of Unions of SA (Saftu), as well as the SA Federation of Trade Unions (Fedusa) and the National Council of Trade Unions (Nactu).

Less union rivalry may not be good news for those employers who have adopted a union divide-and-rule approach, because union cooperation will now strengthen their bargaining power. In most circumstances, however, union rivalry creates an atmosphere of labour tension that, amongst other things, affects productivity, and therefore it is likely that employers would prefer the benefit of labour peace rather than a strategic advantage over rival unions.

# Impact of Job Security and Loss of Income on Strike Action

## *Cause*

Strikes have become so much a part of negotiations between employees and employers in South Africa that we even have a so-called 'strike season' that extends from approximately May to September.

The question that now arises, given the loss of one season due to the pandemic in 2020, is will we see a change in the approach by trade unions in dealing with wage negotiation deadlocks?

While there is much debate about what a return to normality will entail, it appears that, at least for the foreseeable future, unions are going to have to reinvent themselves, because their bread and butter comes from strikes and the results they bring. As it is, most of the three million South Africans who had lost their jobs by mid-2021 due to the pandemic were blue-collar union members, and the majority of these will by now have given up their memberships because of an inability to pay their dues.[7]

Even prior to the pandemic a different reality started to set in amongst union members, namely that you can strike or negotiate yourself out of a job, as the awareness dawned that a union constituency tends to shrink from one year's negotiations to the next. Workers also realised that due to the no-work-no-pay principle that applies during strike action, you can strike yourself poorer, as an increase in employee debt challenges has shown.

## *Effect*

A push-back from workers against strike action will place a higher responsibility on union negotiators to approach wage negotiations with the aim to reach a negotiated settlement in the absence of strike action. This in turn will mean that workers' expectations will be tempered as job security will rank higher than a double-digit wage increase.

The strike season may be dampened further due to the Code of Practice on Collective Bargaining, Industrial Action and Picketing, issued by Nedlac in December 2018, which

---

7    Hinxman, 2021

was created to provide practical guidance on collective bargaining, the resolution of disputes of mutual interest, and resorting to industrial action.

While the impact of the pandemic on employment and the Code and its application may curb the overuse of strike action linked to wage negotiations, an increase in strike action may occur in response to retrenchments and non-payment of salaries. Workers and unions have learnt during the pandemic that alternative employment opportunities are scarce and litigation can end up in drawn-out and expensive legal processes, and that strike action, or a threat thereof, under these circumstances yield the best results.

Again, with cause and effect in mind, employers have shown that their response to a strike or union delaying tactics in response to the issuing of a section 189 notice is the offering of voluntary severance packages or an application for business rescue or voluntary liquidation. With the latter in mind, there need to be a stronger focus by unions on an employer's sustainability, as there is an increasing risk that employees will be out on the street without a retrenchment package when a company is pushed over the edge due to union strong-arm tactics.

## Post-Covid-19 and the Impact on Trade Unions: Responding to the New World of Work

The pandemic gave unions increased exposure to the new world of work. Suddenly unions had to conduct online training for shop stewards, negotiate through virtual mediums, and communicate with and mobilise workers through the internet and social media.

As the pandemic manages to fast-track 4IR, the survival of unions will depend on their approach to it. The logistical challenge for most unions will be capacity to dedicate staff to focus on 4IR matters, and to conduct research on the latest developments in the new world of work.

Likewise, unions require capacity to participate in and contribute to national and sector-related 4IR forums. At the same time, unions need to stay in touch with 4IR developments at individual workplaces to prevent a disconnect between the union and its members.

South African unions can learn from trade unions in Germany, where the mainstream unions are focusing on 4IR opportunities and not only discussing risks. These opportunities arise from new types of work that will result from technological innovation and digitalisation.

The guiding theme of German trade unions are 'Decent Work by Design.' This means that the employees and trade unions are involved in, and can co-determine, the definition of the objectives of artificial intelligence (AI) systems that influence working conditions and employment prospects, as well as further training and continuing education options. Designing binding processes for the timely involvement of unions is a crucial factor for the successful use of AI systems in the workplace. Furthermore, trade unions have a duty to ensure that the right to privacy is protected. In this case, even the possibility of surveillance by new technical systems is decisive.[8]

As much as unions need to position themselves to have control over the introduction of technology, they also need to be sensitive regarding how their actions and relationships with employers will influence automation. Poor labour relations can be a trigger for an employer, especially the manufacturing and mining sectors, to move toward automation to eliminate the impact industrial action can have on production and safety. This, at least, is something unions have total control over.

## Digital and Cyber Unions and their Links to Youth

While unions have been struggling to organise workers in a typical employment category, a bigger challenge is the organising of workers in the new jobs created through digitalisation in the era of 4IR.

The first so-called 4IR union was the YouTubers Union established in 2018, which focuses on YouTube content creators. The YouTubers Union occasionally uses the support of the influential German metalworkers' union, IG Metall, when they need the platform of a traditional union, especially to apply pressure on European governments.

There are, however, major developments in the US regarding the creation of cyber or digital trade unions focusing on platform workers and those in the gig economy. Examples are the US-based Podcaster Union, the Internet Creators Guild, and the American Influencers Council, all of which were specifically created to support and protect gig workers.

Digital unions mainly use social media to communicate with their members and to apply pressure on employers during campaigns for better remuneration and working conditions.

Given their ageing membership base and their representivity of just over 20% of South African workers, trade unions will have to reposition and modernise themselves to attract millennials and gen-Zers as members. These generations will be more interested in belonging to cyber or digital unions with whom they can interact via

---

8    Hoffman, 2019

social media and the internet. Traditional IR services will not be in great demand; rather, helping to fund further studies and negotiating benefits related to achieving a work-life balance will attract these generations.

Furthermore, unions are struggling to be proactive in their approach to dealing with the current and pending impact of climate change on employment. Unions have been in denial about the impact of climate change; they have commissioned research and talked the talk, but in terms of concrete proactive work that reckons with the impact of climate change, not much has happened.[9] This is something that is of interest to gen-Z and is another reason why unions need to mobilise this generation to champion the cause and increase the relevance of unions in this debate.

# Rendering an Individual Service

Another advantage the pandemic brought for trade unions was that, in the absence of collective bargaining that was deferred, lockdown regulations taught them how to deal with increasing individual member issues and queries.

In view of the rise in flexible employment practices, the impact of technology on the new world of work, the break-up of conglomerates into smaller companies, and collective bargaining slowly diminishing, unions will have to develop an individual member service model.

The rendering of an individual service will also open a new area for union growth which is already showing potential, and which has to be harnessed at management level. This is the level just above the traditional trade union membership level, which falls outside collective bargaining structures. These are workers who are promoted to that level who retained their union membership, while members of management and professionals are feeling increasingly vulnerable and are experiencing the need to be protected by a trade union.

# Conclusion

The Marikana tragedy and the great recession of 2008 substantially altered the South African industrial relations landscape. The disruption of industrial relations by Covid-19 and 4IR will be far more radical, with a mix of negative and positive consequences.

The preferred post-Covid-19 industrial relations dispensation still has to go through unstable phases, which means that labour unrest will not disappear overnight. However, ongoing social dialogue between industrial relations role-players at the workplace level and industry forums, as well as between social partners at Nedlac,

---

9    Benya, 2021

remains the key to stable labour relations. As Winston Churchill remarked: "To jaw-jaw is always better than to war-war."[10]

However, time to achieve a turnaround in industrial relations is limited, because rising levels of frustration of the unemployed, especially the youth, follow closely on the heels of labour unrest.

---

10  Churchill, n.d.

# 7.3 Is it Time for a New IR Dispensation in the New World of Work?

## Johan Botes

~~~~~~~~~~~~~~~~~~~~~~~~~~~~~~~~~~~~~~~~~~~~~~~~~~~~~~~~~~~~~~~~~~~~~~~~~

*"Forget normal... since the pandemic, everything is up for re-examination."*
Prof Margaret Heffernan, University of Bath

*"COVID has caused the world to adapt to a new way of working and some people believe it may be hard, even undesirable, to put the genie back in the bottle."*
Susan Eandi, Head of Baker McKenzie's Global Employment and Labor Law practice group for North America

# Introduction

In 1913, Henry Ford introduced the moving assembly line to his Ford Motor Company manufacturing plant, which revolutionised manufacturing. The increase in productivity was dramatic, but so was the staff turnover. Employees struggled to cope with the increased pace and demands occasioned by the introduction of this technology. If the factory wanted to increase its staff complement by 100 in 1913, it had to hire 963 employees to factor in the high staff turnover.

Not prone to flinching at challenges, Ford responded by doubling wages. He introduced a $5 a day wage in 1914, which unsurprisingly had a positive impact on the company's staff retention rate. But the double wage offer came with unique conditions. Employees had to agree to adopt healthy and "moral" lifestyles if they wanted the benefit of the $5/day wage.

Ford set up a sociology department to monitor compliance to the set standards for employees and their families. Company investigators would make unannounced calls at employees' residences to gather information about their living conditions and lifestyle. Hit the sauce too hard or regularly, and you would immediately be disqualified from earning the $5 wage.

Ford's social experiment halted in the early 1920s for two main reasons. Firstly, it became increasingly costly to maintain the programme in the light of heightened competition from other vehicle manufacturers. Secondly, there was significant push-back from staff to the home visits by inspectors and the stringent "moral" code imposed.

# The post-Covid World

The impact of Covid-19 on the world of work is arguably even more dramatic than the introduction of the assembly line by Ford more than a century ago. Job losses as a result of the pandemic were estimated to be in the region of 255 million globally during 2020.[1] As if this was not enough, in the style of late night infomercials... but wait, there's more!

Trade union membership continues to decline, with employees growing more disillusioned with organised labour.[2] Students and other new entrants into the work environment have shown that they are adept at engineering meaningful change without the assistance of trade unions. The #FeesMustFall movement resulted in the insourcing of outsourced workers[3] as a consequence of student and worker protest, with little meaningful leadership or coordination from organised labour.

The dramatic increase of gig or irregular work has had a significant impact on the modern workplace. With one study estimating that 162 million workers are engaged in gig work, it is clear that more businesses are absorbing the perceived benefits of such workers. The ability to supplement the current workforce with giggers with special skills for specific projects, using them to manage labour costs and dealing with seasonal demands, are compelling reasons for many organisations to place greater reliance on gig workers to meet labour demands.

Social media has further opened a new frontier for worker activism that has reduced the need for unhappy employees to picket or strike to express their dissatisfaction with workplace policies or practices. Social media campaigns are used with great success by employee groups, shareholders or stakeholder activists to bring about industrial change.[4] Employees (and, at stages, businesses) participate in protests and demand societal reform when global or local injustice makes headlines, as evidenced by the outrage expressed in the recent #BlackLivesMatter protests.

The interconnectivity between the workplace and society has arguably never been as visible as during the current times. Social conflicts and disruption spill into the workplace in a manner last seen during anti-apartheid strikes, work stoppages and civil disobedience. Employees, customers, shareholders and other stakeholders are demanding that organisations take a stance in respect of various societal ails bedevilling the world. Companies are under pressure to consider their impact on problems such as racism, unemployment, income disparity and meaningful jobs, with

---

1   United Nations, 2021.
2   Cloete, 2021.
3   Employment Relations Exchange (ERX), 2017.
4   Nathoo, 2020.

leading businesses turning this challenge into a competitive advantage by creating workplaces with purposeful engagement or "noble purpose".[5] As Hubert Joly stated in *How to Lead in the Stakeholder Era: Focus on purpose and people. The profits will follow* "For business to be part of the solution to our collective challenges, we leaders must see companies not as soulless moneymaking entities but as "human organizations" made of individuals working together in support of a shared goal. This goal must contribute to the common good by making a positive difference in people's lives."[6]

If the industrial relations training or framework developed in the '90s are still driving your workplace practices, you better be working in a government department or other form of protected employment, as those are the only places where typical traditional industrial relations practices may miraculously survive. Outside the public sector, trade unionism is on the wane. Employees are no longer satisfied to be the beneficiaries of a collective bargaining agreement that grants them across-the-board wage increases or benefits. Employees listen to Spotify, the world-changing music streaming service, which provides listeners with endless playlists individually tailored to the specific user, every single day. Staff are used to cellular phones that unlock based on the software that recognises their own, unique facial features. Their medical aid service provider rewards them every week for their personal health, driving and spending performance of the past week. They can perform their banking transactions online or via an app, and if they have to call their financial institution, voice recognition software identifies and authenticates the caller. Whilst it is estimated that around 36% of the global workforce comprises Gen-Z employees[7], they are certainly not the only ones converted to the benefits of individualisation and specialisation of services offered to them.

With the incredibly high degree of personalisation in their regular lives, why would employees then be satisfied with the fruits of a union official, who they are unlikely to see again for another year, and who negotiated a two or three page wage agreement wherein everyone is treated exactly the same? Employees want a personalised work experience; they want to feel connected and valued as individuals, and are no longer content with the slogans that ushered us into workplace democracy. "An injury to one is an injury to all" still looks good on a placard in the picket line, and may garner a few likes and retweets on social media, but it is unlikely to speak to the soul of a new generation of employees. Employees of the modern workforce are concerned with societal issues and want to work in an environment where they feel that they are making a meaningful contribution to the greater issues afflicting our globe. Businesses can no longer claim to be winning at industrial relations by relying on

---

5   Joly, 2021; McLeod, 2016.
6   Ibid.
7   Kerrigan, 2019.

traditional indicators such as the average days lost due to strike action, or number of grievances filed or disputes declared. Indicators such as staff turnover and employee engagement are the more critical markers of organisational effectiveness.[8]

# The post-Covid Workplace

The pandemic certainly forced many organisations to consider (and reconsider) their staffing levels. By July 2020, it was estimated that over three million South African workers had already lost their jobs as a result of Covid[9], although the International Labour Organisation predicts a strong recovery post vaccination. "While there is still a high degree of uncertainty for 2021, the ILO estimates projected that most countries could see a relatively strong recovery in the second half the year, as COVID-19 vaccination programmes take effect. ILO put forward three scenarios: a baseline estimate showing a 3 per cent decline; a pessimistic forecast indicating a 4.6 per cent loss, and in the most optimistic scenario, a 1.3 per cent decrease in working hours through this year."[10] Managing headcount on the road to recovery may spell the difference to a business between competitiveness where staffing is optimum, an inability to capitalise on increased demand, or disaster where costs associated with an increased employee count cannot be offset when demand picks up at a slower rate than anticipated.

A recent survey conducted by *Fortune 500* among the CEOs of 2020's Fortune 500 list looked at how their companies dealt with the pandemic and how the CEOs are planning for the future. The majority of CEOs predicted that business travel and a continued physical presence in the office will never return to the levels seen before Covid-19. The accelerated technological transformation of their organisations, experienced by three quarters of the CEOs surveyed, was cited as the main reason for this changing trend. Most companies have already stated a plan to implement a hybrid model in the workplace – staff will work in the office on certain days and at home for two or three days of each week, sharing office space.

In the *Fortune 500* survey, the number one concern of 60% of the CEOs during the pandemic was how they would keep employees safe and productive. Yet more than half of the companies also expected to employ slightly fewer employees post-pandemic than they did in early 2020, and there was an increasing trend towards restructurings and redundancies as the lockdowns took hold. This continues to add pressure to the increasing global unemployment problem.

---

8    Smith, 2019.
9    BusinessTech, 2020.
10   United Nations, 2021.

The pandemic has certainly brought into focus the issue of optimal staffing. When production and services slowed down, employers were forced to critically evaluate headcount. Whilst redundancies abounded, many employers were also planning for the eventual upturn in business. To that end, creative solutions to job losses found favour. With a significantly diminished likelihood of securing alternative employment in the short term, many employees were more receptive to alternative work arrangements in an effort to stave off redundancies. Such arrangements included salary cuts, deferring bonus payments and other benefits, and even agreeing to a period of unpaid leave in an effort to retain employment. Employers that managed to unlock the solution to retaining staff at a cost suited to the business found not only a repayment in employment loyalty when work started streaming in again, but also had the benefit of trained and experienced staff at the ready when production ramped up.

A survey by *WIRED* and Baker McKenzie[11] noted how companies expressed the importance of being able to hire external help because they needed the talent or wanted to address specific bottlenecks in the modern workplace, whilst also addressing concerns about the inflexibility of traditional staffing solutions. Making use of irregular workforce solutions introduces various organisational risks. The lines between conventional full-time employees, agency workers, gig workers and independent contractors are alarmingly blurred in the modern workplace – with all indications being that this trend will continue in the post-Covid workplace. The friction between orthodox workplace structures and communication methods and layered, multi-faceted staffing options warrants attention. The survey noted that companies should adopt a purposeful, conscious strategy to address new frictionless communications tools, and they should nurture attention capital (an employee's ability to focus on value creating work)[12] amongst their workforces.

Respondents expressed a deep-seated ambivalence about the frictionless era. Notably, 64% of participants agreed that a flat organisational structure led to more innovation and 53% said that a frictionless workforce increased creativity and innovation by bringing together diverse views, skills and cultures. However, 51% acknowledged that a frictionless workplace, such as hot-desking, weakened cohesion and corporate culture. Further, 43% respondents agreed that the increased use of freelancers was creating a fragmented workplace culture, which was burdening the organisation. When it came to technology, 75% of survey participants said that frictionless internal communications (email, chat, video calls, document sharing and professional social media) helped their organisation be responsive and agile, but four out of ten participants thought these same tools could cause distraction and burnout. Almost three-quarters (74%) said that companies needed rules to avoid an always-on work culture.

---

11    Wired, 2019; Botes, 2019.
12    Botes, 2019.

# Working from Home

Working from home has clearly impacted employee relations. Whilst workers generally value the flexibility that the forced change in working arrangements brought about, downsides abound as well.[13] 44% of South African surveyed by Boston Consulting Group[14] indicated that they would switch to an arrangement where they only work from home. One study[15] has shown that whilst employees working from home increased their performance by 13%, they were 50% less likely to be promoted than their office-bound colleagues. Certain studies have also reported that workers feel disconnected and businesses have experienced a lack of engagement amongst employees working from home. Although not unique to those working from home, employees often cite the blurring of lines between home and private lives as a concern in such surveys. Various countries (France, Italy, Slovakia and the Philippines) have introduced legislation outlawing the obligation for employees to be contactable or connected after hours. Progressive companies have implemented policies to allow employees to disengage after hours. Notable first movers include Volkswagen, Allianz, Telekom, Bayer, Daimler and Henkel.[16]

# Impact on Employee Relations

The disruptive factors inherent in the changing modern workforce doubtlessly impacts the employee relations climate and strategy of organisations. Even businesses with strong trade union penetration can ill afford to manage their employee relations by relying on the strategies used in the first two decades of democratic South Africa. Plans aimed at ensuring labour peace will be insufficient to deal with fractured trade unions and declining union membership, social media campaigns, stakeholder activism and the war for talent. World-class businesses recognise the need to create value and meaning for their staff[17] – issues that do not feature on any typical list of trade union collective bargaining demands.

Sadly, it appears that long gone are the days when an organisation could rely on the average trade union to have its finger on the pulse of workplace issues and actively engage with businesses to find meaningful solutions. Promising signs indicate the growth of a small number of trade unions appreciating the need to re-invent themselves to meet the changing requirements of the workplace and their members base, and taking steps to provide a modern service offering. Regrettably, many trade unions remain bogged down with strategies that see issues such as the annual

---

13    Strack, Kovács-Ondrejkovic, Baier, Antebi, Kavanagh, & López Gobernado, 2021.
14    Ibid.
15    Bloom, Liang, Roberts & Ying, 2015.
16    Babel, 2019.
17    Carlisi, Hemerling, Kilmann, Meese & Shipman, 2017.

distributive collective bargaining process, aimed at securing an across-the-board salary increase for their members, and representation of their members in disputes, as critical. Businesses that focus on keeping the trade union happy may find that they succeed in doing so, but still lose talented staff to competitors and are unable to attract and retain the right applicants for work. Employees want to be recognised as individuals and demand workplace plans that recognise and reward their unique contributions, whilst ensuring fairness across the employee population.

Employers should consider a change in their employee relations strategy that moves from a primary focus on collective engagement to recognition of the needs of smaller interest groups, or, where possible, individual employees. Employee engagement surveys, individual feedback sessions, career planning, performance management, employee goal and expectation setting, anonymised feedback channels and exit interviews are useful tools in the arsenal of the modern people practitioner and line manager. These and other communication vehicles are likely to be a more accurate barometer of the employee relations climate than considering the number of days lost due to industrial action, number of grievances filed or labour disputes declared. In this era of high employee mobility – even when taking account of the dramatic unemployment rate – staff appear to be more inclined to vote with their feet (or social media account) than filing a grievance or demanding that their trade union resolve the issue with the employer.

With businesses used to differentiating employment policies and strategies to attract and retain executives, these principles may find application in dealing with more junior staff as well. Younger workers also want to participate in longer term incentives, talk to their line manager to raise issues (rather than to have to file a grievance or declare a dispute), get individualised performance feedback, and take part in creating meaningful work goals for themselves. The traditional collective labour relationships are ill-fitted for this purpose and are more appropriate than the carrot and stick approach to managing staff. This approach is not ideal for employees at all ends of the spectrum and in-between who seek "... meaning, connection, and joy in their work, as well as the desire to contribute, develop, and achieve".[18]

## Reconsidering Employee Relations Strategies

Businesses that desire to steal a march on their competitors in the post-pandemic world should consider the following:

- *Achieve the correct workforce composition*
  - Critically consider the composition of the workforce, creating a structure

---

18   Carlisi, Hemerling, Kilmann, Meese & Shipman, 2017.

that draws on the various forms of staffing solutions that are appropriate to the business, with due regard to the benefits and drawbacks of traditional and flexible workforce options.

- *Treat people like individuals*

  ◦ Design an employee relations strategy that is appropriate to the workforce solutions favoured by the business, but is ideally biased towards the relationship with the individual employee or smaller groups of staff.

  ◦ Where engagement with organised labour is prescribed or effective, focus on unlocking meaning for individual employees rather than creating solutions that will treat people similarly.

- *Listen*

  ◦ Create opportunities for feedback and information from staff and stakeholders outside (or in addition to) the traditional upward communication channels.

  ◦ Find workplace-appropriate mechanisms to regularly test the employee relations climate, being nimble to adjust employee relations strategies to tailor the fast-changing views of society as reflected in the workplace.

- *Create meaning*

  ◦ Create purpose for employees by communicating an understanding of what the business is and the reason for its existence, then linking that to the function of the teams and individuals.

  ◦ Embed this meaning through meaningful leadership modelling.

# Legal Landscape

In 2015, the South African Labour Relations Act[19] introduced additional protection to vulnerable employees (earning below the statutory earnings threshold) working for labour brokers (temporary employment services) on limited duration contacts or doing part-time work. The enhanced measures aim to eradicate disparate treatment between agency workers, fixed- and part-term employees, and staff on open-ended or permanent employment contracts. The Employment Equity Act[20] further prohibits unfair discrimination in respect of terms and conditions of employment. The legal framework thus seems to adequately protect the rights of irregular workers, but does it really provide sufficient cover against unscrupulous employment practices?

---

19  Republic of South Africa Government Gazette, 1987, 66 of 1995 - sections 198A - D.
20  Republic of South Africa Government Gazette, 1987, 75 of 1997, section 6(4).

The International Labour Organisation adopted the Home Work Convention (No 177) in 1997, which aims "...to improve the situation of home workers". It compels member countries to adopt a national policy to promote equality of treatment of home workers on listed grounds. These grounds include remuneration, occupational health and safety, social security protection, access to training and maternity protection. Only 12 countries have ratified this convention to date, and South Africa is not one of them. It is an indictment that a country with a progressive employment law landscape is not signing up to improve the rights of home workers, especially when considering all the current signs pointing towards a greater migration to flexible working arrangements. Ratifying the convention and amending current legislation to comply in full with this convention will send a strong signal to the global market about our commitment to regulate flexible working arrangements. Whilst it may sound counter-intuitive to seek regulation when the move is towards flexibility, the greater need is for legal certainty. Global businesses keen on investing in foreign markets are more likely to value certainty, even where it means there is greater regulation of a flexible workforce.

## Conclusion

Henry Ford was a rabid anti-unionist.[21] Tactics he implemented to keep the unions out of his business a century ago will certainly not pass constitutional muster in South Africa, neither are they desirable. However, the new world of work has seen a shift away from the traditional workplace relationship with organised labour towards a worker preference for individual attention and interaction. With unions struggling to maintain, let alone increase, membership, many face an existential crisis, with few showing meaningful signs that they are rethinking their purpose and adapting to the demands of Gen-Z. Businesses that still back their relationship with organised labour as the key driver of their employee relations framework run the risk of failing to attract or retain talent who have different needs and expectations of their employers. More than half of job seekers surveyed said they will not consider an offer from a company that does not share their views on diversity and inclusion, for example. [22] Companies that are able to correctly identify the right workforce mix when considering the various staffing options available to them, and then find ways of communicating with their staff in an effort to create meaning for them, are at a strategic advantage to their competitors in the new world of work. The employee relations dispensation of the past is unlikely to sustain business and is arguably incapable of creating organisations with meaning in the post-COVID workplace.

---

21  People's World, 2014.
22  Strack et.al., 2021.

# 7.4 Is it Time for a New Employee Relations Dispensation in the Future World of Work?

## Akona Makoboka

In this context, an employee relations system refers to the precepts and protocols for determining the nature and framework for both individual and collective employment relationships primarily between employers and employees and also trade unions. Employee relations incorporates both "societal values (e.g., freedom of association, a sense of group solidarity, search for maximized profits) and techniques (e.g., methods of negotiation, work organization, consultation and dispute resolution)".[1]

Few topics in contemporary labour law have generated more literature than the future world of work and the so-called 'gig economy' and/or 'platform economy'. The future of work is a subject as captivating as it is disquieting. We are at the heart of a paradigm shift as attitudes to work continue to evolve. The bread and butter of a conventional employment relationship in terms of the concept of 'master-servant relations' and the 'command-and-control concept' are proving obsolete. Everything that is a standard feature of an employment contract in terms of regulated working time, predictable office location, long-service awards, and secured benefits in a hierarchical organisation where consistency of treatment is the backbone of all things employee relations, is changing rapidly. Companies, employees and unions are faced with antiquated laws that no longer serve the current realities. Davidov succinctly argued that the "regulation that we use – the legal instruments and techniques – have lost their harmonization with the goal they are supposed to advance"[2]. The result is an incongruity that creates a great chasm between employees who need protection and those who enjoy the protection without adequate justification.

The dawn of the new world of work has contributed to thought leadership in respect of how labour law can be reconfigured to extend the scope of its protections beyond the concept of a 'standard employment relationship', which is fast becoming outdated.[3]

The trajectory has been set and speaks to the following over-arching themes which briefly summarise the new reality of work. These themes will be examined in the context of the current versus the future employee relations dispensation:

---

1    Trebilcock, 1998.
2    Davidoff, 2016
3    Franca & Doherty, 2020.

i. New forms of work and employment situations.

ii. Diverse working conditions, shifting time variables and the dispersed workplace.

iii. The emergence of multi-faceted performance management processes.

iv. Activism versus trade unionism.

v. The social dynamics and the employer's duty of care.

## New Forms of Work and Employment Situations

In this changing world of work, traditional work models are staring down the barrel of more flexible alternatives as the labour market evolves and diversifies. Crowdsourcing and job-sharing are taking the world by storm, as companies also look to source independent talent from the cloud via freelancing platforms. As per the ILO, "the world of work has seen continuous evolution, including the growth of diverse forms of employment and contractual arrangements in labour markets across the world"[4]. Independence of employment speaks to individual choice, which in turn lends itself to multi-activity by employees through various concurrent or consecutive jobs and several income streams.

Permissible multiple employment immediately speaks to the need to rethink the inclusion of moonlighting clauses in employment contracts and the terms and conditions thereof, as juxtaposed with the form of employment that is prevailing. Moonlighting clauses have been standard for many years, but they now have a limited shelf-life. Whilst this comes with certain freedoms for employees, it is not without risk for both parties who need to become au fait with conflict of interest provisions and intellectual property protections respectively. Reasonableness will have to take centre stage to prevent needless litigation. An employee relations shift towards managing outcomes as opposed to actual time spent will assist to ease the angst of potentially relinquishing this added protection.

The new world of work also calls into question the nature of restrictive covenants such as non-compete or non-solicitation agreements that are housed in employment contracts with the intention that they survive termination of employment. Non-standard or multiple forms of employment being taken on by a single employee mean that there could be concurrent, and prospectively overlapping work functions being conducted by one employee within the same industry and possibly with a competing business. This can become a very fine line to traverse in non-standard forms of employment – especially where an employee works on a part-time basis and can render services elsewhere for the remainder of their time. This is in stark contrast to the standard form of permanent and singular employment where the basic determination is well

---

4   World Economic Forum, 2020.

set in law as being a balancing of employee interests versus protecting legitimate company proprietary interests. We do know that generally speaking, restraint of trade provisions are often analysed in terms of inter alia, the reasonableness of duration of the restraint, geographic scope of applicability and the existence of protectable proprietary interest(s), all under the  lens of not being contrary to public policy. Also, restraint of trade provisions tend to have greater enforceability when the employee in question is more senior in an organisation. This is largely due to the exacerbated risk of direct exposure to trade secrets and/or confidential information and key strategies that could pose risk to the employer's business should they fall in the hands of a competitor firm. Accordingly, due consideration now needs to be given to what happens when remote working and flexible working renders the geographic scope and the accompanying duration thereof meaningless, especially because atypical work is not limited to junior roles only. Will restrictive covenants in their current form serve the intended purpose? Likely not.

The new world of work shows a reality where an individual can be physically located within South Africa or a particular province, but their work may be directed to a location outside of the country or province. Employee relations strategies and the drafting of the respective contractual agreements need to find the sweet spot that will not only protect the employer, but also not unduly prevent the employee from making a living. With globalisation at the fore and the fading borders in respect of business enterprises, there is likely a school of thought that will speak to the notion that the legitimate business interest being protected is not mutually exclusive to the physical location of the individual, and that the crux is the work being performed. One would be inclined to suggest that a one-size-fits-all approach may not serve the interests of the employer, and will certainly require that restrictive covenants be tailored according to risk, seniority of the employee, the extent of the exposure to confidential and proprietary business information, the extent of tenure, and possibly the form of employment – as well as location.

Just touching very briefly on this topic opens up the myriad complexities that need to be addressed in terms of work being performed remotely in multiple locations whilst transcending jurisdictional boundaries. What becomes critical to success is ensuring that employment agreements are not only compliant, but exceedingly clear to ensure the true consensus of parties. Perhaps the balance then lies in the identification of key roles within the business where there is diminished risk in this respect. What is quite clear is that the rigid employee relations ways of old will prove somewhat ineffective in the management of this situation, which will require defined parameters that are easily understood, protective of both the company and the employee, and importantly, will serve to further the interests of the business.

# Diverse Working Conditions, Shifting Time Variables and the Dispersed Workplace

New technologies allow for more flexible workplaces, as well as an expansion in the definition of 'the workplace', where working hours vary widely and work done is not confined to particular company premises[5]. With more flexible working hours comes greater freedom in scheduling and choice of location, which is favourable for employees. Whilst that is the reality, the current definition of a workplace, as per section 213 of the Labour Relations Act[6] (LRA), is "...(c) in all other instances [it] means the place or places where the employees of an employer work. If an employer carries on or conducts two or more operations that are independent of one another by reason of their size, function or organisation, the place or places where employees work in connection with each independent operation, constitutes the workplace for that operation". The Constitutional Court in AMCU and Others v Chamber of Mines of South Africa and Others held that: "Two things are immediately notable about the way the statute defines "workplace". The first is its focus on employees as a collective, while the second is the relative immateriality of location.[7] Further, the Basic Conditions of Employment Act (BCEA)[8] defines "workplace" as "any place where employees work", thus lending credence to the notion that collectivism plays a key role. This has implications in terms of the Occupational Health and Safety Act[9] (OHSA), as well as in respect of the health and safety of employees.

The BCEA, viewed in conjunction with other labour legislation such as the Employment Equity Act (EEA)[10] and Skills Development Act (SDA)[11], include the definition of an employee similar to the one found in section 213 of the LRA, which reads: "(a) any person, excluding an independent contractor, who works for another person or for the State and who receives, or is entitled to receive, any remuneration; and (b) any other person who in any manner assists in carrying on or conducting the business of an employer." The challenge is that many applicable protections are only geared towards employees who earn below the earnings threshold of R211,596.30 ZAR per annum, as prescribed by the BCEA. It is clear that there are several categories of workers that could be left out in the cold per strict interpretation of the current legislation.

The question becomes whether companies will adopt an employee relations strategy that is rooted in a 'wait and see' approach, (this would be largely dependent on what

---

5    World Economic Forum, 2020
6    Act No. 66 of 1995.
7    [2017] 7 BLLR 641:24.
8    Act No.75 of 1997.
9    Act No.85 1993.
10    Act No. 55 of 1998.
11    Act No. 97 of 1998.

will likely be a long wait for the development and promulgation of jurisprudence in this regard), or whether companies will look to be proactively prescriptive within current legislative guidelines and espouse a business-centric approach around these issues.

New collaborative management models are needed within the world of work, as opposed to the traditional command-and-control management models that provided key certainties in the face of predictabilities in the employee relations climate. The ask of companies that wish to stay relevant and commercially viable is the recognition of the fact that the introduction of increased employee autonomy and flexibility means that companies can no longer demand passive obedience from their employees. This is a direct result of employees' futures no longer being linked to one company. This is a pivotal aspect as ER has traditionally been based on the principle of subordination and loyalty. Boundaries in companies are far more permeable, "where work—and people—move inside and outside more freely".[12] This in itself implies a paradigm shift in terms of labour law.

Companies must now expect challenges from employees on policies and governance, where employer decisions emanating therefrom simply do not make sense. The ideology has historically been to regulate as much as possible in a policy or code of conduct that employees would read and abide by, whilst leaving a gap for employer prerogative in respect of certain decisions. The future shows a different picture, where some employers will be challenged every step of the way regardless of what a policy says – especially where there are residual, unintended discriminatory or negative consequences for workers. Whilst there is a great degree of uncertainty and moving parts, it would serve companies well to remember that an imbalance of power places the employee at a disadvantage when it comes to bargaining power and resources, and due to this imbalance, the function of labour law is to protect employees and assist them in redressing the imbalance.

## The Emergence of Multi-faceted Performance Management Processes

The traditional differences between permanent and atypical labour will continue to fade away. "Atypical will become the new typical, which has both positive and negative connotations."[13] This will require suitable performance management processes in work environments that are likely to be hybrid for the foreseeable future. Fairness must always be central to managing performance, as an adverse end may be an incapacity termination on the basis of poor performance. What is clear is that whether in recruitment, training, education, guidance or evaluation, technology can stand to benefit the individual and the organisation alike when properly applied.

---

12    Spreitzer, et al., 2017.
13    De Vos, 2018.

Hybridity potentially provides the dual benefits of remote working in terms of flexibility, increased productivity, and employee satisfaction alongside the key assets of traditional work offices, in the form of "smoother coordination, informal networking, stronger cultural socialization, greater creativity, and face-to-face collaboration".[14] It must be said, however, that a key feature of hybridity is that employees have different access to resources and different levels of visibility, thus potentially impacting performance appraisals and growth prospects in the company.

The Code of Good Practice[15] and the substantive and procedural fairness elements of assessing performance have not changed, and are unlikely to do so in the near future. What will always be under scrutiny is the reasonableness and clarity of any action taken by an employer according to the prevailing circumstances. The Code of Good Practice should continue to form a compass to guide the actions to be undertaken in crafting a new business reality in terms of employer expectations. It is the role of employee relations function to assess these policies to proactively address any unintended discrimination or subconscious bias from seeping through in application.

As an example, employees who work remotely can be disadvantaged by diminished access to information and a weaker technological setup, which can make it more difficult to demonstrate their competence. Therefore, the design of policies and procedures should not provide an unfair advantage due to KPIs that do not align with resource accessibility, or evaluations that do not account for differences in visibility levels. Without clearly prioritised and achievable goals that account for an agile and consultative process in line with the ever-changing new world of work, performance management will be difficult.

Great caution should be taken to ensure that digital platforms are leveraged where necessary to provide adequate feedback, and to ensure that such feedback is documented in a bid to discharge the employer's obligation to show their awareness of the standard set, the achievement/non-achievement of that standard, and the awareness thereof per the LRA. The new world of work increases the need to rethink how organisations manage, evaluate and reward workers.

## Activism versus Trade Unionism

"The LRA guarantees employees the right to join trade unions and participate in their activities, affords representative trade unions a set of organisational rights, establishes collective bargaining structures, recognises and gives effect to collective agreements, and upholds the right to strike."[16] The legislation creates these rights to act as a counter-balancing measure to the power of employers.

---

14  Mortensen & Haas, 2021.
15  Schedule 8 – Labour Relations Act.
16  Botha & Fourie, 2019, p. 181.

Trade unions in South Africa have been a bit slow off the mark in respect of clearly outlining their approach to the new world of work and their strategic intent insofar as the challenges of organising and representing gig workers. What is evident from other territories is that there is burgeoning activism and new formats of institutional collective voices, and action by gig workers where the trade unions are lending support.[17] This forms something of a conundrum as this new activism and collective action is ad hoc and difficult to sustain due to its very nature of mushrooming in different workplaces for different issues, and having not been co-ordinated by the same individuals. This challenge is precisely the strength of trade unions, however they are faced with the unprecedented difficulty of trying to organise across different forms of employment, different workplaces (some of which are numerous or even individual homes), and different employment conditions, all without definitive legislative protections.

In the short-term, unions will have to make choices in respect of whether they want to oppose the new ways of working in a bid to protect what is current, or whether they wish to steer the transformation to ensure the defence of worker rights in the new dispensation. Do trade unions intend to upskill themselves and create secure digital platforms upon which they can engage with members, or will they continue to adopt approaches that are not useful, such as protesting that a section 189 consultation in terms of the LRA is procedurally inept due to it being conducted on the digital platform of Zoom, as we saw in the Food and Allied Workers Union (FAWU) v South African Breweries (Pty) Ltd[18] labour court case? These are important considerations in terms of the activism required to establish new paths in respect of employee representation and bargaining.

As work patterns bypass the employment contract, consultation and bargaining will either naturally fade away, or will have to be re-institutionalised. The prevailing ambivalence in the trade union space should not signal that the employee relations strategy is to stop communicating and engaging with employees and trade unions. It certainly does not mean that a concerted effort to create platforms and channels for feedback, queries and engagement – especially digitally – should not be made by employers. Employers need to be conscious that platform workers or atypical workers assemble and organise online, irrespective of their personal legal status, country or jurisdiction. It is this assembly and engagement through informal network unions that can be a catalyst for any decided action and/or protest to address burning issues. As we have seen, this course of action can be equally as damaging as a physical picket outside of employers' premises.

---

17   Franca & Doherty, 2020.
18   Food and Allied Workers Union (FAWU) v South African Breweries (Pty) Ltd (SAB) and Another (J435/20) [2020] ZALCJHB 92; (2020) 41 ILJ 2652 (LC).

# Social Dynamics and the Employer's Duty of Care

The new world of work comes with inherent vulnerability for employees. The flexible working conditions associated with the gig economy and permanent employment, for that matter, may have physical and psychological impacts on employees, including work-related stress, loneliness and financial instability.[19] We are already familiar with stress, burn-out and bore-out as the peripheral phenomena of an evolution that has shifted the workload problem from the physical to the mental.[20] Highly competitive labour markets can adversely affect the earning potential and bargaining power of workers. There should always be cognisance of two potentially vast realities in terms of high-skill workers who can select alternate work arrangements at will, and low-skill workers who cannot afford the luxury of being selective because they struggle to make a living and are thus at the mercy of employers.

Non-standard hours of work may blur the lines between work and family life. The ability to work anywhere and anytime leads to a tendency to incessantly work, resulting in a failure to disconnect and exacerbated stress levels.[21] For full-time permanent employees, firms may see flexible schedules as onerous, resulting in stigma and employees feeling pressure to intensify their work effort.[22] Work-life balance is teetering on being non-existent in some workplaces, which will inevitably drive up absenteeism and ill health. Recently, the European Parliament passed a legislative initiative on the right to disconnect. The initiative recommends implementing an EU directive that allows those who work digitally to disconnect outside their working hours without facing any adverse consequences. The right to disconnect is a bid to ensure that the employee's ability to focus on value-creating work does not diminish due to an "always online" environment. Whilst our law has not progressed to this degree, the question remains as to whether employers have a general view of how many hours employees are working on a daily and weekly basis, and how this measures up against the current (albeit insufficient) prescripts of the BCEA and other related global legislation.

Mechanisms to provide readily available support to employees for health and well-being needs to be a key priority for companies. Distinguishing between the types of employees as a requirement to access wellness assistance is a particularly poor practice that needs to be eradicated, lest an employer finds themselves litigating a matter regarding vicarious liability when something adverse has happened.

---

19    Anwar & Graham, 2021.
20    De Vos, 2018.
21    Spreitzer, et al., 2017.
22    Spreitzer, et al., 2017.

The personalisation of labour rights is an important instrument for social inclusion. The vulnerability of certain categories of workers should not be seen as an opportunity to replace labour protection in the workplace, including the regulation of working time and the protection of physical and mental health of workers against the risks of fatigue and burnout, with securing stability of income. Every employer should be protecting human dignity at the workplace.[23]

## Conclusion

The new world of work profoundly affects the traditional configuration of work and employment. It introduces dimensions of flexibility in favour of autonomy, but at the expense of security. It moves the "goalposts between employees and the self-employed, between paid and unpaid work, between work and non-economic activity, between workers and companies and between workers and consumers".[24] If rights to healthcare, training, education and support are only acquired through regular or standard employment, the new world of work may represent a large-scale threat to economic activity as opposed to an opportunity to be properly leveraged. This would indeed be counterproductive.

Companies have always looked to the LRA and BCEA for guidance to determine what rights and benefits employees are legally entitled to. In the current space where South African legislation has not caught up with developments, companies may need to look across the shores for guidance where jurisprudence has already started to form, and to apply their minds to what is best suited for the business and its employees. The legislation will likely continue to dictate minimum standards, but there is nothing precluding any company from charting its own trajectory and going over and above in a legally compliant and creative manner, in a bid to ensure business success. What is clear is that the general ways of old in employee relations have little to no place in the future world of work.

---

23  De Stefano, 2018.
24  De Vos, 2018.

## Chapter 8

# The New Diversity, Equity and Inclusion (DEI) Realities and Challenges

### Kurt April

# Introduction

## The World of Work

Issues of workforce diversity, equity and inclusion remain some of the biggest challenges facing societies, organisations and individuals the world over. Heart-walls and mindset walls, coupled with a fear of loss of privilege and relevance, too often define many and serve to divide and rouse anger among various groups and societies. This is also true for South Africa. Twenty seven years on since the advent of democracy in South Africa and, besides voting politically, very little has changed for many of the most marginalised in the country. With good education and relevant workplace skills, some find opportunities in the workplace where none existed before (albeit among a multitude of challenges and enduring social/workplace scripts, which have served to maintain the status quo in terms of career progression, access to real organisational power, and opportunities aligned with the population demographics in the country), but the majority carry on with lives that are causing them to slowly lose hope in the promise of 1994.

Formally, *diversity* is seen as all the ways in which people differ. It is recognising and embracing the existence of many visible differences (e.g., genders and the gender-fluid; races and ethnicities; nationalities; variously-abled people; different age groups; skills; sexual orientations; languages; sometimes spiritual orientations and religions), and invisible dimensions (e.g., spiritual orientations and religions; thinking styles; psychometric profiles; experiences and different tenures; leadership styles; philosophical views – conservative vs. liberal; socioeconomic class; education backgrounds and different educational disciplines; learning agilities; value systems;

personal purposes; different upbringings; various heritages, beliefs and perspectives; and individual differences). Each visible and invisible dimension can render someone a diverse minority in a workplace or social setting, for example from a rural area but working with urban residents in a big city, even if they were part of a diverse majority along another dimension (e.g., being African Black in Africa).[1]

*Equity* is the fair treatment, access, opportunity and advancement for all people, while at the same time striving to eliminate barriers that have prevented everyone from participating equally in achieving the organisation's and stakeholders' goals. Often there is confusion as to whether organisations should provide 'equality' or 'equity' in the workplace, therefore I will help elucidate the difference here. 'Equality' means that each employee or employee group of people is given the same resources or opportunities. This would make sense if there were no historical advantages for some over others, i.e., balanced educational, social and economic systems, and all individuals and groups started from the same base, but that is not the case the world over and in South Africa, given its enduring colonial and Apartheid legacies. 'Equity', however, recognises that each employee or specific employee group has different circumstances and starting educational, social and economic positions, and allocates the requisite resources and opportunities needed to reach an equal outcome. Dressel explains that, "The route to achieving equity will not be accomplished through treating everyone equally. It will be achieved by treating everyone justly according to their [specific] circumstances".[2] 'Justice' can take 'equity' one step further by fixing the social, legal and workplace systems in ways that lead to long-term, sustainable equitable access and opportunities for generations to come.

*Inclusion*, though, is about creating a workplace environment that values and integrates each person's differences in ways that make individuals and groups feel welcome, respected and valued to fully participate. So, you can see how, even when an organisation has lots of diversity in its employee, supplier and stakeholder base, it may not be practicing equitable participation, or even deem different employees equally credible in workplace and business settings, nor making employees feel like they are supported or belong.

## Underlying Philosophies Shaping Organisational Perspectives and Approaches

There are three underlying philosophical sources which organisations draw from to inform their diversity and inclusion (D&I) approaches[3]:

---

1   Daya & April, 2021.
2   Dressel, 2014.
3   April & Forster, 2020, p. 135-137.

The *sociological perspective* relies on the concept of learned behaviour over time, and argues that, as humans, we spend most of our lives trying to differentiate ourselves from others by changing ourselves physically (hairstyles, lipstick, clothes, earrings, tattoos and branding, etc.); educationally (schooling, tertiary and professional qualifications, continuous learning, etc.); and otherwise (different cars and colours of cars, watches, restaurants, brands of cell phones, suburbs, etc.), so that we may gain social favour/capital and economic favour/capital in the future. We will even create rules and structures (and internalise them) to sustain our power. Social capital, together with conscious exclusion, and the economically dominant group's cultural norms in an organisation are known to be identified as highly influential to career-progression opportunities and access, with unspoken expectations to assimilate to mainstream cultural norms.

The extent to which diverse economic minorities participate in such cultural integration has previously been identified as a significant factor affecting progression.[4] As a result, those in the dominant/privileged groupings consciously and unconsciously fight notions of "being equal" because their separateness and differentiation are spurred on by their desire to obtain and hold onto such social and economic power. Therefore, organisations following this approach argue that humans will not willingly give up their hard worked-for power, and therefore have to mandate for equity, equitable access to resources and opportunities, tolerance for and understanding of others, and the collective unlearning of prejudices by way of organisational policies and compliance rules/disciplinary committees, D&I training workshops, and facilitation initiatives. Countries like South Africa and Malaysia do, and other countries (e.g., New Zealand, Canada and the USA) have done, the same with employment equity laws and affirmative-action policies, and insist that in-country organisations become legally compliant. They have to visibly manage risks related to diversity, equity and inclusion. Within organisations, such initiatives are usually overseen by HR departments and/or specialised D&I functions, and the responsibility is generalised, in non-threatening ways, for people to come to terms with their prejudices. Additionally, the South African government has instituted a far-reaching programme of Broad-Based Black Economic Empowerment (B-BBEE), which attempts to move diversity from being a political ideal to a practical business mandate through legally enforcing equity in the value chains and supply chains, as well as ownership, employee mix, and training and development within organisations.

The *psychological perspective* relies upon psychological coping strategies that are developed to deal with separation, and argues that, as we grow up, there are 'less acceptable' aspects of ourselves that we are forced to give up or suppress, either by parents or the community/society in which we find ourselves. However, we

---

4    Myeza & April, 2021.

are attracted, negatively or positively, to this denied aspect of ourselves in others, and when we see these aspects allowed to exist overtly in other people, especially those who are different from us, they "press our buttons" (we have psychic scars around these denied and projected aspects, according to both Freud and Jung). The pathway for development, from this perspective, is to re-own the projected aspect, and reintegrate it into ourselves by doing courageous self-work; understanding personal meaning-making processes (committing to more self-aware pathways that encourage eudemonic choices and the full functioning of the person); engaging in self-awareness initiatives; understanding and noticing transference in our behaviour (not to continue to make current choices and evaluation of others in relation to our parents or previously significant people from earlier times in our lives); growing in emotional maturity (which is different from emotional intelligence, i.e., emotional intelligence is understanding human emotions, your own and others, whereas emotional maturity is the application of this understanding when engaging with others); learning to forgive ourselves and others; and developing the capability to rigorously interrogate our own reaction formation and mental models (particularly about others). The responsibility for such work lies with individuals as it is deeply personal work, often complemented through coaching, in which individuals begin to accept their own internal diversity (acceptance of who you really are authentically), and therefore are more able to accept the external diversity they see outside of themselves (extending grace and compassion to others and moving beyond our shame).

The *spiritual perspective* stems from separation from God/The One/Oneness/Being/Universe. Essentially, this perspective challenges one to see others as one's God or higher power sees others, and asks us to consider how we wish to treat them if God or a higher power also exists within them (i.e., simply put, we cannot continue to discriminate against others if God exists within them, because then we would be discriminating against God). It requires cultivating a healthy enough relationship with ourselves to start engaging others in more mature ways (i.e., with deep respect and dignity). This perspective therefore seeks cohesion and relationship alignment by getting individuals, teams, customers and stakeholders to dialogue about their values and purposes (encouraging character congruency through finding coherence between their espoused values and their lived values). In transformational leadership literature, such an orientation is often expressed as servant leadership or stewardship, in which organisations strive to make others powerful and mentor them to become leaders over time, engaging in collective meaning-making and social contribution towards the common good (being purveyors of hope through action). The orientation of this perspective, from both individuals and the organisation itself, is toward contribution, supporting others, and working with others towards the evidence of things not yet seen in their lives.

All three of these perspectives promote a positive orientation to equity, respect, meaning-making, tolerance, integration, values and purpose. It should be obvious, though, that only focusing on diversity is not enough. However, each of these perspectives can also throw up possibilities for conflicts and disagreements, as diverse perspectives and differences of interpretation can also be sources of conflict, disharmony, as well as challenge, both at work and in society at large. For instance, workplace harassment is often the result of deteriorating political and social contexts in countries or regions, and cannot be viewed in isolation from broader trends of sexism, racism, xenophobia and, in particular, growing anti-Semitic, anti-Muslim-, anti-Black, and anti-Asian sentiments across the globe. Intersectional approaches are what are necessary for making headway toward equity. In addition, compliance initiatives, solely according to the sociological perspective, while being absolutely necessary to address historical imbalances, tend to build resistance – it does not take very long within workplaces before organisations start complaining about the cost that such compliance is adding to their operational costs. Additionally, many internal employees start complaining – those not being affirmed feel left out, claim reverse discrimination, engage in confused collaborative-disingenuous relationships with those being affirmed, and some even start psychologically withdrawing from their companies (translating into less effort). Meanwhile, those being affirmed feel that their credibility is being called into question, that they have to be many times as good as others to feel credible, and that they are carrying the burden of their entire marginalised or atypical group (i.e., feeling that if they fail, their employers and the employees not being affirmed will write-off their entire group as incapable).

In South Africa, there is a clear need to broaden our thinking and expand the practice around diversity, equity and inclusion (DEI); it cannot remain a tick-box exercise for meeting legislative requirements, without invoking the other two perspectives, i.e., psychological and spiritual. There might be much to learn from global organisations that are further down the DEI lifecycle than most South African organisations, i.e., they have understood and interrogated the diversity logic for their policies and procedures to meet the demands of their changing environments; drawn in the best DEI practices regionally and internationally to link their business models to these; already integrated DEI practices into the strategic fabric of their organisations; aligned their resources and infrastructures to enable inclusive workplace cultures and greater stakeholder engagement; tailored their human capital practices to align with the DEI-business logic; and put in place measurement approaches and tools for monitoring adherence and progress to the DEI-business logic, as captured in Figure 1:

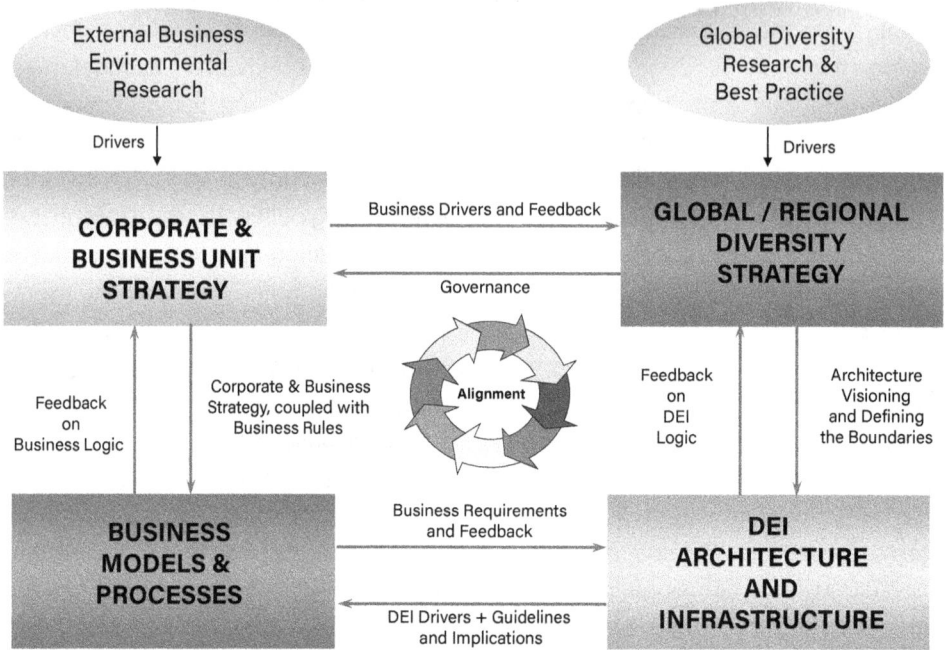

*Figure 8.1: Diversity, equity and inclusion organisational integration*

Many South African organisations lack the action steps for securing a workable DEI journey over time. Below is a proposed 7-step framework for making progress on the DEI-Business front:

**Step 7: Secure Financial, Infrastructural & Human Resources**

Identify the resources and infrastructure required to successfully deliver your DEI-Business Strategy & Plan.
Ensure that you have the short-term financial resources in place to be able to deliver the action plan (and future budget for the DEI journey).
Start identifying and proposing for your future, long-term financial resources to deliver your DEI-Business Strategy & Plan.
Ensure that you identify credible internal- and external people for delivering your DEI-Business Strategy & Plan.

**Step 6: Build and Map Stakeholder Engagement**

Develop a detailed stakeholder ecosystem group map (employees, management, vendors, suppliers, clients, customers, government)
Identify all of the key- and other stakeholders in each stakeholder group (names and connections into the organisation and other part of the ecosystem)
Graph and rate the: (1) importance of each stakeholder, and (2) value to the organisation
Identify the stakeholders necessary for the delivery of your DEI-Business Strategy & Plan.
Identify which key stakeholders need influencing to positively move forward the DEI-Business Strategy & Plan.
Develop a detailed communications plan targeted at your key stakeholders.

**Step 5: Develop an Action Plan including Measurement**

Build a clear delivery plan with milestones and deadlines.
Be clear about how you are going to measure progress – technology, tools, measures (single or multiple), linked to pay/bonuses.
Nominate (sometimes hire) accountable individuals for both monitoring and ensuring delivery of those deadlines and milestones.

**Step 4: Establish the DEI Vision and Goals**

Set a timeline for the DEI-Business Journey – be clear about the progress you want to make, against set dates over time. Articulate the vision and goals for the DEI journey.

**Step 3: Establish Leadership and Accountability**

Confirm the Board and Executive Committee commitment to diversity, equity & inclusion as critical to the business.
Set up an independent/external Advisory Committee of experts on DEI to help shape the strategy and monitor the direction.
Identify a senior leader who will take ownership of the work on DEI (either a CEO, CFO, Chief Diversity Officer, or Human Resource Executive.
Establish Diversity Councils per department and region – hold them accountable and responsible for progress.

**Step 2: Build the Business Case for change**

Explain why diversity matters in terms of the: commercial case, legal case, and moral case
Align the business case with your DEI logic

**Step 1: Assess the Internal & External Environment**

Review recruitment, selection, retention, training and development opportunities, turnover, promotion rates by DEI criteria (e.g., race/ethnicity, gender identification, psychological profiles, sexual orientation, education, values, socio-economic status/background, life experiences, skills, language, diverse-abilities, etc.).
Gather data on employee perceptions & experiences through surveys, focus groups, stories, interviews, videos.
Review what your vendors, suppliers, competitors and clients are doing on diversity, equity & inclusion. Benchmark your position relative to best practices, per region, nationally and internationally (your industry sector and others you can learn from).

PROGRESS

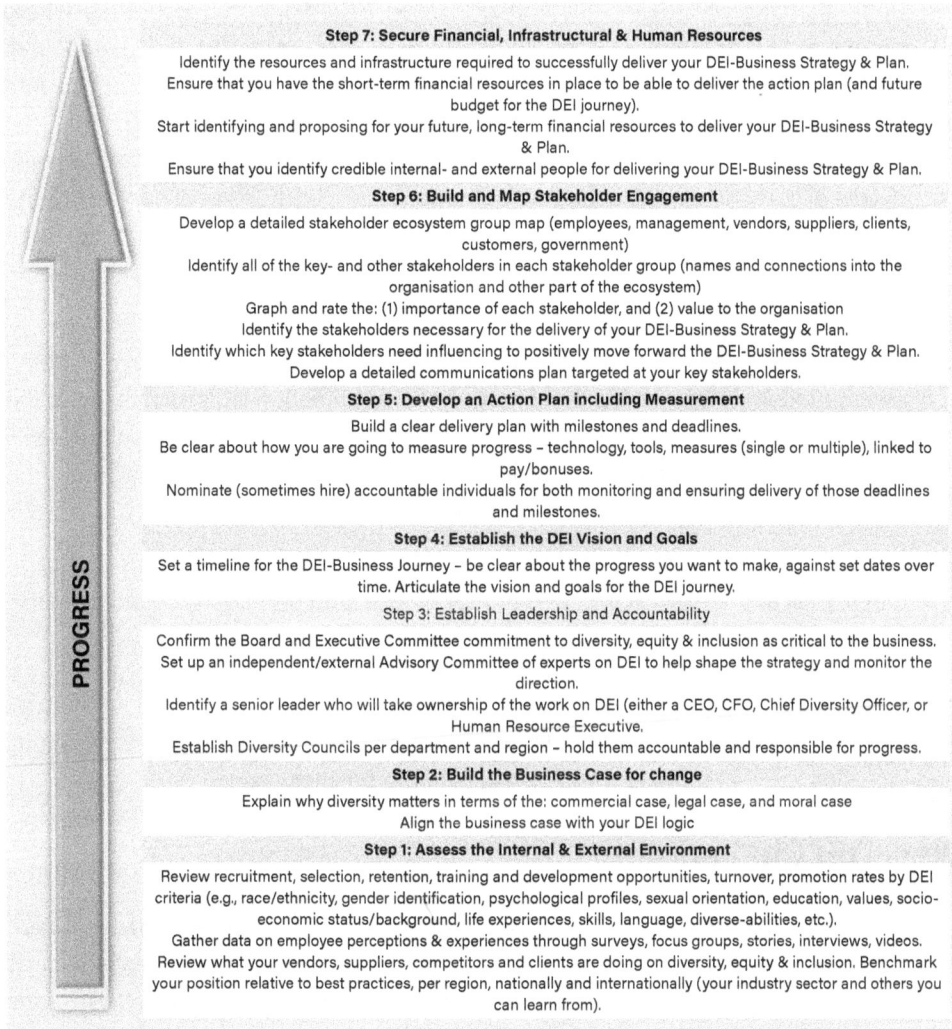

*Figure 8.2: 7-Step Framework for Making Progress (adapted from the KPMG model)*

# Diversity, Equity and Inclusion Business Case

For organisations, there are a number of workplace forces and threats globally and locally that cause them to engage with issues of diversity, equity and inclusion. As a result, forward-thinking organisations purposefully set out to build a three-legged business case to engage with these forces:

- Considered dimensions of the *commercial case*: Cost of staffing; access to new customers; the return on using various and different recruitment agencies that have networks in underserved communities; increased productivity; new products and services through higher levels of innovation and creativity; better understanding of stakeholder constituencies in regions and countries where organisations operate; greater understanding that happy and engaged staff affect performance and profit; cost of staff relocation; being able to tap into the scarce talent pool available and the various forms in which they come; the need to retain talent through their personal organisational journeys and the life cycles of companies; the changing demographics and mobility of people around the world; and because it has been statistically shown that more inclusive organisations perform better than less-inclusive organisations on a number of business measures.

- Considered dimensions of the *legal case*: Cost of litigation; employees being aware of their rights; the burden of proof of discrimination legislation around the globe shifting to being the responsibility of employers; poor and good industrial relations; brand damage; cost of internal investigations; cost of dislocation in teams; and difficulty in attracting prospective employees.

- Considered dimensions of the *moral case*: The right thing to do; dignity of employees and stakeholders: respect for others' traditions and practices; sense of connection and belonging; engagement and community cohesiveness; as well as alignment of personal and organisational values and purposes.

Forward-thinking organisations understand the need to approach diversity, equity and inclusion from all three of the constructs of the business case.

## New DEI Challenges

For South African organisations, the drive for greater equity through Affirmative Action and B-BBEE should continue, however the scope of the DEI efforts of organisations needs to be a lot broader and more strategic in their approach. Below are suggestions for just a few new areas to address the enduring DEI challenges and obstacles encountered by many in their workplaces. The reason for listing only a few is quite purposeful, because history has proven that long lists of issues and challenges to address causes a watering down of action, as opposed to a consolidation of action, resources and people, to really move the needle on DEI realities and challenges.

## Lived Experiences through Storytelling Approaches

Narratives and storytelling serve to counter the perception production of the unknown person and of the danger emanating from them, in particular, countering the incitement and ongoing production of fear and how the unknown person and groups (such as Black people in South Africa) are continuously tainted as prone to violence or being violent/aggressive in nature; countering the notion that being under-resourced and poor go hand-in-hand with crime; countering the tendency to link everything to racism and Apartheid; countering the idea that Camissa/Coloured/mixed race people just want to laugh, get drunk and do not want to take up senior accountable roles; countering the idea that Indian/Asian people are just out for the money and the show of it; countering the notion that all White people are racists and are not engaged in reparative acts; and so forth. Since narratives are socially produced along particular cultural and socially-oriented lines, people position themselves within the structure of narratives and stories according to their mental models/personal scripts and life circumstances. Additionally, the diverse range, or lack thereof, of people's lived experiences set limits on what is possible in their minds, the narratives that they are able to tell, and the narratives that they are able to entertain from others.

Discourse positions always create subjectivities – real and perceived – and are how constructive and destructive ideologies are created. Interpretive repertoires are therefore important to understand and shift, as they are the lenses and perspectives which people use to describe their lives and also the means by which they continue to produce ideas of social integration or social disintegration. Organisations can use narrative inquiry and the storytelling approach to provide the necessary psychological safety for people to explore their feelings of exclusion and inclusion, related to belonging and connectedness; feelings of credibility, respect and disrespect, fairness, empowerment and disempowerment, when and around whom they are able to act authentically or when they are covering; the ways in which they position themselves in relation to power and those in authority; and how the focus on one individual or group over themselves make them feel and behave.

Tapia and Polonskaia explained that, "Storytelling goes to the heart of trust. Authentic, relevant stories move us from intellectually transmitting information to emotionally inspiring transcendent trust. Powerful stories inspire us to connect, to contribute, and to include".[5] High-trusting relationships lead to stronger outcomes[6], while low levels of trust[7] promote loneliness, maladjustment (aggression) and an unwillingness to cooperate with others. Research tells us that trusting work environments are more productive as people have higher levels of conscious engagement, they tend to make less errors and collaborate better, creativity and innovativeness are enhanced, and employees report higher levels of belonging and subjective happiness. By being given opportunities (one-on-one, in focus groups, in large workshops, in shared written forms) for sharing their lived experiences, employees gain insight into the lives, challenges and hopes of others, but also grow in empathy and actioned compassion for colleagues and others (as well as for their own struggles and challenges, i.e., a type of self-compassion emerges too). The use of storytelling to share and explore each other's lived experiences engenders reciprocal empathy (an appreciation that

---

5    Tapia & Polonskaia, 2020, p. 35.
6    Brown, Gray, McHardy, & Taylor, 2015.
7    Rotenberg, 2020.

pcoplo's lived experiences are very different), and is probably the most powerful transformative tool, when facilitated well, or when the participants are given the proper, non-violent communication techniques, e.g., Socratic dialogue and listening techniques, in their attempts to create more inclusive workplaces and communities. When individuals and those in authority develop trusting relationships, and those in authority prove themselves trustworthy, decision-making tends to move more quickly, employees take greater risks, and people feel better about their work environments.

## Focus on Black and White Fatigue

Inequality, particularly economic equality, for Black people has persisted over centuries. In 2019, Stats SA[8] released the *Multidimensional Inequality Trends Report*, which highlighted that, while efforts to build a better South Africa have been consistent and slowly led to positive change, the country on the whole remains deeply unequal, e.g., unemployment remains highest among African Black South Africans (31%) and Camissa/Coloured South Africans (23%), whilst being significantly lower among Indians (11%) and White people (6%). As far as gender is concerned, women are paid less than men who have the same level of education as them. In terms of spending power and disposable income, White South Africans are still the biggest earners and spenders of any racial group, with Indians spending half as much, Camissa/Coloured people spending close to a quarter of Whites, and African Blacks one tenth of what a White South African spends. Beyond race, the richest 10% in South Africa account for more than half of all household expenditure. Even in modern-day South Africa, a country with the highest GDP on the African continent, only 11% of people have access to the internet at home, 28% own a private vehicle, and 17% have access to medical insurance/aid. The majority of White and Indian South Africans use private healthcare facilities, while most African Blacks and Camissa/Coloured people use the less-resourced public/government healthcare facilities (known for their inefficiencies and high volumes of patients).

For the majority of Black people, it is just tiring to carry on in their current lifestyles and work experiences, and this tiredness has been felt across generations of Black people in the country, which ultimately affects not just individuals, but also communities and society. Additionally, racism and constantly having to defend one's humanness can eventually erode an individual's resilience and will to live. Winters defined Black fatigue as repeated variations of stress that result in extreme exhaustion and causes mental, physical and spiritual maladies that are passed down from generation to generation.[9] Black people (African Black, Camissa/Coloured, Indian/Asian) in South Africa have, over their entire lives, needed to deal with the myriad of accumulated pain,

8    Stats SA, 2019.
9    Winters, 2020.

as well as unjust and inequitable experiences that are relentless and too often lead to ongoing marginalisation and a continual questioning of their (positional) credibility in the workplace. Many White people claim to not have much understanding as to why Black people claim to be fatigued when the country's affirmative action and Broad-Based Black Economic Empowerment policies appear to be favouring Black people, particularly in jobs in the government- and state-owned enterprises.

During the Covid-19 pandemic, it became evident that Black people, and Black women in particular, were the most negatively affected by disruptive lockdowns, temporal and permanent shutting of businesses and workplaces, as well as suffered the most under wage cuts and wage abandonment. Many know that being Black and human is not the same as being White and human and having the luxury of not having to consider or think about one's whiteness or earned/unearned privileges. Organisations have an opportunity to provide 'voice' to Black fatigue and allow Black individuals to authentically share what it is like to walk in their shoes each day; to speak about the overt and micro-aggressions experienced in the workplace daily; to educate about the effects of implicit biases on others; to let others know what it feels like to constantly feel undervalued, invisible and disrespected; to allow others to know what it is like to wake up every day and having to prove (every day) that you are capable and human, in order to encourage empathic and compassionate responses to such an existence (beyond merely the White gaze).

White people in South Africa have also voiced their own concerns about the toll of White fatigue – individuals having to constantly apologise for Apartheid, explain how they are not racist and that carrying the shame of the actions, and non-action, of their parents and grandparents during formalised oppressive systems in the country also results in mental rumination and stressful work engagements (always feeling under suspicion). "Young white individuals, in particular, find it frustrating not being able to engage in discourse and debates about historical issues of the country, especially issues to do with race. Many white people, particularly young ones, are encouraged by their parents or superiors to just "move on" with the business of the future and not care about what happened in the past. This "let bygones be bygones" attitude has cultivated a generation of ahistorical people who do not understand the significance of someone denying that Apartheid was a crime against humanity or tweeting that not everything about colonialism was that bad. The consequences of not understanding what Apartheid was and how you benefited from an inherently racist system are devastating ... White parents and educators, in my experience, are woefully equipped to talk to young white people about Apartheid. They become defensive, ashamed or angry when you raise the topic of our past".[10] "I find it greatly encouraging to see white people organising themselves into learning groups and addressing the topic

---

10   Basson, 2020.

of whiteness and white privilege. These individuals are doing the inner work that I believe is so vital to transformation – that is, educating themselves about how rank, power, and privilege play out in so many aspects of their lives".[11]

Hook[12] critiqued Robin DiAngelo's influential concept of White fragility and stated that it does not go far enough in accounting for three central aspects of White anxiety as it occurs in the (post-) apartheid South African context. He utilised Lacanian psychoanalytic theory to sketch a paradigm of anxiety, with one of the implications being that beneath the racist defensiveness of post-apartheid whiteness, an ambiguous mode of unconscious identification racial otherness might indeed be at play. Organisations need to help and equip all employees to talk about race and race experiences; how to deal with one's reluctance to delve into the uncomfortable experiences and perspectives of others, and not to shy away from it; what it means to be an ally; and how to engage in allyship for all those diverse and atypical individuals who live marginalised lives. In genuinely wanting to minimise or even eradicate fatigue, Human Resource and Legal Departments in organisations have roles to play in dismantling structural racism. Organisations can purpose to amplify, through face-to-face and online means, the voices and experiences of those who are fatigued. Organisations can also find projects and outlets for the thousands of individuals across the country, Black and White, who want to contribute to a more equitable country, but simply do not know how. There is a massive opportunity for forward-thinking organisations to drive social innovations that will make tangible differences in people's lives, and thereby provide constructive outlets for people's intent-to-action.

## Inclusive Leadership

Ignoring the conversation about diversity, equity and inclusion is no longer an option for leaders anywhere in the world. DEI management literature suggests that support from senior leadership of an organisation is key for the success of its DEI governance structures, policies, initiatives and access to resources. "A strong leadership commitment enhances the profile of diversity management, elevating it to a significant strategic priority. Furthermore, when leaders act as role models and diversity champions, they lend legitimacy to diversity goals and concerns in the eyes of other organisational actors including line managers and non-managerial employees. As a result, support from the top leadership cascades down to all levels and functions of the organisation, creating a sense of importance and urgency to achieve a culture of diversity, [equity] and inclusion in the organisation."[13]

---

11   Molefi, 2017, p. 105.
12   Hook, 2020, p. 612.
13   Lewis & Tatli, 2020, p. 42-43.

In South Africa, leadership roles and people in positions of senior and executive leadership lack diversity in terms of demographic diversity dimensions such as race and ethnicity, gender and gender fluidity, sexual orientation, social class and educational background, and do not accurately reflect the values and worldviews of the multiple cultures that exist in the country nor its varied customer base. Inclusive leaders must have the cultural flexibility and adaptability to role-model, inspire, mentor and guide people who represent the whole rainbow nation. They have an initial responsibility to continuously do better through feedback to learn to understand their own attitudes, biases and behaviours and their impact on others, and commit to improving their own knowledge, self-awareness, skills and behaviours to better support their colleagues, employees and organisations. The role of inclusive leaders is the role of advocacy, and they must have the courage to recognise and highlight the commonalities among people, while at the same time celebrate the differences among people (to be, but also to facilitate, the bridge between the two).

Research highlights that successful inclusive leaders are "dedicated to the thriving of others (especially those who have struggled proportionately more to be heard and valued), they honour and value input, nurture purpose in others, and encourage authenticity for those who fear the repercussions of being authentic ... they are passionate about challenging whatever obstacles to potential and performance they can ... they take a strong stand against bias, even in its most subtle forms, and they understand where and when they can step in and use their voice ... and think about systemic reasons for why [things are] occurring".[14] Given that resources are often scarce or overstretched in South Africa, leaders must find ways to inspire people to work together to solve their mutual concerns, the mutual concerns of their organisations' stakeholders, and to change those aspects of society that are inequitable. In particular, leaders must address the barriers and challenges that perpetuate inequity and especially economic discrepancy among the different people residing in South Africa (locals, foreigners, immigrants and refugees).

It is time to make the commitment and start having courageous conversations to deeply change the workplace cultures and organisational orientations – inwardly and outwardly. This will demonstrate the need for, and rebuild the sense of, national community (which cannot be left up to sporting events only) and mutual responsibility (business, the government and civil society) for making a difference in the lives of all who reside in the country, and reiterate our interdependency on each other as humans. Inclusive leadership, in an emerging economy like South Africa, requires a reorientation toward social activism and responsibility for the public good (something that cannot be left only up to the national government). Businesses and organisations must engage in solving many of the country's problems through their access to

---

14    Brown, 2019, p. 4.

financial and other resources, networks (locally and globally), project expertise, experience in governance, ability to grow financial resources, and demonstrated expertise in delivery.

## Conclusion

South African workplaces have opportunities to broaden their scope of engagement in diversity, equity and inclusion – at the individual, team and organisational levels. The idea is not to 'do something' to those with whom we work and who are different to us or see the world differently to us, but rather to with work with them, to help each other, and to remain in a relationship with them to realise more equitable and inclusive environments for all. The ideas put forward in this chapter are an invitation for the reader to engage with complex practices that would take South African organisations beyond their narrow focus on only affirmative action and B-BBEE, remembering, though, that the early stages of practically engaging with these ideas can be awkward and prone to failure, but that perseverance and co-creation can ultimately move the needle for many leaders, employees and customers in very real ways.

Chapter 9

# Increasing Social Capital Through Employee Engagement, Employee Experience and Belonging: The Spar[1] Ltd Story

**Thuli Tabudi**

## People: The Key to Competitive Advantage

We are all aware of organisations that have pioneered certain innovations, only for their competitors to catch up overnight, and in some instances, even beat them at their own game. Grafton[2] asserted that people are the only element in an organisation's strategy that can never be copied, thus putting employees at the heart of organisational success may be the winning strategy that organisations need. She further contended that the inimitable nature of people's capabilities makes employees a living strategy that can become the competitive advantage of an organisation.

Even in instances where an organisation can poach employees from their competitors, unless the culture in the organisation is favourable, it is likely that employees will find themselves getting frustrated when their new environment does not measure up to the culture to which they are accustomed. This is because employees are affected by their environment, and if it is not conducive, even the most competent recruit will feel disengaged and end up resigning.

---

1   The SPAR Group is a wholesale company with its origins in the Netherlands and a presence in South Africa since 1963. The Group includes six distribution centres (South Rand, North Rand, Lowveld, Western Cape, Eastern Cape, KwaZulu-Natal) in the various provinces and a Central Office that is based in KwaZulu-Natal.
2   Grafton, 2000.

# Engagement through Individual and Organisational Alignment

The workplace plays an important role in an individual's life as it facilitates the fulfilment of their economic, social and psychological needs. People join organisations with their own aspirations, therefore in selecting an employer, individuals will try to ensure that the company aligns with their own values and beliefs.

Having said that, the reality is that not all work seekers have the luxury of choosing a preferred company, and at times individuals may be forced to take the next available position, even if the organisation's values are not aligned to theirs. Hence, by their very design, organisations attract a plethora of individuals with diverse backgrounds, beliefs, values, needs and expectations, and with this multi-faceted workforce comes the need to create a common purpose. Failure on the part of the organisation to create an alignment between individual and organisational goals will result in a dysfunctional organisation. It is for this reason that organisations need to clearly define their goals and strategies, and assist employees to understand how they can align with, and contribute to, these.

## Social Capital: The Strategic Execution Imperative

Great strategies are relatively easy to craft, especially if one has the money to employ the services of a highly competent strategist. Such a strategist could easily engage the executive team and after asking a lot of incisive and strategic questions, come up with an impressive strategy. That said, the strategist's task would be done, and they would deservedly submit their invoice and wait patiently for their pay cheque. This part of the task would probably be the easiest hurdle, with the biggest task being to get the buy-in of the entire organisation.

A strategy, if not implemented, is just a nicely written document that looks good on a noticeboard. Great organisations understand that the executive team can never bring a strategy to life without mobilising every employee to be a true ambassador.

Gratton[3] talked about the fact that individuals are not machines who are programmed to deliver in a rational and predetermined manner; they have hopes and fears, they laugh and cry, they have a soul, and they have dreams. An organisation's priority, therefore, is to ensure that each one of their employees:

- understands the bigger picture;
- knows what their role in the bigger picture is;

---

3   Gratton, 2000.

- is aware of the environment in which the organisation trades, with all its complexities; and

- appreciates the importance of working together as a team.

By harnessing the strengths of all employees through this process of alignment, organisations can facilitate successful strategic execution, ensuring a consistent competitive advantage.[4]

## Increasing Social Capital, The SPAR Group Ltd Way

Social capital is defined as the networks of relationships among people who live and work in a particular society, enabling that society to function effectively.[5] In the work context, the biggest challenge is to align diverse individuals and ensure that they work together as a team, which is no mean feat. When employees work well together, it ensures that the organisation becomes successful through the collective efforts of all the employees. This working together of individuals does not happen by chance or overnight, and is a combination of organisational practices that contribute to ensuring that every individual is engaged and contributing to the performance of the company. At the foundation of successful, long-term relationships are several essential building blocks such as a great organisational culture, conducive leadership style and employee growth.

## Social Capital Drivers

Social capital is the by-product of several processes, which, when functioning properly, ensure that employees within an organisation work well together. Listed below are the elements that drive the social capital at SPAR to ensure that the employees' experience and engagement levels are optimised whilst fostering a sense of belonging.

## Organisational Culture

In the words of Peter Drucker[6], culture eats strategy for breakfast, and what differentiates great organisations from their counterparts is the culture that permeates through their organisations.

SPAR believes that employees are an internal market that needs to be "marketed to" first in order to drive the business strategy. Creating and maintaining a culture that ensures employees remain fully engaged is viewed as a business imperative; it is for

---

4    Trooboff et al., 1995.

5    Wikipedia, 2021.

6    Drucker, 2006.

this reason that a lot of hard work goes towards ensuring that levels of motivation are high, and a great deal of focus is paid to ensuring that staff at all levels of the organisation are engaged.

Culture surveys are conducted annually to identify those stumbling blocks that negatively impact the company culture. The objective of the culture survey is to minimise or eliminate any issues that are identified as impeding the culture of the organisation. The results of the survey are used to devise action plans that are then used to implement improvement plans so that the year-on-year progress can be measured on an ongoing basis. Having a great culture that is conducive to delivering exceptional service to customers is a business objective that is viewed by senior management as an important pillar in driving the strategy. These action plans are shared with employees so that everyone is aware of the focus areas, as problems cannot all be resolved at once. That said, it does not mean that every issue that is identified can be addressed, which is shared with employees so that their expectations are realistic and those things that the organisation cannot change, are discussed.

## Leadership

The right leadership in an organisation can give direction and mobilise employees to translate the strategy into deliverables. A great leader is one who uses their influence and position to create a space where people can thrive and become the best that they can be. They have the ability to share the vision of the organisation and are able to enthuse every employee to spring to action and play their part in leapfrogging the organisation forward. Much has been said and written about change and the importance for leaders – wherever they might be – to adapt to the changes that are taking place around them.[7]

SPAR's leadership philosophy is that of authenticity and it is important that employees are treated with respect. The company values the principles of accessibility in leaders to ensure that employees can build good relationships with their leaders. Teamwork is an important element of meeting the needs of customers, and like any sports team, the success of the team can be attributed to the quality of the leadership they have. Every leader is tasked with driving the objectives of the organisation by ensuring that each employee is executing their job to the best of their ability. As the saying goes, companies must take care of their employees and the employees will take care of the business. SPAR continues to focus on the development of its leaders to ensure that they are doing a great job at unlocking every employee's potential and creating a learning environment.

---

7    Coats & Codrington, 2015.

## Company Values

Values are standards that define what is good and just in an organisation. Simply put, core values answer the question, "How do we ensure that the way we act aligns with our objectives and drives shareholder value"? Values are deeply embedded and are important for sharing and teaching a shared sense of beliefs within an organisation. Values give anybody who visits the organisation a sense of what is really happening and reveal the company's true DNA.

Values, when used correctly, can support the overall business strategy as they give a clear direction of what is important to the organisation. Company values need to be integrated into people processes such as recruitment, selection, performance management, succession planning and rewards so that they become entrenched and drive the correct behaviour.

SPAR has three values upon which its unique culture is built: family, passion and entrepreneurship. At the core of the organisation's make-up is the ethos that places significant emphasis on creating a sense of family, since the retailers, who are the customers, are independent stores who chose to join the SPAR family. It is for this reason that SPAR places a lot of value in ensuring that divisions provide the feeling of working in a family business. The *family* value talks to the sense of belonging, relationships and teamwork that is needed to deliver the service to retailers. The value of *passion* focuses on the commitment, authenticity, enthusiasm and enjoyment with which every person is expected to approach their work. The *entrepreneurship* value drives the innovation, ownership, leadership and focus that is expected from employees as they engage in their day-to-day activities.

SPAR believes in the family value so much, that as a result, employees' families are integrated into the SPAR family in many ways. One such way is by having family days in the divisions, where employees get to invite their families to the workplace and celebrate family day with their loved ones and colleagues. Children of junior employees are also assisted financially in their tertiary studies. In this way, SPAR is able to assist the employee during what is one of the most expensive periods in any young person's life.

During the Covid-19 pandemic, the company invested a lot of money on making the pandemic more bearable for employees. In the initial stages of the pandemic when the country was in total lockdown, this included ensuring that staff were given extra support. The organisation, being in the food industry, was declared an essential service, which necessitated that the SPAR provide private transport to staff when there was a lot of uncertainty surrounding Covid-19. The reasoning behind the decision was to support employees who were reliant on public transport by giving them one less thing to worry when little was known about precautionary measures to ensure personal safety.

When the government's vaccination rollout got underway, a decision was taken by management to make Covid-19 vaccines accessible to staff by introducing workplace vaccinations. This enabled staff to get the vaccines without travelling long distances and included availing funds to employ companies to administer vaccines at all the national divisions. The occupational health clinics that are present in the divisions were on hand to deal with any cases of Covid-19 in the workplace and give support to those who tested positive at any given stage. These efforts spoke to the values of passion and family.

Driving values is a serious business objective, with specific activities planned in each division during the year to facilitate this. These include creating fun activities that are aimed at educating staff and celebrating SPAR's values, thereby ensuring that driving the company's values is a shared responsibility. These activities are imperative in keeping the values and the culture alive, whilst ensuring that employees continue to have fun whilst performing their duties.

## Staff Empowerment

Leaders may be the architects of organisational goals, but employees are the executors, and it is important that the people tasked with making the strategies come to life are empowered. It would be impossible for leaders to hope that they could supervise every task in the organisation, as they simply would not have the know-how, nor the capacity. Great leaders ensure that they articulate the organisational goals well and help set individual objectives that support departmental and organisational goals.

They then need to capacitate every team member to ensure that they have what it takes to perform the allocated tasks and then continuously manage performance. Employees need to receive a clear message that their leaders have all the faith in them to execute their responsibilities effectively and can, at any given time, rely on their superiors' support.

Empowering employees means that team members are given the power to make decisions in line with their responsibilities and are held accountable for the results. When employees feel empowered, they strive to show their leaders that they can be trusted to perform well. On the contrary, when a leader constantly checks on their subordinates and strips them of any decision-making abilities, the unintended result is employees who do not go the extra mile and simply do the bare minimum. This places an additional burden on the leader as they must do their own job and still find time to micro-manage everyone else, which can be exhausting. Leaders who build empowered teams free themselves from mundane tasks and create space to focus on strategic issues.

Staff empowerment is an important element of SPAR's leadership philosophy, and it is for this reason that entrepreneurship is one of the core values. The premise is that the individual who does the job knows it best and should therefore be empowered to make decisions relating to their work in line with the guidelines given. This orientation encourages people to be innovative in their work, constantly implement continuous improvement, and find solutions to problems. By ensuring that staff are given the necessary power to make decisions within the scope of their jobs, the company ensures that they are committed to their customers and teams. This talks to the passion that the company seeks to instil in every one of its employees to ensure that they want to do what they need to do, whilst at the same time enjoying their work.

## Communication

It is often said that as organisations become bigger, communication becomes harder. Perhaps this is because the senior team is no longer able to call impromptu meetings to share news with the staff. That said, when the organisation grows, the leadership team needs to ensure that there is a communication strategy that is aimed at keeping employees informed about what is happening within the organisation. Such a strategy has got to be multi-dimensional, focusing on one-on-one communication, team meetings, sharing the vision, providing feedback, as well as celebrating the successes of the organisation.

SPAR recognises the importance of communication in driving the business strategy, therefore every effort is made to ensure that communication is effective. This does not mean that it is easy to get it right. On the contrary, communication is one of the issues that is a focus area for improvement following the recent culture survey. The communication strategy includes formal channels such as onboarding, newsletters, e-mails, town hall meetings, surveys, instant messaging, webinars, blogs, industrial theatre and staff functions, as well as informal channels such as departmental meetings, one-on-one sessions, and intradepartmental meetings, to name a few. Further to this, television screens are placed at strategic places in all the divisions to communicate important information to employees. They are also used to celebrate special events in people's lives, such as birthdays and any special achievements.

The Covid-19 pandemic introduced a different set of challenges that impacted on communication, in presenting the impossibility of gathering many people in one place. Focus had to be given to other alternative means of communicating, including having virtual meetings to ensure effective communication continued, even though some team members were working from home. A lot of time was invested in designing communication strategies to educate employees about the pandemic, as well as governance policies relating to various aspects of the pandemic.

Every division has an Industrial Psychologist, and together with the occupational health team, this team of experts had their hands full trying to give support to employees, especially those who tested positive for Covid-19. This also extended to counselling those who lost colleagues and loved ones, and allaying fears as positive case numbers rose at work.

## Growth Opportunities

It is universally accepted that employees do not only join organisations for financial benefit, but they also seek meaning in what they do and aspire to realise their full potential. Individuals want to grow within organisations, therefore it is imperative for a company to create an environment that allows people to thrive.

Companies need to ensure that they invest in training and development to ensure that they have a skilled workforce. Training should not only incorporate a focus on competencies that enable a person to do their job, but also further development to allow individuals to acquire skills that enable them to advance. In understanding that people join organisations with their own aspirations, companies need to ensure that they have the necessary processes that promote people advancement. These include induction, on-the-job training, mentoring, coaching, formal education, performance management, career paths, manpower planning and succession planning.

SPAR is a firm believer in developing employees, which is evidenced through the various programmes that are offered at different levels of the organisation. These range from learnerships to short courses, leadership development programmes, diplomas and degrees. The culture of learning is encouraged throughout the organisation, with leaders often leading the pack by undertaking executive and formal academic developmental programmes themselves.

## Fun at Work

People spend most of their time at work and it goes without saying that relationships and friendships develop. These relationships, if positive, further contribute to the enjoyment that people feel when they are at work. To create this positive atmosphere, the employer must work hard to ensure that people get on well and that they feel cared for. The company is responsible for ensuring that people work hard and achieve the organisational objectives, but at the same time, should help them have fun at work.

For SPAR, this means ensuring that good relationships exist between employees and their leaders, and between employees and their colleagues. This includes planning events that promote fun at work, which range from sports to cultural activities, team building, celebrations and rituals that give the organisation its identity. Social evenings and celebrations (such as Youth Day, Women's Day and Heritage Day) sees people dress up and festivities are built around that.

While the Covid-19 pandemic forced an abrupt end to "in-person" fun, the SPAR teams have become incredibly creative in managing to take many of these events online and creating a sense of shared fun in different ways, albeit remotely.

## Employee Recognition

Human beings thrive in an environment where they are treated fairly and are recognised for their contribution. Organisations are responsible for ensuring that employees are compensated fairly and that they comply with all the relevant legislation. As per Maslow's Hierarchy of Needs, when one's basic needs are not met, it becomes impossible for one to achieve the higher order needs. When an organisation takes care of meeting its employees' lower order needs, it allows them to work hard to achieve their higher order needs.

When employees work hard, they hope that their superiors will notice this and recognise them accordingly. Recognition can happen in several ways, ranging from informal to formal notice. At times it is a simple 'thank you' for a job well done, to publicly acknowledging someone's contribution in a project instead of a senior leader taking all the credit. It can also be about remunerating the person and giving them a performance-related increase in recognition of their hard work.

Organisations are tasked with ensuring that they put systems and processes in place that ensure that employees are rewarded and recognised accordingly. This includes ensuring that managers are properly equipped to handle performance management, including poor performance. Managers play a vital role in driving employee recognition, therefore they need to balance the need to reprimand individuals and to praise them when they have done well. Leaders are often accused of turning a blind eye to superior performance but taking a hard line when there are performance defects. Positive reinforcement is important to ensure that leaders promote the kind of behaviour that is desirable by providing recognition to employees. This not only affirms the employee, but it encourages them to strive to do even better next time in the hope that they will be recognised again.

SPAR looks after its employees by paying competitive packages, which also ensures that the company attracts the right calibre of employees and keeps them engaged. This includes ensuring that salary surveys are conducted and that the benefits that are offered are market related. In addition to monetary rewards, fun and staff development are presented as a package to promote excellence and offer recognition. A case in point is the drivers' competition, which is held annually and sees divisions choose drivers in different categories to compete at national competitions held across the country with prizes to be won. This promotes camaraderie as employees get to meet colleagues from other divisions whilst promoting driver excellence. Those who win such competitions are revered within the organisation and are viewed as role models, whilst those who do not win are still recognised for getting to the final stages of the competition.

## Conclusion

It is evident that whilst organisations compete on many levels, the one element that can lead to an unparalleled competitive advantage is the people. As has been explored above, employees are affected by the organisational culture, thus it is important for management to see it as a business imperative. When management pays attention to ensuring that the culture that permeates the organisation is a positive one, they will benefit from a motivated and productive workforce that is fully aligned to the organisation's purpose and passionate about the pursuit of its visions and purpose, ensuring the successful achievement of its strategic objectives.

## Chapter 10

# Bringing The Human Back into the Workplace: Changing Perspectives on Employee Health and Well-being

**Dr Dieter Veldsman & Ninette van Aarde**

*"Being human always points, and is directed, to something or someone, other than oneself – be it a meaning to fulfil or another human being to encounter."*

Viktor E. Frankl

# Introduction

As organisations prepare for the post Covid-19 workplace, the changing needs and expectations of employers and employees will set the tone for a revised employment relationship. The pandemic has left many employees disappointed with the level of support, care and understanding shown by employers as they have struggled to balance their personal and professional priorities. Others have seen and experienced authentic efforts from employers to view their employees within their contexts and have considered a more humanistic approach towards engagement. Regardless of approach, the impact of the pandemic on the psychological contract will forever change the way and manner in which we work. This movement has prompted a definitive shift towards a more human-centric approach in people practices, being more about the "human" and less about the process and policy worlds which tend to dictate modern practice. This shift towards human-centric and experience-based approaches were discussed earlier in this book; this chapter will build upon this argument through the lens of holistic human well-being in the modern workplace.

The purpose of this chapter is to propose a more holistic and human-centred approach towards employee health and well-being, and aims to draw upon current research and practical experiences within Momentum Metropolitan Holdings, a multi-national insurance business of 16,000+ employees. The chapter will start by providing a brief overview of employee well-being as a concept, how the term has evolved within organisations, and the current trends we see within the industry. The chapter will also discuss the methods and processes applied within Momentum Metropolitan in an attempt to show how authentic well-being impacts the employee experience and creates a sense of belonging.

# A Brief History of Wellness and Well-being

Modern definitions of wellness and well-being often utilise the terms interchangeably. This is problematic, however, as the roots of the two terms are vastly different and this leads to some confusion in terms of the scope and parameters associated with both wellness and well-being. Wellness as a term finds its roots predominantly in the medical sciences, and as such, a big focus is associated with physical health and lifestyle. Well-being is a more holistic concept and finds its origins in both medical sciences and psychology, and sees physical wellness as one sub-dimension of overall well-being. These definitions are not clearly differentiated and factors such as context, geography and orientation towards the objective of wellness or well-being seem to influence the understanding of the term.

A significant shift in how wellness was positioned came as a result of the work done by Dunn[1], who is considered one of the founding fathers of the wellness movement. Dunn was one of the first scholars who positioned wellness as a continuous journey to optimise individual functioning in a particular environment. This shifted the perception that wellness is something that is attained versus something that we should continuously be in pursuit of. The World Health Organisation (WHO) utilised this definition and formalised wellness to be a "positive, holistic concept that relates to a multi-faceted approach towards flourishing in different contexts"[2] This definition is important given that it positions wellness to not only be the absence of disease, but rather to be a pursuit of positive outcomes. This was in line with the original work done by Dunn in 1959 and set the tone for the wellness movement that continues to influence the current world of work.[3]

We have also seen wellness being interpreted differently, depending on geographical location. European definitions tend to focus more on a sense of "feeling well", which has a larger focus on pleasure and immediate gratification. This has given rise to the wellness tourism industry, which today is estimated to be worth more than $1 trillion. More eastern-oriented definitions tend to have a larger focus on the spiritual connotation to wellness, even though given its lucrative nature, the tourism well-being destination opportunities have also influenced this perspective in modern times. Insurance organisations have also played a big part in commercialising wellness.

---

1   Dunn, 1959.
2   World Health Organization, 1997, p.1.
3   Dunn, 1959.

Physical wellness reward programmes are commonplace, with individuals being rewarded for behaviour that leads to good physical health. Yet these programmes tend to overlook mental health concerns, as their main purpose is to reduce risk and promote physical wellness.

The founding of the positive psychology movement also influenced the conceptualisation of well-being. Well-being began to be more broadly defined in terms of a positive outcome that is influenced by various factors associated with an individual's pursuit for purpose, happiness and joy. Well-being also seems to be associated with a continuous journey towards a state, rather than reaching a particular goal. In this definition, there is a strong focus on body, mind and spirit as three parts of the equation, and all are equally important to achieve equilibrium. This definition seems to be more consistently used in academic literature and has strong origins in both psychology and medical sciences. This definition became popular in the 1980s, but was utilised predominantly from a psychological perspective through the seminal work by Diener[4] on subjective well-being. This defined the term in light of the experience that human-beings utilise to evaluate their lives across specific domains. Hettler[5] had already made some inroads with regards to these dimensions as part of the work of the National Wellness Institute (our argument is that these actually refer to well-being):

1. Physical health (body, nutrition, healthy habits).

2. Emotional (feelings, emotions, cognitions).

3. Employment (work, skills, finances, planning).

4. Spiritual (sensitivity, values, self-esteem).

5. Social (family, friendships, community).

6. Intellectual (creativity, cognitive, knowledge, independence).

In 1977, Travis published *The Wellness Workbook*[6], which translated the original dimensions defined by Hettler into more practical techniques that individuals could apply in their own lives. These techniques largely focused on fostering self-awareness and positioned wellness as the responsibility of the individual to manage. This definition aligns to work done later by Ryan and Deci[7] on hedonia and eudaimonia. Hedonia is the pursuit of immediate sensory pleasure, happiness and enjoyment, while eudaimonia relates to the consequences of growth and the pursuit of self-actualisation. Within this perspective, the balance and equilibrium between body,

---

4    Diener, 1984.
5    Hettler, 1976.
6    Travis, 1977.
7    Ryan and Deci, 2001.

mind and spirit is seen as the ultimate goal which can only be attained through a focused holistic approach that balances these different elements. Ardell (1979) disputed the focus on the spiritual element of wellness and positioned wellness to rather be a focus on body and mind. This perspective gained favour in the late 1980s.[8] The approach neglected the spiritual domain of well-being, however, and very little attention was paid to factors such as mental health, which were left largely to clinical and health practitioners to resolve.

As Figure 1 below indicates, wellness and well-being have been important subjects for the past 50 years, and various scholars have contributed towards our current understanding of the concepts. Even though there are vast overlaps between how the terms 'well-being' and 'wellness' are utilised, distinct differences do exist. Below, Table 1 indicates the similarities and differences between the two.

| | Wellbeing involves mind and body, disputing the spiritual element | Positioned dimensions of wellness (or well-being) physical health, emotional, employment, spiritual, social and intellectual | Built on the work of Hettler 1976 creating practical techniques focused on self-awareness, positioning wellness as the responsibility of the individual | Positioned subjective well-being referring to the experience that human-beings utilise to evaluate their lives across specific domains | Positive, holistic concept that relates to a multi-faceted approach towards flourishing in different contexts | Hedonia the pursuit of immediate sensory pleasure, happiness and enjoyment and Eudaimonia relating to the consequences of growth and pursuit of self-actualisation |
|---|---|---|---|---|---|---|
| Continuous journey to optimise individual functioning | | | | | | |
| Dunn 1959 | Ardell 1976 | Hettler 1976 | Travis 1977 | Diener 1984 | WHO 1997 | Ryan & Deci 2001 |

Figure 4.1: A timeline demonstrating the development of the wellness and well-being literature

Table 4.1: Wellness and well-being – similarities and differences[9]

| Wellness | | Well-being |
|---|---|---|
| Keen focus on physical wellness with strong origins in medical sciences. | **Origin** | Keen focus on mind, body, and spirit, with strong origins in both psychology and medical sciences. |
| Goal of wellness is to make informed lifestyle choices to feel well, which leads to healthier habits. | **Outcome** | Level of well-being exists on a continuum between a high level of well-being and illness, with individuals continuously moving along this continuum. |

---

8    Ardell, 1979.

9    Veldsman & van Aarde, 2021.

| Wellness | | Well-being |
|---|---|---|
| Responsibility lies with individuals to manage their own wellness through the choices they make. | **Responsibility** | Responsibility lies with individuals to manage their own well-being. As such, self-awareness is important to better understand the specific aspects of one's own well-being journey. |
| Measured in comparison with others on set scales. | **Measurement** | Measured in terms of outcomes associated with happiness, joy and contentment. |

For the purpose of this article, we will refer to wellness purely within the context of physical health and lifestyle choices. Well-being will refer to a more inclusive and holistic approach, with physical wellness seen as a sub-dimension of overall human well-being. It is important to differentiate between the terms, as from an organisational perspective, this has influenced the focus, priorities and resources allocated to support both wellness and well-being.

## Well-being Enters the Workplace and World of Work

Well-being in the workplace is usually associated with employee assistance programmes. The origin of these programmes can be traced back to the post World War 2 era; they came into existence largely to support the rising trend of social problems, which led to the inability of employees to work and organisations to be productive. Even though these programmes have evolved over the past 50 years, unfortunately a number of challenges still exist with regards to the effectiveness and stigma associated with them. To a large extent, these programmes aim to resolve psychological challenges that have already occurred and as such tend to be largely reactive in nature. The programmes also suffer from stigmatisation, with most employees believing that if their manager knew that they utilised these services it would have a detrimental impact on their career prospects. A recent study by Veldsman and van Aarde[10] shows that in general, most of these programmes only have a 10% utilisation rate, with most employees not even being aware of the services offered to them by their employer. In addition, the Covid pandemic highlighted that the scope and services of these solutions tend to be too narrow. The challenge of anonymity also exists, with some employees believing that these support services are not really confidential and would place them in a vulnerable position. At an organisational level, leaders often question the investment made into these programmes by focusing on irrelevant metrics of success such as utilisation or licensing fees. These metrics most often disappoint, and as such devalue the perceptions held with regards to the relevance of these programmes in the organisation.

---

10   Veldsman & van Aarde, 2021.

Despite the above, most medium to large employers have some form of in-house or outsourced well-being and employee assistance programme. These services largely focus on psychological support for employees from a short-term intervention perspective, and aim to provide containment and debriefing services. Longer-term support services usually fall outside the scope of these programmes and largely act as an "in the moment" support or briefing service. Physical wellness has also become more popular, with employee assistance programmes promoting a "healthy body, healthy mind" mentality that is largely driven through education and communication campaigns and interventions such as sport clubs, gym memberships and fitness classes. From a financial perspective, a number of organisations have expanded their employee assistance programmes to include access to financial guidance and services in an attempt to promote financial well-being as an avenue to ensuring holistic well-being. These services include aspects of budgeting, financial advice, short-term loans and other related financial solutions, depending on the needs of the workforce.

## Repositioning Employee Well-being on the Strategic Agenda

As the impact of Covid-19 reached organisations and the world of work, the well-being of employees became a critical priority beyond employee assistance. A survey conducted by The Chartered Institute of Personnel and Development (CIPD) in 2021 confirmed that employers are shifting from a reactive approach to well-being to a more pro-active approach.[11] Two-thirds (75%) of respondents believe that well-being is on the executive agenda, however noted that the focus is predominantly on mental health. A study conducted by Mindset Management during the pandemic in 2020 indicated that the strongest drivers of well-being in organisations were more focused on social and relational factors such as trust, teamwork, confidence to ask support from managers and teams, and the flexibility to care for others. Work aspects also play into employee well-being such as clarity of work expectations of individuals and teams, as well as the ability to focus on work.

These results confirm the view that well-being goes beyond employee assistance offerings and that employees require organisations to broaden their view of employee well-being. This also indicates that employee well-being and engagement should be seen as two sides of the same coin. The notion here is that employees need to be well in order to be engaged, productive and contribute towards organisational outcomes. This relationship has been expressed in well-known models such as the Job-Resources and Demands Model by Bakker and Demerouti[12], and local models

---

11   CIPD, 2021.
12   Bakker and Demerouti, 2007.

such as the Organisational Human Factor Benchmark developed by Afriforte.[13] These models have also shown a link between employee well-being and performance, with factors such as managerial and organisational support playing a mediating role. Even though all this evidence exists that investing in employee well-being is a positive investment for an organisation, most battle to tangibly put practices in place that go beyond the traditional employee assistance programmes. This is largely due to a lack of resources, but also because the perception still exists that well-being falls within the ambit of human resource management departments and is not a direct responsibility of line management. Although Covid-19 has started to change this perception, it remains to be seen if organisations take this seriously enough to embed employee well-being into the strategic agenda in the long-term.

Organisational sustainability has also become a key consideration. The Covid-19 pandemic highlighted the gaps in knowledge, and in some instances organisations were left stranded when key individuals fell ill. This posed a question in terms of the importance of holistic well-being to ensure organisational continuity in the short-term and organisational sustainability in the longer term. In this context, the focus on holistic well-being is a necessity for organisations as opposed to a 'nice to have' practice that forms part of the employee value proposition.

## From Theory to Practice: The Momentum Metropolitan (MMH) Case

Momentum Metropolitan is a multi-national financial services provider with 16,000+ people across Africa, the United Kingdom and India. As part of a revised five-year people strategy, the organisation initiated a new focus on the scope, positioning and visibility of their well-being solutions. This formed part of a broader strategic perspective of "Thinkhumanfirst", which was a philosophical stance on the importance and relevance of people practices in the organisation. This philosophy also positioned a strong human-centric approach towards work, which had to be articulated in its approach and execution of well-being initiatives and how the organisation engaged with its employees. The strategy was crafted in 2018 before the Covid-19 pandemic, yet it set the tone for how employee well-being was driven during the pandemic and beyond.

The next section of this chapter will provide an overview of the process and positioning of the "Thinkhumanfirst" people strategy, with a specific focus on well-being practices and how it was implemented within Momentum Metropolitan from 2018 to 2021.

---

13   Afriforte, n.d.

## Understanding the Environmental Context

In 2010, Momentum Metropolitan was formed as a result of a merger between Momentum and Metropolitan, with the goal to form the largest end-to-end insurance provider in South Africa. A tough operating environment coupled with unsuccessful investments and leadership changes led to a steady decline in business performance post the merger, with the Board taking action in 2018 by bringing in a new CEO and executive team to spearhead a "Reset and Grow" turnaround strategy. This strategy included a new strategic mandate, a revised target operating model, and significant cost-cutting initiatives aimed at streamlining the business' focus and direction.

From an employee perspective, at the time the climate and culture surveys indicated high levels of disengagement, employees suffering from mental fatigue and emotional overload, and to a large extent burnout risks. The purpose of the people strategy was not only to support the "Reset and Grow" strategy, but also to re-energise the workforce and ensure that the organisation had the required energy and drive to focus on organisational outcomes. From a well-being perspective, an employee assistance programme had been in existence since 2016, but was predominantly focused on financial, mental and physical well-being. Financial well-being, being a core component of the Momentum Metropolitan business, was driven through access to financial services, advice and products for employees. Physical wellness was driven through constant education and communication campaigns, as well as access to organisational wellness and rewards products that promoted healthy lifestyle and habits. A network of psychological support services was also available and in place, yet at the time this was not yet well socialised or established, with utilisation largely driven through human capital referrals and support. A decision was made to establish an organisational and people effectiveness division as part of Group Human Capital, with a specific mandate to focus on employee well-being and value proposition.

# Humanising the Employee People Persona

To refocus the employee well-being proposition, the HR team undertook an exercise to better understand the employee profile of the organisation. Demographic data, workforce trends, focus groups and semi-structured interviews were utilised to create persona profiles that were a representation of who the employees were within the organisation. This enabled the team to better understand the needs, wants and desired experiences from these profiles so that employee well-being practices could be focused, targeted and relevant. Five profiles emerged, which formed the basis for the conceptualisation of the well-being strategy and offering, while still taking current hygiene needs and factors into consideration:

*Table 4.2: Employee people persona matrix*

| What is their name? | Who are they? | What is their context? | What do they want from work? | What do they expect from an employer? | What are their key relationships? |
|---|---|---|---|---|---|
| Iminathi | 25 year old, African, Female, Millennial. She earns less than R12,500 per month. She has a Matric and works at the semi-skilled level of work. | She supports her Mom and her younger sister and is the only employed person in her family. She requests a salary advance at least once a year. She has the weight of expectation knowing she needs to step up quickly and prove herself. | She is ambitious, determined and looking to make a real difference. She expects a fast moving, social and accessible workplace. | Her loyalty is to the purpose of the organisation. She wants to be valued and heard. She believes respect is earned and values leaders who can listen. | She reports into a white male Baby Boomer leader who is part of 2300 employees retiring over the next 10 years. |
| Marvin | 40 year old, Coloured, Male, Gen X.<br><br>He has a Diploma and works at the skilled level of work. | He has a young child and trying to manage his work/life balance to be there for his child. | As a first time manager he is ambitious but also needs family time. Trying to balance both is tough. He needs to be set-up for success as a leader but the flexibility to be a good dad. | His little one is starting school and fees are a big factor in his financial equation. He needs help budgeting and managing his day to day finance. Though his title is not important to him, his development as a leader is. Accessibility to his organisation is important and he wants to make difference. | He manages a team of young Millennials and is trying to keep up with the demands of his team. |

| What is their name? | Who are they? | What is their context? | What do they want from work? | What do they expect from an employer? | What are their key relationships? |
|---|---|---|---|---|---|
| Carol | 52 year old, White, Female, Baby Boomer.<br><br>She has a Diploma and works at the skilled level of work | She is a mom and her kids are out of the house at university. She needs to support her children's studies while trying to save enough for retirement. | She craves security and stability in her work while being allowed to train up those below her. She also wants to feel like when she retires she leaves some kind of legacy behind. | She does not have enough money for her retirement and worries about the time she has left to save. She needs help to balance her finances. Respect for her contribution is important to her while loyalty runs deep. Her development focus is on deep skills in her area of expertise. | She forms part of a team that have all worked for the organisation for 15+ years. |
| Marius | 42 year old, White, Male, Gen Xer.<br><br>Works at the transitional leadership level of work | They need to manage their health, balance their family commitments and feed their ambitious goals simultaneously. | They both carry the weight of the organisation on their shoulder and are stretched in terms of work and mental load. Their challenge is retaining staff, transferring the vision and passion they see into a work force where purpose trumps profits and delivering on strategy through their people. | They are custodians of culture and are expected to strategically lead with an execution orientation. Despite a lot of change, ambiguity and re-alignment, they both are engaged and bought into the organisational vision. Their organisational commitment is high and they are passionate. | They both lead a predominantly black, female, Millennial workforce |
| Kagiso | 45 year old, Black, Male, Gen Xer.<br><br>Works at the transitional leadership level of work. | | | | |

These personas were instrumental to help the decision-making process of where to invest critical resources in the context of a holistically developed well-being framework and model.

# Adopting a Holistic Approach Towards Human Well-being

Once the personas were conceptualised, they were utilised to drive internal and external research to understand the needs from a well-being perspective for these employees. Data were validated through triangulation methods and ensuring that the balance between industry and organisational specific context remained intact. Based upon this exercise, the following employee well-being model was conceptualised and validated with key stakeholders:

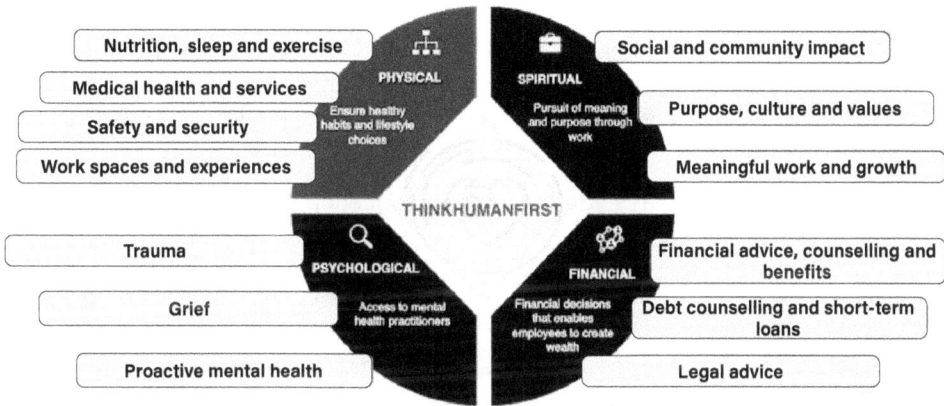

Figure 4.2: Think human first

The model defined holistic well-being in terms of four dimensions. The **physical wellness dimension** focused on "ensuring healthy habits and lifestyle choices". This dimension was operationalised through four key focus areas:

- *Nutrition, sleep and exercise:* This focus area was largely driven through education and campaigns to inform and help employees make the right decisions. Access to specialist services such as gym memberships and loyalty and rewards programmes was also included in this focus area. Rest was a key consideration given the context of the organisation, which was integrated into defined "time off" and "right to disconnect" approaches that were adopted at a business unit (BU) level.

- *Medical health and services:* Access to free medical advice through a digital mobile solution called Hello Doctor was put in place. This focus area included regular medicals as well as pilot programmes to monitor physical wellness and access to wearable technologies and monitors.

- *Safety and security:* Physical safety was a key focus given the current environmental context. Two key initiatives dominated this area with regards to a safety alert solution that gave each employee access to an emergency response service if they were threatened or in harm's way. The zero tolerance stance on gender-based violence (GBV) led to the creation of relationships with safety houses, special leave for GBV-related matters, a duplicate bank account to ensure financial freedom, as well as broad-based education on what GBV is and how to support employees in that situation.

- *Work spaces and experiences:* This focus area focused specifically on the creation of an engaging workplace and led to a reconceptualisation of the organisational spatial strategy and the role of the office in the way of work.

The **psychological dimension** encapsulated the traditional employee assistance programme whilst also extending it to include the following:

- A specific focus on dealing with trauma and grief by establishing support groups across the organisation.

- Proactive mental health solutions through education and destigmatising mental illness in the organisation.

- Inclusion of the entire family structure in solutions to shift towards seeing each human within their context of life as opposed to a narrow workplace only view. This shift proved instrumental to the success of the programme during lockdown and enforced remote working.

The **spiritual dimension** placed a strong focus on social impact and the difference that the organisation makes on the communities within which it operates. This was accentuated through corporate social investment programmes as well as volunteering platforms and opportunities for employees to give back to the communities. A strong focus within this dimension was to articulate the purpose and the desired culture of the organisation, and to put the necessary artefacts in place for the culture to lead to authentic lived experiences. A strong focus on meaningful work and growth also resulted in new principles being enforced around organisational and job design, as well as the creation of a strong career development orientation. The notion that "you join us for a job, but stay for a career" was made practical through a strong focus on experiential learning and talent management.

The **financial dimension** provided a strong focus on financial education whilst also providing employees with access to a broad range of financial products to ensure the financial well-being of themselves and their direct family members. Internally this also led to a re-evaluation of the remuneration philosophy and how this is operationalised in terms of remuneration practices and principles. This also entailed access to legal services to support employees with basic advice for legal matters.

## Implementing a Rhythm of Well-being Practices

The model was introduced to the organisation over a period of time. A set rhythm was initiated that balanced education and communication with manager training, as well as quarterly reviews of service adoption (not pure utilisation) and evaluating these services in line with the employee people persona requirements. Well-being was also included on the Board agenda, with the quarterly CEO's report detailing well-being related initiatives. A monthly dashboard was provided to each business unit which showcased trends regarding type of services being adopted, increases/decreases in numbers, and other insights. It was important to establish a set rhythm to introduce the programme over time, depending on the environmental context and business needs, as opposed to a broad-based approach. Visibility of the programme was paramount and the rebranding of the programme to "Wise and Well" played a big part in repositioning where and how well-being fits into the broader employee value proposition.

## Remaining Relevant, Being Practical and Demonstrating Impact

The programme was also continuously evaluated to ensure its relevance and that certain services were enhanced or decommissioned, whilst new solutions were introduced over time.  A guiding factor for the evaluation of all solutions was their relevance to the holistic well-being narrative, the personas, and the organisational strategic intent. From an accessibility perspective, the programme also evolved to ensure a multi-channel approach that allowed employees to access well-being services digitally and anonymously at any time and from anywhere. This was instrumental in ensuring that confidentiality and anonymity concerns were addressed, leading to an increase in solution adoption.

Employee well-being insights were also introduced as part of broader people data analytics and used as inputs to better understand the relationships between well-being trends and organisational impact. These were utilised to further enhance the strategic positioning of well-being as a key enabler of organisational success.

# Implications for the Future

As this chapter demonstrates, the post-Covid workplace will adopt a more human-centric approach towards well-being practices that considers the needs of employees from multiple perspectives. A clear distinction between wellness and well-being is also required, with more investment and focus on well-being as a holistic, multi-dimensional concept that focuses on a proactive approach towards human flourishing. Well-being will become a key differentiator for organisations as the ever-changing world of work demands more from their workforce, and traditional employee assistance programmes will need to evolve if they are to remain relevant. We believe that well-being will play an important part in the employer/employee relationship going forward, and organisations will have to be able to demonstrate their commitment towards the well-being of their employees through their people practices and investment in enabling resources.

# Chapter 11

# The New Challenges for HR: The Governance of Ethics for the 2020s and Beyond

**Penny Milner-Smyth**

# Introduction

The dawn of the 2020s saw an extraordinary convergence of socio-economic, political, health and environmental developments, which was destined to have a profound impact on the organisational governance agenda.

The ensuing new era of governance is one in which legal and regulatory compliance has become a minimum requirement of organisations, and in which the far higher standard of ethical leadership has been recognised as of overarching importance.

The shift has both increased the strategic significance of the Human Resources role, and extended its scope. Achieving the required impact demands that the profession draws upon knowledge from diverse disciplines and incorporates this into its competencies and contributions.

This chapter will:

- identify the global trends shaping the organisational governance agenda;
- explain the expanded scope of organisational governance in the 2020s;
- explore new sources of insight for the HR role; and
- examine implications for future HR practices and programmes.

# Global Trends Shaping the Organisational Governance Agenda

To appreciate the significant step change in governance required of organisations, one needs to revisit certain trends that were emerging as the 21st century moved from its teens into its twenties. The early 2020 outbreak of a highly infectious coronavirus strain, Covid-19, was to temporarily mask, but ultimately magnify, the need for the fundamental change demanded by these developments.

As 2020 dawned it was clear that in many previously stable countries, citizens dissatisfied with and disillusioned by the status quo were demanding change, and the consequences were being felt from the ballot box to the boardroom.

An unprecedented number of countries had seen national protests against perceived misuse of political power. Wild card candidates from little known parties were voted into public office having campaigned on a commitment to clean government. Deposed leaders were being held accountable and ill-gotten gains confiscated.

Corruption was identified as a leading cause of global social instability, driving involuntary mass migration, financing terror activities, obstructing justice and perpetuating poverty. Slavery, so long outlawed, was assessed as being more prevalent than ever before.

For the first time in modern history, more CEOs were fired for ethical lapses than for financial performance failings. Employees protested against their employers on ethical grounds – against product development with potential harmful applications and against internal policies discrepant with stated values.

Insiders, outraged at what they believed to be unethical practices in their organisations, leaked compromising information into the public domain, often in quantities so large that it took teams of investigative journalists to analyse. Others made use of external whistleblowing facilities provided by regulatory bodies to bring the law to bear on errant employers.

Individual and business reputations established over decades continued to be destroyed in minutes under the stark social media spotlight, and corporate ethical failures obliterated investment values in the course of single days of trading.

Around the world, legislation designed to facilitate and protect whistleblowers was introduced and strengthened, with regulatory bodies incentivising disclosures by insiders in order to protect the investor and consumer from unethical corporate conduct.

Laws that made bribery by a business or its agents a corporate criminal offence were introduced by more countries, and those in existence delivered enforcement actions with stinging reputational and financial consequences for the businesses concerned.

Charges of deceptive marketing were brought against brands for failing to fulfil their public ethics pledges, and a generation of environmentally-conscious children turned the tables on their parents and presidents – demanding that they implement measures to limit the adverse effect of human activity on the environment.

The month of July is typically the hottest in the global year, but it began to be associated with successive annual declarations as the hottest on record. Simultaneously, planning to limit the adverse operational consequences of extreme weather events became a priority item on many corporate risk registers.

Powerful sovereign wealth funds developed a reputation for shifting investments towards ethically-run corporations and away from sectors causing social and environmental harm.

In 2019, nearly half of all global pay was earned by just 10% of workers, while the lowest paid 50% received only 6.4% of total global pay. Poorer countries were found to have higher levels of pay inequality than richer nations; in sub-Saharan Africa, the bottom 50% of workers received only 3.3% of total pay.[1] This disparity was exacerbated by the economic impacts of the Covid-19 pandemic, which pushed unemployment levels in this region even higher.

The persistence of poverty and wealth disparities in a world characterised by simultaneous abundance and deprivation cast the current practice of capitalism in a poor light, and the continuing cancer of corruption increased doubt as to the merits of democracy.

In an historic development, the powerful Business Roundtable, which has issued corporate governance guidelines in the US since 1978, removed its long-standing reference to the primacy of the shareholder. In a new 'Statement on the Purpose of a Corporation', 181 CEOs of some of the world's largest corporations committed to leading their companies for the benefit of all stakeholders – customers, employees, suppliers, communities and shareholders (notably listed last).[2]

It's no wonder that a survey at the turn of the decade found that 93% of CEOS surveyed across 130 countries believe that business has a responsibility to deliver a positive social impact beyond the pursuit of profit.[3]

---

1   International Labour Organisation, 2018.
2   Business Roundtable, 2019.
3   YPO Global Leadership Survey, 2019.

In short, at the dawn of 2020, no leader with a commitment to their organisation's future success could ignore the inextricable link between the stability and sustainability of the world on one hand, and that of business on the other. It had become clear that fundamental changes needed to be made to the way that organisations, the world over, operate.

Given that it is people who lead and serve organisations, this profound repurposing of the role of the organisation would of necessity require that HR professionals similarly redefine the scope and nature of their contributions. It was to be only a few months into 2020 that the Covid-10 pandemic unexpectedly catapulted the HR management role to the top of the organisational sustainability agenda.

## The New Scope of Organisation Governance: The Extended Enterprise

The boardroom of the 2020s was to see the introduction and development of an increasingly rich language to describe sustainability goals. Just as executives had familiarised themselves with the 2030 Sustainable Development Goals (SDGs)[4], they scrambled to understand what was meant by the 2050 net-zero carbon targets.

Whether it comes to be known by another name or not, there is one concept that will define the future scope of organisation governance – the extended enterprise. Often referred to as an ecosystem model, the concept of the extended enterprise in the governance context calls for:

- the concerted use of influence to promote ethical conduct and legal compliance throughout the organisation's supply-chain;

- a life-cycle approach to responsibility for the organisation's outputs and their impacts; and

- an appreciative and collaborative approach to other stakeholders in the eco-system, including civil society organisations, sector representative bodies and all levels of government.

Can an organisation make a positive societal contribution through its choice of partners and suppliers? Undoubtedly, for it is through the procurement and delivery of goods and services that every organisation has impact well beyond its direct activities.

---

4    United Nations, 2015.

What interested and influential stakeholders have identified is the fact that organisational purchasing power and supplier relationships can be a lever for the alleviation of adverse socio-economic impacts and realities.

In South Africa, as an example, black economic empowerment legislation requires businesses to take the empowerment status of their direct suppliers into consideration when awarding contracts. In another example, the country's Protected Disclosures Act, which seeks to facilitate the reporting of unethical and corrupt conduct in organisations, was amended in 2017[5] with a requirement that direct suppliers are informed of the avenues they can follow if they or their employees need to report wrongdoing by the customer business.

Fuelling the focus on governance of the extended enterprise is the reality that organisations around the world are being judged according to the company they keep:

- Outraged consumers are boycotting brands when harmful practices in the production of their raw materials are exposed.

- Governments and their regulatory bodies are holding corporates criminally liable for the actions of their third-parties, for example when their agents flout anti-bribery laws or their suppliers make use of forced labour in contravention of anti-slavery legislation.

In the language of the extended enterprise, direct suppliers are also known as first-tier suppliers, while those that supply them are an organisation's second-tier suppliers, and so on. It is the governance expectation in the application of the extended enterprise concept that a business accepts their obligation to know the origins of all the inputs that they use, right back to the source of raw materials.

Having mapped their supply chains, often extending across countries and even continents, organisations are in a position to start the process of assessing the extent to which they are contributing to the fostering and perpetuation of harmful business practices.

When it comes to the sourcing of raw materials, the relationship between business and civil society organisations has undergone a profound shift. They are working together in previously inconceivable co-operative partnerships to address the adverse social realities that cause a given community to be vulnerable to exploitative working conditions.

---

5    The Government Gazette of South Africa, 2017.

Where a number of manufacturers participate in a supply chain with origins tainted by human rights violations, they too are working together and applying the influence and resources of their entire sector to social remediation programmes.

In the establishment of new direct supply arrangements, the selection and contracting process will increasingly involve commitments to, and ongoing evidence of, good governance on the part of suppliers. Newly appointed suppliers are being required to attest that they are requiring the same ethical and legal standards of their own suppliers.

A seemingly simple illustration can be found in the practice of corporate compliance with foreign anti-bribery legislation. Companies subject to the UK Bribery Act or the US Foreign Corrupt Practices Act are likely to have anti-bribery training programmes in place for their own employees and require the same of their suppliers as a condition of selection. If not, the suppliers may have to agree that their employees will participate in the customer's anti-bribery programme.

Beyond the specific example of anti-bribery practices, selected suppliers will be required to provide evidence of screening their own suppliers for legal compliance and a commitment to ethical business practices.

If the expanded scope of HR was not evident at the turn of the decade, the extended enterprise concept was soon to dominate the HR agenda in an unexpected way. The social distancing, self-isolation and quarantine requirements required to limit the spread of Covid-19 caused a sudden and dramatic proliferation in the number of organisational 'operating sites'. Every employee who possibly could was required to continue working without presenting themselves for duty at their formal place of work. What's more, the physical and mental health of every employee became an overriding business and HR priority.

The extended enterprise concept requires that organisations not merely reduce the extent of their negative impacts on the broader environment in which they operate, but that they exert a positive impact on the actions of those over whom they have influence.

A significant implication of the extended enterprise concept for the new HR role is the need to contribute:

- beyond the application of regulations applicable to the organisation's specific sector; and

- beyond compliance with the national laws and governance codes of the country in which the organisation is domiciled.

This contribution will be achieved by drawing on both existing and new sources of knowledge and guidance.

# New Sources of Insight for the Expanded HR Role

Rather than being daunted by the prospect of a role elevated in strategic importance that moreover extends into the supply chain, the future HR leader can draw upon a host of helpful insights from unexpected sources and diverse disciplines.

In this section I present and summarise key sources of recent and emerging knowledge with practical implications for the leadership of ethics in organisation.

# Guidance From International and Multilateral Organisations

International governmental and multilateral organisations are an essential source of guidance for the new HR role, with application both within the ethical organisation and across its supply chain.

The United Nations (UN) pursues the common goals of 193 member states, which together with two observer countries represent the entire world. It works in pursuit of global sustainability, world peace and human well-being, with goals as varied and complex as the world we live in. HR practitioners are at least familiar with one of the UN agencies, the International Labour Organisation, whose mandate is the pursuit of social justice and the promotion of decent work.

Other UN agencies and international organisations whose outputs need to be referred to and applied in the new ethical organisation and extended enterprise context include:

*The UN Development Programme (UNDP) and the Sustainable Development Goals (SDGs)*[6]

The UNDP is a specialist UN development agency that works across the world to fight poverty, reduce inequality, and promote sustainable development. The SDGs are 17 global goals agreed in 2015 for attainment by 2030, and stated as aspirations such as No Poverty, Quality Education, Gender Equality, Decent Work and Economic Growth, Responsible Consumption and Production, and Climate Action.

---

6    United Nations, 2020.

Today's HR leader needs to make regular reference to the targets and measurement indicators attached to the 17 SDGs, and use a wide range of UNDP tools to influence the alignment of organisational strategies with their attainment.

*The United Nations (UN) and the UN Convention against Corruption (UNCAC)[7]*

The UN Convention against Corruption (UNCAC) was the first legally binding multinational instrument against corruption. It requires state parties to enact legislation that criminalises certain corrupt acts, including both domestic and foreign bribery and the associated offences of money laundering and the obstruction of justice. Of particular value to the HR leader is the chapter of the convention that deals with anti-corruption measures directed at both the public and private sectors.

*The Organisation for Economic Cooperation and Development (OECD) and its Anti-Bribery Convention[8]*

The OECD is a forum where governments of 36 democracies with market economies, together with over 70 non-member economies, work together to promote economic growth, prosperity and sustainable development. Its Anti-Bribery Convention requires parties to criminalise the bribery of foreign public officials in international business transactions. Of particular value to the HR practitioner are the OECD Anti-Bribery Conventions Guidelines for Multinational Enterprises.[9]

*The World Economic Forum (WEF) and its focus on stakeholder capitalism*

The 2020 annual meeting of the WEF in Davos refocused the attention of both business and governments on the concept of 'stakeholder capitalism', and shifted away from the dominant 'shareholder capitalism' paradigm. The stakeholder capitalism conceptualisation of business is that its purpose is not to produce profit, but rather to produce profitable solutions to the challenges facing the planet and its people.

In a significant contribution that aims to make tangible the objectives of a business driven by stakeholder capitalism, the WEF published a resource in September 2020 which provides a blueprint to organisational leaders: *Measuring Stakeholder Capitalism: Towards Common Metrics and Consistent Reporting of Sustainable Value Creation.*[10]

---

7    United Nations Office on Drugs and Crime, 2004.
8    OECD, n.d.
9    OECD, 2011.
10   World Economic Forum, 2020.

This white paper is built upon four pillars or principles, Governance, Planet, People and Prosperity. In turn, it lays out comprehensive metrics, applicable across all business contexts, which should drive the efforts of every organisation to deliver shared, sustainable value. As a resource that integrates the principles and objectives of the SDGs into a business roadmap, and as the product of a far-reaching consultation process, this WEF publication should sit at the top of the HR pile of resources.

From this overview of the work of just a few international organisations, it is evident that they can be a source of powerful insights for HR leaders in their quest to impact the strategic agenda of the organisations they serve.

## Foreign Bribery Legislation and Related Guidance Documents

As is apparent from the discussion of the work and programmes of international organisations, high importance is being attached to combatting corruption. While bribery within a country is a crime the world over, it was for many decades the case that these laws did not extend to bribery committed in business dealings with and in foreign countries.

While a number of countries today have anti-foreign bribery laws, the better known of these are the US Foreign Corrupt Practices Act and the more recent UK Bribery Act. Put simply, these Acts say that if you do business in the US or UK and you or your agents engage in bribery anywhere in the world, they can impose criminal and civil penalties that will negate the value of the ill-gotten gains – or withdraw your licence to operate there.

Enforcement is achieved using a wide array of measures. In addition to orders of profit disgorgement and fines, individual executives are being held accountable. Companies are incentivised to self-disclose instances of bribery in their dealings and to cooperate fully with government investigators. In return they can receive some remission on the extent of the penalties imposed.

The guidance documents issued by the relevant regulators of this legislation are of particular value to the HR leader. These are essentially blueprints for the establishment of ethically-run organisations and carry a great deal of weight when presented in the boardroom.[11, 12]

---

11    US Department of Justice Criminal Division, 2020.
12    Transparency International UK, 2012.

## Research, Best Practices and Partnerships with Civil Society Organisations

The historically uneasy, if not adversarial, relationship between civil society organisations and the corporate world is undergoing a fundamental change of mutual benefit.

The rigorous and readily accessible research and publications of Transparency International, the pre-eminent anti-corruption civil society organisation, are today an invaluable resource for those working in pursuit of corporate compliance with foreign bribery laws.[13] Similarly, Anti-Slavery International is just one of many organisations that exists to fight human trafficking and forced and child labour.[14] Once a company maps its full supply chain back to the source of raw materials or original inputs, evidence of unethical business practices is more likely to be found. In significant instances, severe human exploitation is revealed.

Examples of products that we now know cannot be guaranteed by manufacturers to be free of child labour include chocolates and rechargeable mobile devices.[15] This child labour is found in the cocoa bean fields of the Ivory Coast and in the artisanal cobalt mines of the Democratic Republic of Congo (cobalt is needed to make the rechargeable batteries which are used by an ever-widening range of products, many of which, like mobile phones, are considered necessities of contemporary life).[16]

In a new, pragmatic partnership approach, companies and entire sectors are working hand-in-hand with civil society organisations, and where they are amendable with governments, to address the prevailing socio-economic circumstances that give rise to this unethical exploitation of vulnerable communities.

Rather than withdrawing from unsavoury supply arrangements and circumstances that they have been an unwitting party to creating, corporations are acknowledging the realities and embarking on long-term programmes to remediate the adverse conditions that have been created.

## New Notions of Cross-Cultural Morality from The Field of Social Anthropology

From the field of social anthropology, new research is highlighting the strong commonality of age-old guiding principles across cultures, and in the process enhancing our understanding of the power of ingrained societal beliefs on behaviour.

---

13   Transparency International UK, 2021.
14   Anti-slavery, 2021.
15   Whoreisky & Siegel, 2019.
16   International Labour Organisation, 2019.

In an important study based on 600 sources in 60 societies, seven so-called co-operative behaviours were found to be prized as morally good across 99.9% of cultures.[17] These behaviours included: help your family, help your group, return favours, be brave, defer to superiors, divide resources and respect others' property.

If we consider just the first three of the seven behaviours, we become aware of the extent to which modern conceptions of ethical conduct in work, for example that nepotism is wrong, can require employees to battle with the impulse to use their access to resources and positions of authority to favour their family members.

## Better Understanding of Brain Function from The Field of Neuroscience

As research techniques have advanced, the field of neuroscience has provided rich evidence of the role that the brain plays in human behaviour. The application of this knowledge for the workplace was first articulated by David Rock in the now classic resource, *Your Brain at Work*.[18]

There is now evidence that dispels widely held myths about the brain. Rather than having unlimited capacity, we have learned that the pre-frontal cortex, the part of the brain essential for judgement and decision-making, is limited in capacity, is easily tired and distracted, and can be significantly impaired when we are overwhelmed by fear and anguish.

In the context of our interactions with others (the key focus of the speciality of social cognitive neuroscience), we find that negative emotions that disrupt the capacity of the pre-frontal cortex are easily aroused by conditions of unpredictability, ambiguity, unfairness, indignity, disrespect, social exclusion and powerlessness. Faced with a workplace in which such conditions are experienced on a persistent basis, employees unable to resign their positions survive by psychologically disengaging – a mental state in which the best interests of the employer are no longer the employee's overriding priority.

The finding that we can only consider a finite number of inputs simultaneously when exercising judgement is partly responsible for the phenomenon of ethical blindness – a temporary inability to see and consider the ethical dimension of a decision.

---

17   Curry, Mullins & Whitehouse, 2019.
18   Rock, 2009.

# Improved Insight into The Role of Cognitive Biases in Decision-Making

The concept of cognitive bias may have been introduced as long ago as 1972, but it has been a subject of continued research and relevance in the field of human judgement and decision-making ever since.[19]

In essence, a cognitive bias can be described as a mental short cut that our minds can take, without our conscious awareness, when we are assessing situations, formulating positions and making decisions. In terms of our survival, it is an adaptive ability that enables us to evaluate and respond at speed to situations that are potentially threatening. In a world of information overload and competing demands, it helps us to make quick judgements without consuming our limited conscious cognitive processing power.

Cognitive biases tend to be imbued with stereotypes, beliefs and societal injunctions that we acquire at an early age and further develop or discard through a lifetime of experiences. Unaware that they are exerting a powerful influence upon our response to a given situation, it is not unusual to find that we retrospectively rationalise conclusions that we were barely conscious of reaching.

A seemingly endless list of cognitive biases today find their way into everyday conversation. Think about the courtesy bias, the optimism bias and the status quo bias, amongst others. For the HR leader seeking to promote ethical decision-making, these are an invaluable source of actionable insights. This can be illustrated with just one example, the reciprocity or reciprocation bias.

The reciprocity bias is a term that describes our impulse to return favours that people do for us. From an evolutionary perspective, this bias would have had survival advantages and it continues to oil the wheels of cordial relationships at home and at work. Considered in the context of workplace ethics, an obvious implication of the reciprocity bias is its potential to compromise impartiality in decision-making, for example, in the context of a supplier selection process.

Before we consider our next source of insight it is appropriate to describe the reactance bias: our tendency to do something different from that which we are asked to do when we perceive an attempt to constrain our freedom and options.

---

19   Kahneman & Frederick, 2002.

# Invaluable New Insights from The Burgeoning Field of Behavioural Economics

In 2017, the Nobel Prize for Economics was awarded to Richard Thaler, who, together with Cass Sunstein, is credited with bringing attention to what is popularly referred to as 'nudge theory'.[20] Thaler and Sunstein are but two of a host of researchers studying the subject of prosocial behaviour: how we can inspire people to behave in their own and in society's best interests.

HR practitioners in ethical organisations are taking the learnings from this fast-growing field and implementing measures that will encourage prosocial decision-making in the workplace, in addition to simply prescribing it through policies and enforcing it with discipline.

# Implications for the New HR Ethics Agenda

The current suite of well-developed HR competencies plays an important ongoing role in minimising people-related risk, promoting compliance with organisational procedures, and facilitating effective performance and good conduct.

Taking the presence of these contributions by the HR function as a given, we will focus on the enhanced expectations of HR in the ethical organisation of the 2020s and beyond.

## Promoting internal transparency and engagement in decision-making

Faced with the prospect of employee protests against policies, programmes and practices that are perceived to be unethical, internal transparency and engagement in decision-making processes is an increased necessity.

A culture of engaging and securing employee support ahead of, rather than in a rear-guard reaction to, an employee public outcry, should be championed and supported by HR.

Effective leadership now requires that the rationale behind decisions and strategies are presented for debate and at the very least explained. It will no longer be possible to simply announce decisions and expect uncritical employee compliance.

---

20   Thaler & Sunstein, 2021.

## Facilitating organisational positions on socio-political issues

The organisation will find itself unable to sustain a position of detached neutrality in relation to contentious social and political issues. Disappointed with their politicians, employees and customers are demanding that businesses clarify their positions and take positive action to influence lawmakers, particularly in the protection and advancement of evolving views on human rights.

By definition, this expectation presents the risk that a business might alienate those employees and customers who hold views contrary to the position it adopts. HR has a significant role to play in reading the evolving social and political mood of the workforce and interpreting this for the organisation's leadership.

The risks and complexities of this new corporate role aside, brands that have taken a public stand on contentious social causes in recent years, such as Nike, have found that many more consumers bought rather than boycotted or burned their products.[21]

Clear positions on social issues can be an important part of the employer value proposition, with indications being that employees are increasingly choosing their employer based on the degree of values alignment they perceive to exist between themselves and the organisation. HR should expect to be questioned on, and defend, the employer's positions on a widening range of social and political issues to a new generation of candidates.

## Creating a speak up culture and facilitating internal disclosures of unethical conduct

In light of the heightened reputation and regulatory risk of insiders making claims and revealing evidence in the public domain, today's leaders cannot afford to be the last to know of unethical conduct in their organisations.

The world over, employees with information they wish to share in the best interests of the organisation and its stakeholders can increasingly rely on the safety afforded by legislation that provides protection for whistleblowers.

A culture that supports the employee fulfilling their duty to bring suspicions or knowledge of ethical and legal risks to their employer's attention is becoming an overriding organisation development priority. When information of unethical activity flows with ease to those responsible for ethical practices in the organisation, issues can be addressed effectively, internally and at an early stage.

---

21  Wingard, 2019.

HR needs to prioritise leadership practices, organisational policies and development activities that will empower employees to speak up and capacitate managers to 'listen up'. Escalation policies to be followed by both employees and supervisors need to be put in place to ensure that reports are appropriately investigated and acted upon. Multi-channel reporting systems, including those that guarantee anonymity, are now a workplace imperative.

Suppliers and their own employees can have a valuable window on unethical activity in a customer's business that is otherwise obscured from the view of its leadership. With reporting systems in place for the use of employees, HR is well placed to fulfil what in South Africa is now a legal obligation: making safe reporting channels available to suppliers who, like employees, now also enjoy a right to non-retaliation.[22]

The ethical risk management contribution of effective HR leadership in this area cannot be overstated: the biennial global study by the Association of Certified Fraud Examiners (ACFE)[23] finds time and again that tip-offs outrank even internal audit and management reviews as the top initial source of occupational fraud detection.

The ACFE report also confirms that the percentage of tip-offs leading to fraud detection rises significantly when an organisation has an ethics hotline in place, and that businesses without an effective hotline suffer far greater losses to fraud schemes that those which do not. It may not be surprising that the largest source of tips are employees, but it is significant that customers and suppliers are the second and third largest reporting groups.

## Revisiting ethics codes and related policies

The primacy of a code of ethics in relation to all other organisation policies is now without question. Ethics has been recognised as the overarching feature of corporate governance, and we have seen that compliance with powerful foreign bribery legislation now obliges this formalisation of commitment to ethical business conduct.

HR should support the devising and revising of the organisational ethics code, and must contribute to the underlying logic and content of a range of supporting policies.

Here are just a few practical examples:

- Understanding that cognitive biases such as the reciprocation effect can unwittingly cause us to lose impartiality in our business dealings with those who show us favour, HR can provide valuable guidance to the organisation's review of its gifts and hospitality policy.

---

22   The Government Gazette of South Africa, 2017.
23   Association of Certified Fraud Examiners, 2020.

- Appreciating the powerful justification ability that enables ethical blindness by those with competing interests, together with the courtesy bias that inhibits people from calling out their conflicted colleagues, HR should champion a shift away from a tick-box approach to the declaration of interests and towards the conscious, ongoing management of conflicts of interest.

- Knowing that deeply embedded societal norms that cross cultures have instilled in humans a strong, unconscious bias towards those who are our kin or our kind, HR must make explicit the requirement that people and procurement decisions in the workplace are made impartially.

## Disincentivising the unethical pursuit of performance targets

The raised risk of regulatory sanction and reputation harm, where business is revealed as having been secured through bribery, calls for a radical rethink of remuneration strategy.

At the same time, our improved understanding of the effect of cognitive biases, and the potential for ethical blindness on judgement and decision-making, demands a review of the role that reward practices are playing in the promotion of unethical conduct. Simply put, the practice of setting otherwise unattainable targets, attaching large incentives to their delivery and then turning a blind eye to how these are met, cannot continue.

Performance management and remuneration strategies of the future will have to ensure that tough targets are not set and incentivised without clear supervisory line of sight over the process of goal attainment. A quantitative approach that focuses solely on outputs will be supplemented by a qualitative review of the extent to which ethical values were applied in the pursuit of outcomes.

## Maintaining employee engagement with the ethics expectation

The organisation in which ethical behaviour becomes the norm rather than the exception is going to be one that maintains an ongoing focus on the topic in the minds of all employees.

We have seen that the exercise of good judgement at a given point in time depends upon the optimal functioning of the brain's pre-frontal cortex, which is limited in its capacity to weigh up different pieces of information simultaneously. The performance of the pre-frontal cortex is prone to disruption by a lack of psychological safety and its operations are easily distracted.

If we want 'the right thing to do' to feature in our employees' day-to-day decision-making, it is necessary for us to create the environmental conditions for this to be possible. Long-forgotten policies and even an annual ethics class have little chance of competing for attention in the noisy contemporary workplace.

These building blocks – policies and education – need to be complemented by a sustained communication programme that sees every appropriate opportunity taken to draw attention to the ethical dimension of performance and conduct at work. An annual ethics focus needs to be complemented by an ongoing campaign that keeps ethics top of mind.

Whatever communication tools are used, however far-flung the organisation's operations, every employee should be reached by regular ethics messaging. In the management of such campaigns, the role that HR needs to fulfil is one that has the same effect as the lighthouse that reliably guides ships to safe harbour, especially under unclear and challenging conditions.

## Promoting pro-social behaviour

As every HR practitioner knows all too well, policies are essential but insufficient measures to ensure compliance with organisational requirements.

Responding to conduct that deviates from reasonable rules consumes a disproportionate amount of HR time and resources. Similarly, responding to on-principle challenges to policy requirements is a tiring inevitability for the HR leader.

Fortunately, insights from the burgeoning fields of behavioural science, including behavioural economics, are providing us with strategies to use that inspire rather than bluntly require compliance.[24] Applying key concepts such as social proof together with nudge theory, the ethical organisation of the future will be one in which there is a concerted effort to:

- increase the ease with which employees can do what is right; and

- increase the difficulty with which employees can do what is wrong.

The difference between the existing approach to requiring compliant conduct and the new approach to inspiring compliance is often referred to as being the difference between mandating and motivating the required behaviour. The future HR function will complement a policy and punishment approach to securing ethical conduct with one that builds upon the emerging evidence of practical ways to inspire it.

---

24  Carsten & The FCPA Blog, 2017.

## The new face of policies and procedures

HR policies and procedures are the foundation of legal compliance, fairness in management practices, and ethical employee conduct in any organisation. In reality, information overload and digital distraction impairs the ability of managers and employees to hold an ever-increasing range of complex requirements front of mind.

In response, HR leaders are today drawing on best practices in effective communication and using readily available technology to facilitate ease of access and understanding of policies, and to promote efficient and compliant adherence to procedures.

Dense and detailed text is being transformed into brain-friendly formats. Eye-catching multi-media documents designed for ease of understanding highlight key points of the policy, often complemented by microlearning video material. Embedding the full policy document and related forms together with links to supplementary reading allows for quick access to detailed requirements and procedures.

Digital workflow technology is being widely used to enable ease and efficiency of employee policy compliance and management approval processes, in turn providing for automated record-keeping and easily reviewed audit trails.

## New learning and development requirements

When it comes to the requirement for ethical conduct and decision-making, it is often the case that employees are expected to come with a pre-established set of ethics that allows for self-management. We now appreciate the need to make ethical expectations explicit and to develop the skills of ethical decision-making at all levels in the organisation.

At the senior levels, executives, managers and supervisors need to have the principles of managing for ethical conduct as a core component of their leadership development. This includes the importance of creating a team culture in which individuals are likely to openly report concerns. Specific training in anti-retaliation is becoming of increased importance in light of laws protecting whistleblowers from occupational detriment.

At every level of the organisation there is a need for anti-corruption awareness training, with a particular focus on anti-bribery and the recognition of conflicts of interest. Training programmes that promote social courage and the concept of being an active bystander are helping employees to overcome their fears of being the bearers of bad news.

## Contributing expertise and positively impacting on the extended enterprise

The HR leader already possesses a wealth of knowledge and skill that can be valuably applied to the benefit of ethics in the extended enterprise.

Well-developed core competencies, including screening, selection, contracting, induction, legal compliance, policy development, conflict handling and negotiation, performance management, coaching and skills development, to name but a few, position HR for a host of contributions that can increase integrity in the supply chain.

A typical starting point is through internal engagement with the organisation's own procurement function. There is a valuable contribution to ethics in the supply chain to be made simply by offering to review supplier application forms, selection processes and service level agreements. Amendments that enhance vendor screening, selection and management may be easily identified from an HR perspective, for example by inserting provisions around employment practices that respect human rights.

Where smaller suppliers lack internal resources, HR can play a role by linking them with trusted third-party HR service providers. The employee induction programmes offered by HR can also be expanded to suppliers and their employees. Extending ethics and specifically anti-bribery training programmes to suppliers who would not otherwise experience these is of overriding importance. Ensuring that suppliers know how to blow the whistle on misconduct they encounter in the course of service delivery to your organisation is essential.

By no means an exhaustive list of potential contributions to supply chain ethics by the HR function, these examples merely serve to illustrate the value to be derived from applying existing competencies to the extended enterprise.

## The cross-functional governance collaboration imperative

The range of support specialists contributing to the establishment and maintenance of an ethical culture will vary depending on the size and structure of an organisation; larger organisations and those in high-risk sectors are increasingly appointing dedicated ethics officers. Playing a critical role in organisation governance can be a function of finance, internal audit, governance, risk and compliance, legal, procurement, IT and, of course, HR. The unique window that each of these functions has into the same organisation, their specialist skills sets, and their limited time and resources must all be harnessed in a cross-functional approach to the establishment, monitoring and maintenance of an ethical culture. Through common goals, horizontal collaboration and alignment of effort, the HR function will be better positioned to deliver on its expanded mandate.

## HR as the organisational behavioural scientist

Having embraced this broader responsibility and incorporated these additional sources of knowledge into its advisory role, the HR department is well-positioned to make a strategic contribution to every facet of organisational decision-making.

We can capture this new strategic position as being that of organisational behavioural scientist. When one reflects, for example, on the marketing missteps by major brands that have caused deep offence to customers on the grounds of perceived prejudice, it is apparent that HR has a role to play in promoting organisation-wide appreciation of the increasingly complex social environment.

# Conclusion

The recognition that future global and organisational sustainability is inextricably linked has led to a reformulation of the role of business in society. In turn, this requires that HR plays a role of raised strategic importance in the leadership of organisational ethics.

This is a role that represents a significant shift for HR, away from its traditional inward facing focus and outwards in an embrace of the extended enterprise. It is one in which compliance with national legislation and sector-specific regulations become bare minimum requirements.

It is a role in which new strategic value is delivered through an understanding of international developments, be these the laws of other countries which have extraterritorial application, or the standards being established by international and multi-lateral organisations.

Its delivery can only be achieved through the application of insights from a wide range of disciplines and through a commitment to working in concert with and across functions in support of a shared vision of an ethical organisation.

Above all, the role of HR in the future must be to promote and foster workplace cultures and practices that increase, simultaneously, the prospects for organisational and global sustainability.

Chapter 12

# Agility and Innovation – The Ultimate Organisational Coping Mechanism

# The Case of Media24

### Shelagh Goodwin

## Introduction

Media24, a 105-year-old media company with deep roots in printed newspapers, magazines and books, had faced declining revenues and profitability for years. This dire position was not unique to Media24 or to South Africa. Globally, media businesses had been struggling to reinvent themselves in the face of massive digital disruption, with varying degrees of success. The Covid-19 pandemic and the lockdowns and economic devastation that followed should have been the last nail in the coffin for this business, yet one year later, Media24 has not only survived, but achieved a turnaround that few could have expected. This chapter explores the role of agility and innovation as the ultimate organisational coping mechanism in times of rapid change. As background, I describe the challenge that faces the media industry, before outlining the business response to the challenges, highlighting the role of agility and innovation as organisational coping mechanisms. Finally, I suggest a framework that may help organisations to apply agility and innovation when confronting their own challenges.

## A Disrupted Industry: The Challenge

To appreciate the challenge that the media industry faced, it is useful to understand the typical business model of media companies. This model has been applied across the world and over the centuries, and consists of three simple steps:

1.   Build an audience through a mass medium or platform, like pamphlets, magazines, newspapers, radio, television or internet.

2.   Sell their attention to advertisers and/or persuade your audience to pay for the content.

3.   Count the beans! (Ensure that the costs of creating and distributing the content on your platform in Step 1 are covered by the revenues generated in Step 2.)

These three steps are the basis of a robust model that continues to succeed, even for social media giants like Facebook, which:

1.   builds its audience through content that its own members generate every day – posts, memes, videos etc.;

2.   sells their attention to advertisers (in the newsfeed and the marketplace); and

3.   covers the cost of its technology platform and generates profits.

The success of this approach shows us that the problem that faced traditional media companies was not the disruption of the basic business model. Rather, the core problem was that their platform – printed newspapers and magazines – became less popular with readers and advertisers, who now had access to almost limitless content and very cheap advertising rates online. And although the number of copies sold declined, the costs of printing and distribution remained largely fixed, which quickly pushed print media businesses into the red. It was the stubborn fixed costs of creating, printing and distributing content that ultimately led to the downfall of media houses that could not adjust their cost structures quickly enough to survive when revenues fell.

In the South African media landscape, 2020 was a terrible year. Two long-standing magazine publishers, Caxton Magazines and Associated Media Publishing, closed their doors. Yet Media24's magazines division not only survived, but reinvented its business model and thrived. Minette Ferreira, the general manager of the magazine business, summed it up as follows: "Suddenly, in 2020, the runway remaining for our four-to-five-year plan evaporated, forcing dramatic change. The lesson I learned most was always to think forward and not look for excuses not to change when you see the sands of time running out."[1] The agility to respond quickly and innovatively to changes in the audience's needs became the ultimate coping mechanism.

Agility and innovation have been linked to organisational resilience, particularly under rapidly changing and complex market conditions. For example, a recent McKinsey study found that resilient companies cut costs faster under adverse conditions

---

1   Gordon, 2021.

and expanded faster when conditions improved.[2] Top performing companies have consistently been identified as more agile and innovative than their competitors. We will now explore the concepts of agility and innovation, what they mean, what drives them, and how organisations can improve their own agility and innovation for sustainable success.

## What Do We Mean by Agility and Innovation?

Global interest in agility and innovation are intense. A Google Scholar search shows over 250 000 results for 'agility' and almost two million results for 'innovation' since the year 2000. This interest seems to be driven by the need to respond to accelerating change of all kinds: political, economic, social, technological and environmental. For example, rapid technological advances in artificial intelligence, cloud-based technology, high-speed mobile internet and the widespread adoption of big data analytics have resulted in unprecedented digital disruption[3], and socially, greater workplace diversity calls on us to embrace multi-culturalism and adapt to a much wider variety of cultural norms. The Covid-19 pandemic, with its attendant lockdowns, added another layer of complexity for organisations that were already dealing with significant disruption, and affected the health and well-being of employees and customers, the functioning of supply chains around the world, as well as economies and unemployment rates. These and other changes called for effective coping mechanisms, because organisations that cope effectively with large-scale and rapid change are more likely to survive and thrive in a changing world than those that do not.

Organisations that thrive in a changing environment are those that respond with more agility and innovation than their competitors. In the next section, I will define agility and innovation in practical terms, sharing examples of agile and innovative strategies, before going on to offer a framework for organisations to develop their own levels of agility and innovation and become more resilient in the face of change.

### Agility

*"Float like a butterfly, sting like a bee. The hands can't hit what the eye can't see."*

This iconic quote from Muhammad Ali is a great definition of agility at the personal level: Ali's ability to "float like a butterfly" refers to his skill in calmly assessing the situation, while "sting like a bee" speaks to his sharply focused attack. "The hands can't hit what the eye can't see" reminds us of his need to be super-aware of his surroundings and opponent at all times. In short, agility at the personal level calls for

---

2    Laczkowski & Mysore, 2019.

3    World Economic Forum, 2018.

awareness of what is happening around us, anticipating what may happen next, and being ready to respond swiftly to any hint of change.

Just as personal agility enables boxers and other sportspeople to outperform their opponents, organisational agility helps businesses to outperform their competitors. In organisational theory, agility can be defined as the capacity to proactively sense and change direction to remain competitive.[4] The keys to agility are the ability to read the environment and trends so as to anticipate or create change ('floating like a butterfly'), and the ability to mobilise resources quickly and decisively to change direction as needed ('stinging like a bee'). True agility moves organisations beyond the level of merely responding quickly to change to the level of anticipating and even creating change. To this extent, agility becomes innovation. Before we explore organisational strategies for agility and innovation, let me clarify what is meant by innovation.

## Innovation

Innovation describes the process of converting ideas into new or improved products, processes and services. Thus, while agility is concerned with our ability to anticipate or create change in response to changes in our environment, innovation determines the actual changes that are implemented. Henry Ford (1863 – 1947), founder of the Ford Motor Company, famously said, "If I had asked the public what they wanted, they would have said a faster horse". Ford showed agility in anticipating the impact that the internal combustion engine would have on personal transport, and innovation in developing and producing the motor car. Of course, he did not invent the first motor car – that was patented by Karl Benz in 1886. Ford's innovation was the production process for the Model T Ford, which included offering the car in one colour only – Japan Black – as this was the cheapest and most durable coating available for cars. (Sadly, there seems to be no evidence for the urban legend that Ford used only black because it was the fastest drying colour!). It is the combination of agility (anticipating or creating and responding to change) and innovation (creating new or improved processes products and services) that enable organisations to cope with large-scale and rapid changes in their environments, to create and seize opportunities quickly, and to anticipate and deal with threats effectively. Now that I have clarified the meanings of agility and innovation, we'll explore what drives these organisational coping mechanisms.

---

4    Pulakos, Kantrowitz & Schneider, 2019.

# What Drives Agility and Innovation in Organisations?

Agility and innovation don't happen by accident. Rather, a combination of individual-, organisational process- and organisational climate-based factors drive agility and innovation in organisations. The good news is that organisations can actively build their capacity for agility and innovation. Below are some of the features of individuals and organisations that can promote agility and innovation.

## Individual characteristics

The capacity for agility and innovation starts with the skills, knowledge and attitudes of individual members. Without the right skills, knowledge and attitude to embrace change and respond with agility and innovation at the individual level, organisational teams and the organisation as a whole are unlikely to develop agile and innovative responses. In Media24, as in most media companies, creativity had always been highly prized, but creativity alone would not be sufficient to ensure resilience, as we saw with other highly creative media organisations falling by the wayside.

One of the most important individual skills for organisational agility and innovation is *learning agility*, which has been described as "knowing what to do when you don't know what to do". This refers to the ability to apply existing knowledge and skills to new situations. People with higher levels of learning agility are good problem solvers, but also good problem finders; they typically seek out problems and enjoy the challenge of new and complex situations.[5] In addition, collaborative or *team learning* is a critical skill for individuals and teams. Collaborative learning includes creating shared mental models, testing models collaboratively, and openly sharing lessons learned from both successes and failures. Team learning emerges consistently as an important driver of innovation.[6]

The sharing and testing of *mental models* within teams helps to increase and strengthen the knowledge base of the organisation. A mental model can best be described as a person's idea of what a particular reality is and how it works; it is an interpretation of what is happening in the real world. Therefore, our mental models define how we understand what is happening around us. When we share the same mental model with others, it is easier to reach consensus about what is happening and what we should do about it. Mental models, together with the subject matter *expertise* that individuals bring, can be seen as the key knowledge requirements for organisational agility and innovation. A mental model that provides a realistic appraisal of market conditions, key trends and organisational capabilities is essential if the organisation is to respond with agility and to innovate. Expert knowledge that

---

5    Hofkes & Busato, 2015.
6    Edmondson, 2019.

is both deep and relevant can enable individuals, teams and organisations to develop useful and adaptive mental models.[7]

Finally, the skills of learning agility and team learning, combined with subject-matter expertise and shared mental models, will be most effectively combined when individuals have an attitude of *openness to change*. Openness to change, and even a preference to seek out or initiate change, is a key underlying attitude that increases the likelihood that individuals, as well as their teams and organisations, will respond to environmental challenges with agility and innovation. Talent – the skills, knowledge and attitudes of individual members – forms the foundation of an organisation's capacity to respond with agility and innovation. However, talent alone is not enough to ensure an agile and innovative response. Two other factors, organisational processes and the organisational climate, both play a significant role in organisational outcomes.

## Organisational processes

An organisational process that seems to be critical for adaptation, and therefore agility and innovation, is the adaptive process as described by Burke et al.[8] The adaptive process is typically part of how teams in agile organisations operate, and is embedded in their organisational culture. The adaptive process has four steps, which can best be described as a cycle, which is repeated as the situation evolves, ensuring that the organisation remains agile.

For Media24 Magazines, the adaptive process started with not making excuses not to change. Then, they planned and executed dramatic changes to the business, including the following:

- Scaling back the frequency of glossies (Fairlady and Sarie moved to six editions per year) and increased cover prices. "These moves placed the onus on us to ensure and improve quality", said Ferreira. "For example, with Fairlady we have upped the number of pages and expanded the content offering; it is easier for consumers to find cash for a luxury purchase every two months." Result? A 20%+ increase in copy sales since August.

- Outsourcing staff and giving editors contracts to produce magazines based on a fee per edition. Result? A flexible cost base for the company and a surge in creativity and the production of niche-interest content, with fantastic sales for stand-alone products.

---

7    Senge et al., 2011.
8    Burke et al., 2006.

- Refocusing the sales teams to sell creative solutions, not just a page ad. Result? Clients are offered opportunities including events, digital and TV, and ad sales have exceeded expectations.[9]

The adaptive process starts with a *situation assessment*, which refers to the gathering and analysis of information about what is happening and what is likely to happen. One or more of the team members scans the environment for cues that may be relevant, based on the knowledge and mental models held by the team. The knowledge, skills and attitudes of individual team members that we have already described may determine how effectively relevant environmental cues are picked up and interpreted. An effective situation assessment enables the team to develop a shared mental model of what is happening, and to develop team situation awareness. In Media24, this combination of a shared mental model and team situation awareness is called 'looking reality in the face'. This is what Ferreira meant when she said don't "look for excuses not to change". Having a clear and shared understanding of the reality that faces the team or organisation – understanding the key problems to be solved and one's current capacity to solve them – is the purpose of the situation assessment and allows the organisation to formulate an appropriate plan.

After the situation has been assessed, the organisation must *formulate a plan*. Planning includes setting the course of action, goals, roles and responsibilities. At a more detailed level, planning may include the prioritisation of tasks, clarification of performance expectations and identifying contingency plans. The change at Media24 Magazines was far-reaching and touched almost every aspect of the business, with a high risk of failure. Planning was critical. The ability to forecast future events and anticipate different scenarios determines how robust the plan is, and how well it will support an agile response. An effective plan is one that is rooted in a clear and shared assessment of reality, is clearly understood and supported by all stakeholders, and provides a practically executable way to close the gap between current and desired reality. Plan execution is the next critical step in the adaptive cycle.

Once the plan has been formulated, *plan execution* becomes the priority. Napoleon Hill's direction to "Plan your work and work your plan"[10] highlights the importance of these two aspects of the adaptive response. Implementing what has been planned is, of course, the key output here, but effective execution is also supported by leadership, monitoring, coordination, communication and backup where needed. An organisation that executes effectively provides strong support to its members, including the safety net provided by mutual performance monitoring. Mutual performance monitoring means that team members have each other's backs, watch for weaknesses and mistakes, and fill in the gaps rather than letting the team fail. For Minette Ferreira and

---

9   Gordon, 2021.
10   Hill, 1969.

her team, coordination and communication helped to ensure that key stakeholders – readers, editors and clients – understood and accepted the changes. An organisational climate of psychological safety, which will be discussed later in this chapter, is an essential enabler of successful plan execution. Psychological safety refers to a climate in which team members can speak up and share their views openly – even about concerns, objections, risks and mistakes – without fear of negative consequences for themselves. Psychological safety is also an important contributor to the last stage of the adaptive cycle, team learning.

One of the most important features of the adaptive process is *team learning*, which is "an ongoing process of reflection and action, characterized by asking questions, seeking feedback, experimenting, reflecting on results, and discussing errors or unexpected outcomes of actions".[11] Organisations that reflect and apply team learning are able to enhance their agility response and become more innovative in future, as even after the successful execution of a plan, they are always looking for ways to improve performance. Thus, as the adaptive organisation goes through the team learning phase, it also prepares to return to the *situation assessment*, continuing the cycle of learning, adaptation, agility and innovation.

Just as psychological safety provides the climate for effective plan execution, it also provides the climate for effective team learning. Furthermore, the link between psychological safety, team learning and innovation is a strong one. We will now explore the role of psychological safety in providing the organisational climate that supports agility and innovation in organisations.

## Organisational climate

Organisational climate refers to the pattern of behaviours, attitudes and feelings that prevail within an organisation, and is related to organisational culture, but may not be as deep-rooted or stable as culture. Organisational climate is often easier to change than culture, and can have a significant impact on the overall agility and innovation of the organisation. A particular element of organisational climate – psychological safety – has enjoyed increasing attention in recent years. [Amy Edmondson's *The Fearless Organization* (2019) gives a very good overview of the notion, with practical guidelines for managers, and is highly recommended reading.] Psychological safety is the shared belief that it is safe to take interpersonal risks in a group.[12] As such, psychological safety influences the degree to which individuals in a group are willing to speak up ('voice'), share ideas, take risks, and acknowledge and learn from mistakes. Speaking up frankly, sharing ideas and being willing to admit mistakes and learn from them describe how team learning happens, and it will come as no surprise

---

11    Edmondson, 1999, p.354.
12    Edmondson, 2019.

that higher levels of psychological safety are linked to higher levels of team learning, agility and innovation.

Edmondson shares a story about how she came upon the notion of psychological safety, which gives insight into how it operates. She was conducting field research in a number of hospitals, assessing the quality of their outcomes (how quickly patients recovered and how many patients recovered) by counting the number of mistakes made in each. In the hospital context, mistakes can be things like giving a patient the wrong dose of medication or prescribing the incorrect medication. She found a very strange thing: those units that reported making the most mistakes were also the units that had the best outcomes. How could you make the most mistakes and still have the best results? Well, she figured out – as you have probably guessed – that there can be a big difference between the number of mistakes made and the number of mistakes reported. It turned out that the units that were honest about their mistakes and reported all of them, achieved better results than the units where mistakes were covered up. And why would you cover up mistakes in a hospital? Well, for pretty much the same reason as you would do so anywhere else: to avoid getting into trouble. The units where people were afraid to admit to mistakes or question the instructions of the doctor (even when the doctor was obviously mistaken) had lower levels of psychological safety and lower levels of performance.

Some assume that psychological safety is all about creating a caring and supportive environment in a team and worry that this may shift focus away from team performance. If it's OK to make mistakes, won't people just slack? It's useful to think about the drive for performance as being like the accelerator on a car, with psychological safety being the brake. Only a fool would attempt to drive a car with an accelerator and no brakes. In Figure 1, this is the Anxiety Zone, and while you may drive very fast for a short time, this is not a sustainable mode for a car or for an organisation. Likewise, only a fool would attempt to drive a car with brakes but no accelerator. In Figure 1, this is the Comfort Zone – very comfortable, but it doesn't get you anywhere. Both the drive for performance and psychological safety are essential elements of a climate that enables agility and innovation. Without both being in place, we end up in the Apathy Zone. But where we focus both on psychological safety and on performance, we arrive in the learning and high-performance zone. This zone is where agility and innovation thrive.

| | | | |
|---|---|---|---|
| High psychological safety | Comfort zone | | Learning & high performance zone | |
| Low psychological safety | Apathy zone | | Anxiety zone | |

| Low standards | High standards |

*Figure 12.1: Psychological safety and performance*

The organisational climate (psychological safety), organisational processes (adaptive process) and individual characteristics (skills, knowledge and attitude) that contribute towards agility and innovation together form part of a practical framework which organisations may use to enhance their own agility and innovation.

# A Practical Framework for Agility and Innovation

We have considered the role of some key individual and organisational factors in building capacity for agility and innovation, but how do these factors relate to each other and come together to deliver results? We propose a practical framework for agility and innovation, which pulls these elements together and can be used to assess and improve your organisation's current level of capacity for agility and innovation. The model is adapted from Burke et al.[13]

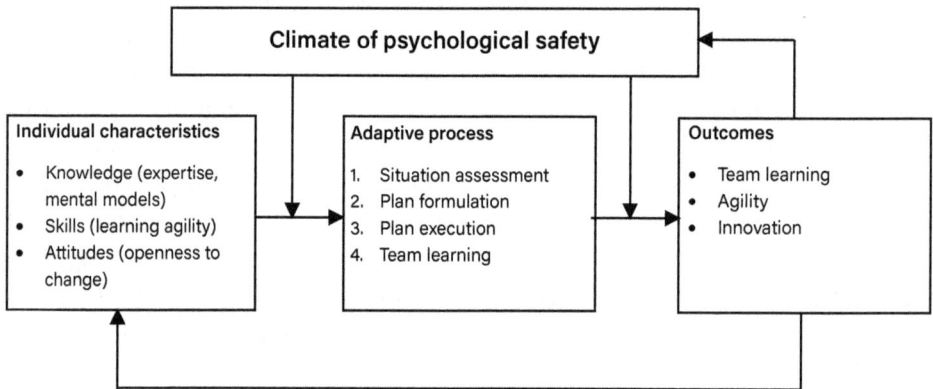

**Climate of psychological safety**

**Individual characteristics**
- Knowledge (expertise, mental models)
- Skills (learning agility)
- Attitudes (openness to change)

**Adaptive process**
1. Situation assessment
2. Plan formulation
3. Plan execution
4. Team learning

**Outcomes**
- Team learning
- Agility
- Innovation

*Figure 12.2: A practical framework for team learning, agility and innovation*

The starting point for the framework is the characteristics of the individuals who work there – the talent. If the individuals have the appropriate knowledge, skills and attitudes to respond with agility and drive innovation, AND if the organisational

---

13   Burke et al., 2006.

climate offers psychological safety, those members are likely to share their knowledge and mental models, to learn as a team, and to embrace change. The appropriateness of the individual characteristics and the climate will determine the degree to which an adaptive organisational process can succeed.

As we have seen, the adaptive process – a way of working that institutionalises adaptation and learning – is critical to the organisation's ability to reinvent itself and stay relevant as the environment changes. Without an institutionalised adaptive process, individual innovators may be able to deliver exciting results, but the organisation's ability to continuously adapt and innovate will be limited. And when the innovator leaves, the organisation's innovative capacity leaves with them.

The path from an adaptive process to the results we seek typically happens through team learning, which in turn leads agility and innovation. The essential pre-condition for team learning is psychological safety.[14] As a team works through the stages of the adaptive process, the level of psychological safety in the team determines the effectiveness of the process and how much learning takes place.

As the adaptive process – learning by doing for organisations – becomes embedded in the culture of the organisation, the outcomes of team learning, innovation and agility are generated. As team learning, innovation and agility are generated, a virtuous cycle is created which:

- reinforces to the organisation's members that their agile individual characteristics, climate of psychological safety and adaptive processes are delivering desirable results; and

- makes the organisation more attractive to individuals who value agility and innovation, which improves its ability to attract and retain agile and innovative individuals.

The dark side of this cycle is the vicious cycle, where in a climate of low psychological safety, people who value agility and innovation first stop speaking up and participating in adaptive processes, and eventually become frustrated and leave. Psychological safety is the key to both engaging and retaining the talented and innovative people who can build a resilient and sustainable organisation.

---

14   Edmondson, 2019.

## Conclusion

Agility and innovation are without doubt the ultimate coping mechanisms for organisations navigating rapid and complex change. In this chapter I have set out what is meant by agility and innovation, and shown with the example of the Media24 Magazines case how individual and organisational characteristics can be combined to ensure resilience in tough times. Setting out what to do to build agility and innovation is easy – the hard part is to have the courage to face reality head-on, and go out and do it.

Chapter 13

# Developing a Growth Mindset – The Route to Flourishing Organisations

Jasmin Pillay

## Falling in Love with a Culture: Where Company and Personal Values First Met

It was 2018 when Microsoft first called me. I must admit, I knew little more about the company than that it was a software firm, however my philosophy of "keep an open mind" prompted me to have a discussion at the very least. So, I had a conversation – seven, in fact. And this is where the magic happened. With each conversation, I fell more in love with Microsoft, and I realised I was experiencing the culture of the company.

But what exactly is this culture that I fell in love with?

## The Microsoft Story: Planting the Roots of a Growth Mindset

Innovation has always been in Microsoft's DNA – from when the company started in April 1975, with a handful of people whose goal was to put a computer in every home. Forty-six years later, with more than 175,000 employees all over the world[1], innovation remains a driving force.

When Satya Nadella became CEO in 2014, Microsoft was successful, yet he recognised that it needed to change – to move from focusing on individual products to solutions that help customers in all areas of their lives: work, learning, play and family.

---

1    Microsoft, 2021.

So, he invited every employee on a quest of discovery to collectively help transform Microsoft's culture: to become a business defined by a growth mindset, where anyone can change, learn and grow, and where potential is nurtured, not pre-determined.

The concept of a growth mindset is not new. It was first penned by Stanford psychology professor, Carol Dweck, in her book *Mindset: The New Psychology of Success*, which explores differences between fixed and growth mindsets, and how mindset can determine success in different areas of people's lives – from school to career to the sports field, and many spaces in between.[2]

Satya was inspired by Dweck's book, both in his personal philosophy, and as a leader.

In an interview with *Bloomberg*, Satya said, "There's this very simple concept that Carol Dweck talks about, which is if you take two people, one of them is a learn-it-all and the other one is a know-it-all. The learn-it-all will always trump the know-it-all in the long run, even if they start with less innate capability.

That is true for boys and girls in schools. It's true for CEOs in their jobs. It's true for every employee at Microsoft. I need to be able to walk out of here this evening and say, 'Where was I too closedminded, or where did I not show the right kind of attitude of growth in my own mind?' If I can get it right, then we're well on our way to having the culture we aspire to."[3]

Microsoft aspires to be a company of learn-it-alls. Satya's vision embodies the entire company, across geographies. "I want everyone inside of Microsoft to take that responsibility. This is not about top-line growth. This is not about bottom-line growth. This is about us individually having a growth mindset", he said in the *Seattle Times*.[4]

At its heart, this approach looks at how we can encourage and enable a growth mindset to take root and flourish. For us, this means obsessing over what matters to our customers, becoming more diverse and inclusive in everything we do, operating as one company instead of multiple siloed businesses, and making a difference in the lives of each other, our customers and the world around us.

This wouldn't be possible without empathy as a core value at the centre of Microsoft's culture. "Our core business is connected with the customers' needs and we will not be able to satisfy them if we don't have a deep sense of empathy", he said. "Empathy is a muscle, so it needs to be exercised."[5]

---

2    Dweck, 2006.
3    Bass, 2016.
4    Day, 2015.
5    Wharton, 2018.

Empathy is an integral part of our ethos, bringing the values that tie our people and the business together to life. We exercise ours by encouraging every individual to practice awareness of our own limitations, triggers and biases, examining these assumptions and seeking input from people of diverse backgrounds in order to challenge ingrained behaviours.

We are also encouraged to build empathy by exercising curiosity, keeping an open mind, asking questions, and actively listening to see and understand a situation from someone else's perspective. Above all, we are asked to demonstrate courage and be brave to ensure that all voices are heard. We do this through an allyship model that acts as a tool for self-reflection to help us better understand our own emotions, make an intentional effort to understand and empathise with others, and hold ourselves accountable to be a sustainable ally by fostering inclusive behaviours.

Harnessing these key attributes and putting them at the centre of what we do requires a focus on behaviours, systems and storytelling. It is well known that behavioural change requires a new way of thinking that is backed up by practice – because we know that practice not only makes perfect, but it also forms habits and creates positive behavioural change.

An example of positive behavioural change is our adjustment to our performance philosophy to focus on impact across three areas: the impact of individual contribution, building on the work of others, and contributing to the success of others. This expands the sphere of impact individuals can have and moves the focus from a fixed to a growth mindset, all the while promoting collaboration.

## Culture as Organisational Glue

Although Microsoft is recognised now for its growth mindset culture, it has been an evolution over the past seven years. Our leaders know our culture binds us together, and is the bedrock of everything we do.

Research backs up the importance people place on the values and culture of the companies they work at, especially in South Africa. A BCG study revealed that South Africa was one of the only countries – in a survey of 209,000 people in 190 countries – where company values rank as the most important consideration for people.[6]

Research also backs up the value of culture in business. A study by Duke University found that the majority of executives see the correlation between culture and business value, with 92% of business executives saying that improving company culture would increase company value.[7]

---

6   Strack, Kovács-Ondrejkovic, Baier, Antebi, Kavanagh & López Gobernado, 2021.
7   Graham, Grennan, Harvey & Rajgopal, 2019.

This is because culture can connect employees to the values of the company through the lived experience, which supports a unified approach and creates a common goal that everyone works towards. At Microsoft we call it "rowing in the same direction". This helps us achieve our people priorities and support our customers, because ultimately these goals should be aligned.

Central to "rowing in the same direction" is creating an environment that fosters empathy, collaboration, diversity and inclusion, giving all employees the opportunity to learn, grow and develop critical digital and work-related skills – continuously.

Building this type of environment and culture is not a point in time, with a start or end, but a continuous reshaping of our mindset to deliver on our mission: **To empower every person and every organisation on the planet to achieve more**.

At Microsoft South Africa, there are those who were part of the company pre- and through its culture transformation and there are those who have joined since. Irrespective of the number of years and our differences (which we welcome), WE – ARE – ALL – IN. Ours is a culture that helps us be better and do better, and support each other along our learning journeys. And we are all committed to closing the distance between our espoused culture and the lived experience for each other and our customers.

This commitment to ongoing learning and improvement is at the heart of Microsoft's culture. "We believe that by applying a growth mindset, we can change the world – empowering every person and every organisation to achieve more", said Microsoft South Africa CEO, Lillian Barnard, in *Business Focus Magazine*.[8]

## Where Leaders are Equals: Joining Hands for Cultural Change

For every Microsoft leader, building culture means being an ally and climbing into the trenches with our teams. No leader sits on the side lines; we do the heavy lifting together, and give our people the tools and platforms they need to foster a growth mindset and embrace ongoing change.

While culture starts at the top, it should not remain there, because culture cannot depend on a single person. Our leadership principles – Creating Clarity, Generating Energy and Delivering Success – are therefore aligned with our mission and culture; they guide our behaviour and they are for everyone.

---

8    Business Focus Magazine, 2019.

How do these principles show up?

We Create Clarity by reflecting on and synthesising the environment to achieve clarity of vision, for our teams and our customers, and then translate that vision into a coherent strategy and plan.

We Generate Energy by being a source of motivation for ourselves and those around us, and we enable an impactful and inclusive environment by building resilience in our teams through curiosity and a willingness to learn.

We Deliver Success by pushing through real and perceived barriers, having a beginner's mind, leaning into uncertainty, and being curious about the perspective of others. And most important is our understanding and measurement of cultural change. We measure change using data and by evolving the way we listen and learn from our teams because we want to know if they see the evidence of positive change in our culture, and what their experiences are.

Our engagement and listening systems are broad: from manager- and leader-led conversations to our Daily Pulse, which provides real-time employee perception data, and our annual engagement survey, a census survey we call the MS Poll, which we use as a tool for managers and teams to better understand issues like engagement, work-life flexibility and career development. We also extract and analyse data from qualitative sources such as Yammer and social sentiment tracking to understand what's in the hearts and minds of employees.

Our leaders communicate openly and regularly to drive our culture and connect with our people. Satya, for instance, uses live events such as monthly Town Hall meetings and Yammer to stay connected with us and encourage two-way dialogue.

In South Africa, Lillian is famous for her "assume you are included" approach, and matches this sentiment with regular company meetings, leader-led inclusive dialogues and more intimate smaller group discussions which we call fireside chats. And her literal and virtual door is always open. This is an approach replicated by our entire leader and manager community, which collectively helps drive and nurture team culture.

## A Growth Mindset in Action: A Focus on Diversity and Inclusion

A core part of this team culture is our commitment to diversity and inclusion. These have always been important, but are becoming ever more critical – especially as key attributes of our growth mindset. Research shows us that employees will consider leaving an organisation for one that is more inclusive, which it is one of their main criteria when deciding to join an organisation or not.[9]

As the definition of diversity continues to expand, human resource practitioners need to adapt for this increasingly diverse employee base, which is critical to business success. As a case in point, the *Harvard Business Review* found that cognitively diverse teams solve problems 60% faster.[10] They are also more profitable and perform better: companies with above-average total diversity had both 19 percentage points higher innovation revenues and 9 percentage points higher EBIT (earnings before interest and taxes) margins, on average.[11]

What this means is that businesses today must support diverse workforces with inclusive digital technology solutions, redesigned processes, and updated workspaces that enable employees to collaborate more effectively in person or when working remotely.

A demonstration of Microsoft's diversity and inclusion in action is through its hackathons. People from all disciplines and backgrounds are encouraged to come up with ideas – often beyond the scope of their day-to-day jobs – and collaborate with their colleagues to bring these ideas to life through proof of concepts.

A wonderful example as an outcome of this is the Xbox adaptive controller, which was designed to help gamers with limited mobility by making user input more accessible. This was possible precisely because of Microsoft's culture, which is driven by a growth mindset and underpinned by inclusivity and empathy.[12]

The idea was born when a Microsoft engineer, Matt Hite, stumbled across a custom gaming controller designed for wounded veterans on Twitter, and came to life when he got in touch with the creator, discovered how inaccessible gaming was for these injured veterans – from triple amputees and quadriplegics to traumatic brain injuries – and how difficult it was to modify equipment for them.

In response, a team of Microsoft employees decided to create a tailored solution at the company's 2015 Ability Summit hackathon. When leaders at the company saw the potential of the device, momentum for the idea and the project began building and different teams got to work on refining the controller – with input from gamers, accessibility advocates and non-profits that work with disabled gamers.

---

9    Eswaran, 2019.
10   Lewis & Reynolds, 2017.
11   Lorenzo & Reeves, 2018.
12   Microsoft, 2018.

The result was a solution that allows users to connect switches, buttons, joysticks and mounts to create a custom controller that suits their unique needs and abilities, and opens up a world of opportunities that didn't exist for these gamers before.

Empathy and allyship are at the heart of this solution; the team made an intentional effort to listen and understand the plight of injured veterans and disabled gamers – and worked to become allies to provide an inclusive solution.

This example illustrates how the company has looked at the behaviours and culture we are encouraging, and how we have put systems in place to determine and measure performance, as well as recognise and reward innovation.

## Bringing Inclusivity into the New World of Work

The whirlwind shift to remote working emphasised the need to enable inclusive workspaces. People with disabilities often require assistive technologies to fully participate and benefit from a remote or emerging hybrid workplace, which combines remote work with the option of going into the office at least part of the time.

The reality is that modern businesses have had the technological tools available to help promote inclusivity for quite some time, but have not yet fully capitalised on them.

Because we have an inherently inclusive mission at Microsoft – to empower everyone on the planet – and diversity and inclusion is core to our business model, we have worked over the years to ensure that technology is at the centre of our efforts to drive inclusivity.

Our efforts have therefore been focused on building inclusivity into our working model, which has been a combination of hybrid and working virtually for years. Pre-pandemic, for instance, our Johannesburg office catered for only one-third of the workforce to be in-office.

Some of the work we have done to encourage and foster greater inclusivity in this environment includes building inclusivity features into our remote working platforms. Microsoft Teams has real-time captioning in meetings and translation in live events so that people with a hearing disability or who speak a different language can participate seamlessly in meetings.

Our culture of inclusivity and diversity through allyship has also opened the door for employees to experiment, innovate and explore new ideas. This is exactly how the Xbox adaptive controller came to be – because employees were given the space to experiment and explore based on their passions, and because of this underlying culture of the whole company being engaged in efforts to drive inclusivity.

Employee resource groups (ERGs) are a key part of our inclusion practices recognising diversity; they provide support, networking opportunities, mentoring, community participation, product input and assistance in activities that promote cultural awareness. This helps embed diversity and inclusivity in our work, and deliver impact through the introduction of more inclusive products.

This then links to our second people priority, which is to evolve our culture with a growth mindset by giving our people the right skills, growing their leadership skills, and building their capability to learn.

Doing so – and recognising and rewarding people for their hard work and innovation – is part of our broader efforts to make Microsoft an exceptional place to work and empower our people at scale.

This is where the role of modern HR – specifically within the context of the new world of work – comes in.

## How Modern HR can Encourage a Growth Mindset in this New World of Work

The pandemic became an unconventional agent of change through mandatory shelter-in-place orders which forced remote work. It spawned a world where dining room tables double as desks, "you're on mute" has become a universal catchphrase for virtual meetings and conference calls, and impromptu coffee breaks with colleagues has been replaced by scheduled virtual catch-ups.

And although these changes have largely become part of our routines, many companies – and their human resources functions in particular – are still trying to navigate the impact these issues and trends have had on their employees, and act as much-needed allies to provide the mental, emotional and practical support that their people need.

Nurturing a growth mindset in this unique time in history, while reimagining new ways of working and doing business and simultaneously placing empathy and allyship at the core of what HR does, has never before been more critical – or complex.

Microsoft's own Work Reworked research, for instance, found that employees view time spent in the office as a powerful way to maintain bonds with their colleagues.[13]

---

13   Microsoft, 2020.

Other research found that nearly 100% of people believe that face-to-face meetings are essential for long-term business relationships because of the power of face-to-face communication: 55% of communication is body language, 38% tone and 7% spoken words.[14]

The value of face-to-face communication perhaps also explains why more than a third of South African business leaders surveyed as part of the Work Reworked research admitted to battling with creating a strong and unified team culture when they first moved to remote work.

This has been a challenge that modern HR divisions have grappled with since the onset of the pandemic. The near-overnight facelift to businesses showed that HR needed to reimagine work for a digital world. It also showed that HR is, and needs to be, an integral part of the business – one that is invested in continuously because of the fundamental role it plays in transformation and change.

HR is the people-focused part of the business that is able to interpret insights and drive change. HR practitioners are stewards of their company's culture, and as such, have a responsibility and an important role to play in embracing empathy and allyship to drive critical culture transformation and a growth mindset.

This is why Microsoft focuses on investing in HR excellence as the cornerstone of this transformation and mindset.

We redesigned our HR model to deliver greater impact by creating a better employee experience and preparing for the future workforce by simplifying processes and making the business more agile. We also actively prioritised using our allyship model to place empathy and understanding at the centre of how we connect with our people and handle issues. This understanding is key to delivering impact, driving a growth mindset and ultimately creating a better employee experience.

# Accelerating Culture Change through Technology

The ability to deliver greater impact, create a better employee experience and simplify processes to prepare for the workforce of the future is underpinned by the transformative power of technology – and Microsoft has used technology extensively to accelerate our culture change in our quest to help people do and achieve more.

---

14   Microsoft, 2020.

We use technology in multiple ways: from screening and hiring talent, right through to retaining and developing our people by enabling digital working and learning from anywhere, on any device. We also use it to create new habits through data-driven insights, as well as to communicate and connect with each other across the company.

Technology can play an unrivalled role in terms of screening talent, because of its capacity to maximise on data and insights, which is especially valuable in the South African context.

The country's major challenges are a contracting economy and widespread unemployment. There is also a digital skills gap – the JCSE-IITPSA ICT Skills Survey shows a chronic shortage of all types of digital skills in the South African ICT sector.[15]

## Technology as an Enabler in Hiring, Retaining and Developing Diverse Talent

Against this backdrop, however, technology can help industries find the right and diverse skills, and expand the talent pipeline more broadly. This includes using LinkedIn and its various capabilities around screening, talent and skills insights.

Because our focus at Microsoft is on being inclusive, we use capabilities such as LinkedIn screening questions to assess an applicant's skill level, as well as Talent Insights to access and visualise real-time data about a candidate's skills – and even whether they have expressed interest in the company. This enables us to source candidates in a more equitable way, based on their proven skills.

We also use Dynamics 365 Human Resources to enhance the employee experience, from personalised onboarding to empowering employees to get the information they need – on their own – through easy-to-use self-service HR tools and Microsoft Teams.

Today's employees are increasingly digitally savvy, and expect to be equipped with the digital tools they need to work from anywhere, on any device, at any time, and that will enable them to accomplish tasks quickly.

This makes it essential – especially in the context of remote and hybrid workplaces – to make HR services a seamless part of people's days, as any of the other tasks on their to-do lists. This is why we introduced our chatbot to help scale our services and handle day-to-day transactional requests, so that our time as HR can be freed up to focus on strategic matters and business partnering.

For example, our data analysis indicated in excess of 200,000 employee requests for visa letters. The introduction of the chatbot meant that these letters could be issued

---

15    Institute of Information Technology Professionals South Africa (IITPSA), 2019.

within five minutes without the intervention of an HR practitioner, saving us time and allowing us to concentrate on what matters most.

## A Growth Mindset in Action: Investing in Employee Experience and Engagement

Technology should serve the same purpose for our employees. In recent years, there has been a proliferation of apps and tools designed to improve productivity and collaboration – like Microsoft Teams – because the modern employee is part of more teams now than ever before.

The challenge comes if these apps and solutions are disparate and create multiple workflows. That is why we use Connectors as a tool to allow our people to connect their accounts, apps, data and devices – including Microsoft 365, Twitter, LinkedIn and OneDrive – to create a seamless workflow that enables collaboration.

A new component of this ecosystem is the employee experience platform we introduced in February 2021. It is a platform that brings together tools for employee engagement, learning, well-being and knowledge discovery directly into the flow of people's work. Its introduction was driven by the recognition of the need to go beyond productivity tools and digitising processes to focus on empowering people and teams to grow, to succeed, and to be their best.

The use of these types of apps, software and tools is helping to foster and harness a growth mindset critical to adapt and succeed in a rapidly shifting world of work.[16]

In this world of work, it is essential to strike the right balance between face-to-face interaction and digital collaboration to keep people connected, as well as to enable them to stay engaged and productive. As the move to remote and hybrid work continues to gain traction, we will see demand for solutions that focus on the daily needs of employees at work grow, particularly around well-being, connection, focus, empowerment, growth and purpose. The demand to enable these needs by supporting corporate culture, knowledge discovery, on-the-job learning and employee well-being will also grow.

By investing in our people and the employee experience, we can directly impact engagement, retention, customer satisfaction and profitability. When people thrive, business thrives; businesses with highly engaged employees enjoy 21% greater profitability.[17]

---

16   Microsoft, 2021.
17   Harter & Mann, 2021.

We are increasingly seeing that learning is a key characteristic of people thriving as part of the employee experience. This prompted us to look at our existing learning approach and modernise it to better empower our people by creating a one-stop shop for their learning needs, available from a single touchpoint.

This one-stop-shop combines Microsoft Learn, which is a free online platform with courses and content designed to help people upskill on cloud technology, and LinkedIn Learning, which enables learning from anywhere, on any device, at any time. These allow employees to easily discover informal and formal learning in their flow of work.

## Where Growth Mindsets meet Data and Analytics to help Employees find Better Ways to Work

The ability to support on-the-job-learning in the face of daily work demands requires data-driven insights that will help people take responsibility for harnessing their own growth mindset, well-being and productivity.

We have seen that by using an understanding of their own unique needs, circumstances and ways of working – driven by data and analytics – employees are able to take charge and design best practices that work for them as individuals.

This intelligence, and the insights generated from it, has been brought into greater focus as people adapt to remote and hybrid working. It allows leaders to understand and support employees and business as a whole in new ways, by exploring behavioural data.

We believe it is critical to provide people with the tools that they need to make these decisions – grounded in intelligence based on their own behaviour. We call this Microsoft Workplace Analytics.

Insights from Workplace Analytics, sent out in a weekly custom analytics email confidential to each employee, gives people the opportunity to analyse their own work style, understand whom they collaborate with the most, and evaluate how much uninterrupted time they have to focus. They may use these data and personalised insights to make changes to their own work style, such as protecting time for breaks, focused work and learning.[18]

I have used my own analytics to make changes to my working style to fit what works best for me. I have found it hugely valuable, and am actively encouraging other employees to use the insights from their analytics to do the same.

---

18   Microsoft, 2021.

Making use of analytics will help employees separate the blurred lines that come with remote and hybrid work, by using rich data that can be made operational. This will be critical going forward as we all will need to be more intentional about separating work from home life.

This is the next chapter in the new world of work: using smart technology intelligently to streamline the employee experience, from facilitating learning and collaboration to using data to find better ways to work and improve productivity.

This needs to be combined with the use of technologies, platforms and tools to keep track of ongoing cultural evolution, and to ensure that positive change within the business sticks and becomes a habit.

We are able to use Microsoft Power BI to visualise our data from all of these sources, and act based on these business intelligence insights to drive real and measurable change and enable a growth mindset.

## Finding the Sweet Spot between Technology and Culture: Lessons we have Learnt

So far, our approach – marrying our growth mindset philosophy, modern HR and technology as an enabler – has yielded key milestones in our quest for cultural change, and has taught us valuable lessons about culture.

The most important of these are: you cannot fake it. Culture has to be authentic and original, and propelled by a purpose-driven mission that is measurable but simple.

You also need to make symbolic changes, which do not necessarily need to be big, but do need to reflect the direction you want to take. These changes need to become habit and who you are, and should be communicated consistently to reinforce positive change and progress.

Communication and understanding is an important part of having all oars in the water and ensuring everyone is rowing in the same direction, as well as checking whether the changes make sense and not being afraid to alter them if they are not.

At the heart of all of this, is humility. A growth mindset culture is not possible without it, and that is embodied in all 175,000 Microsoft employees worldwide. Our people let the quality of their work and passion speak for itself, as they strive to do more and be more – and help others do the same.

This is the culture I fell in love with nearly three years ago, and one I want to continue to be an active part of for many more to come.

## Chapter 14

# Preparing The HR Leader for the Future: Capabilities and Ongoing Development

**Wilhelm Crous**

~~~~~~~~~~~~~~~~~~~~~~~~~~~~~~~~~~~~~~~~~~~~~~~~~~~~~~~~~~~~~~~~~~~~~~~~~~~~~~~~~~~~~~~

*"There are decades that nothing happens, and there are weeks where decades happen."*

Vladimir Ilyich Lenin

# Introduction

The confluence of the Covid-19 fallout and the Fourth Industrial Revolution has caused widespread disruption and even hardship across the world, which is specifically playing out in the workplace. Paul Norman made the point that, "These forces have brought *being human* back to the centre". This has major implications for the HR department, as it calls for a new HR agenda.

In this chapter, the present day and future challenges to the world of work will be highlighted, and a possible scenario of future HR jobs will be addressed. The HR capabilities and requirements to be future-fit and ideas around the education and development of HR practitioners will also be discussed.

## Challenges for the HR Professional

The challenges and opportunities that the Human Resource Management profession and related disciplines are facing are unprecedented in the history of this profession:

- Health and wellness: deterioration is evident across virtually all mental health indicators (burnout, anxiety, suicide, stress, languishing, etc.). The effects of the loss of life, illness, tremendous uncertainty and insecurities will play out for years to come in the form of post-traumatic stress and other mental health disorders.

---

1    Norman, 2022.

- New hybrid work and organisation structures: It appears that going forward, most office workers will prefer some configuration of hybrid work arrangements. The reality, however, is that managing hybrid formats is more complex than an all-in-office organisation or even a 100% remote arrangement. Ongoing research and experimentation will be required to figure out the optimal format for each organisation, which will require bespoke solutions.

- Diversity and inclusion: It could be argued that diversity and inclusion have always been on the agenda of the HR department, yet the Black Lives Matter movement and other initiatives have put the spotlight back on this issue. The fact is that far more must be done to move beyond traditional diversity issues based on gender and race. In this respect, Professor Kurt April has provided an all-encompassing description of diversity which should be addressed in Organisations:[2]

  "Diversity is seen as all the ways in which people differ and recognising and embracing the existence of many visible differences (e.g., genders and the gender-fluid; races and ethnicities; nationalities; variously-abled people; age groups; skills; sexual orientations; languages; sometimes spiritual orientations and religions), and invisible dimensions (e.g., spiritual orientations and religions; thinking styles; psychometric profiles; experiences and different tenures; leadership styles; philosophical views – conservative vs. liberal; socioeconomic class; education backgrounds and different educational disciplines; learning agilities; value systems; personal purposes; different upbringings; various heritages, beliefs and perspectives; and individual differences)".

- The impact of digitisation, AI, automation and robotics in the world of work: Digitalisation has made it possible for organisations to quickly function remotely and/or hybridly. At the same time, it also calls for the rapid upskilling and reskilling of workforces to improve their digital literacy. Organisations are increasingly utilising AI and automation to streamline processes, eliminate mundane work, and improve functionality. According to the *Work Ahead Report* from Cognizant,[3] businesses are progressively applying AI to redesign business processes for human/machine teaming, taking on challenges that neither could do efficiently alone. They see AI/automation as a means to achieve higher levels of human performance: "Executives see that AI is about human augmentation rather than substitution, and that humans and machines will reach new value thresholds, unobtainable in isolation." The report also stresses that, "A view of employees as more simplistic labour 'resources' is giving way to a richer, more complex version of their value". We can therefore talk of a more *people-centric, human-led,* technical dispensation.

---

2   April, 2022.
3   Pring & Davis, 2021.

- *ESG challenges:* The greater emphasis on the environment, the green economy and sustainability is gaining momentum at an exponential rate. Climate change and the impact of "green" technologies will in itself cause further disruption to organisations. Organisations will have to redesign operational and work practices in order to reduce their carbon footprints, which means that jobs will have to be redesigned to reduce or eliminate carbon output.

Covid-19 has shone a spotlight on tremendous inequality and poverty levels, especially in South Africa and Africa. The looting and uprising in KZN and parts of Gauteng can partially be attributed to this reality. According to the IMF,[4] since the early 2000s, South Africa's Gini coefficient of 63 has stayed at that level, with the top 20% of the population holding over 68% of income and the bottom 40% of the population holding only 7% of income. Income per capita has decreased since 2012, while an unemployment rate of around 40% has created a hopeless situation for those without jobs.

Organisations, led by their HR departments, will have to go beyond the traditional CSI initiatives to address these inequality and poverty levels. This is where the concept of humanitarian work comes to the fore. Humanitarian Work Psychology (HWP) is already recognised as a subset of Industrial and Organisational Psychology, which makes humane work a sustainable reality in and for communities and society at large. An overview of the HWP landscape is provided in Figure 14.1 below.

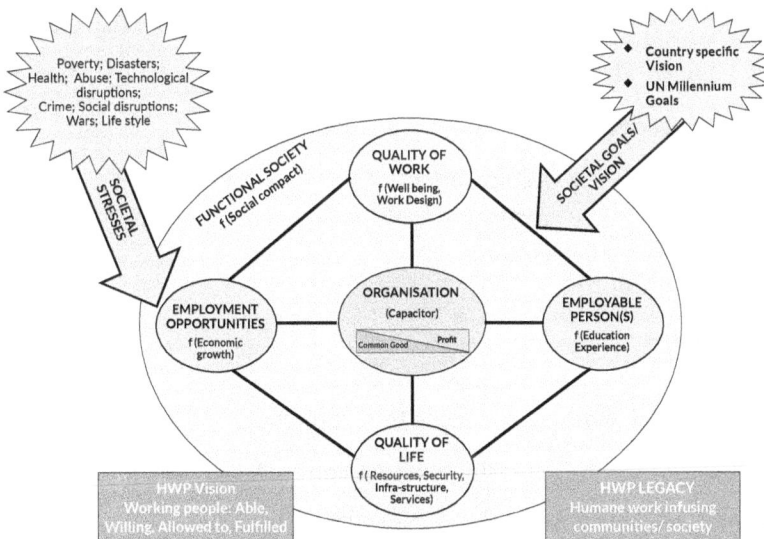

*Figure 14.1: Overview of the HWP Landscape[5]*

Note: f = function of

---

4    International Monetary Fund (IMF), 2020.
5    SIOPSA, 2021.

The HR profession will, similarly to the Industrial-Organisational Psychologists (IOPs), have to view humanitarian work as a priority in order to create a more humane, decent and equal society. With so many new priorities at stake, the chances are that governance and especially ethical conduct could land on the back burner, yet even more emphasis should be placed on ethical practices and conduct, which should be part and parcel of the organisation's DNA. Chapter 11 provides all the necessary guidelines in this regard for HR.

- *Creating real purpose and meaning in organisations:* People are inspired if they can connect to a higher order, goal or purpose that leads to meaningful work. The business case for purpose-led organisations is clear. The HR department should strongly influence leadership to instil a purpose driven-culture, into which the majority of employees will buy and commit to.

The impact of the challenges above calls for a relook at the HR ecosystem. Processes can be enhanced and simplified with AI and automation, and upskilling and reskilling should be done constantly. Simplified performance management systems which are continuous, outcomes-focused and based on trust should be implemented. Focus and respect for every individual's specific needs should be paramount. All of these aspects and much more have been comprehensively addressed in the other chapters of this book.

In addition to the broad challenges described above, there are immediate priorities that HR leaders will need to focus on. According to research by Gartner,[6] these are:

- building critical skills and competencies;
- organisational design and change management;
- current and future leadership bench;
- future of work; and
- diversity, equity and inclusion.

These priorities are broadly driven by:

- hybrid work that is driving business transformation;
- rising turnover that is increasing competition for talent; and
- mounting pressure to make progress on DEI.

---

6    Gartner, 2021.

# HR Jobs of the Future

The Cognizant Centre for the Future of Work, in joint partnership with Future Workplace, has conducted extensive research relating to HR jobs of the future. A total of 21 jobs were identified (see Figure 14.2 below) that could be realised between 2020 and 2030.[7] As with so many other aspects of the future of work, some of these jobs have now been fast forwarded due to the impact of Covid-19 and the new world of work.

THE ROAD TO 2030

## The 10-year journey

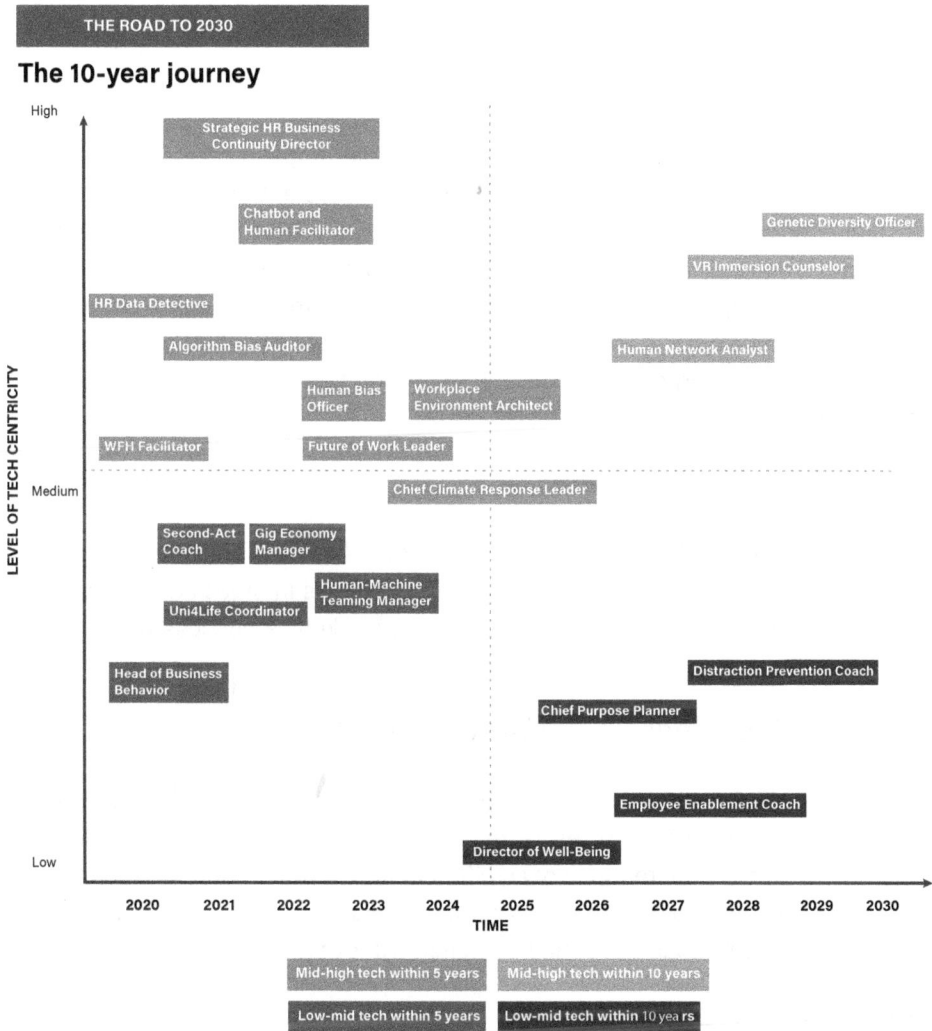

Figure 14.2: 21 HR Jobs of the Future

Short descriptions of a selected group are provided below:

---

7    Brown, Meister, Styr & Pring, 2020.

## HR Data Detective

The HR Data Detective sources, sifts and investigates people data from multiple sources, including human capital management and HR information system data, employee surveys, time-tracking and learning management systems, benefit portals, compensation and succession planning. The Data Detective will also transform unstructured information – such as employee sentiment, text, video or voice inputs – into usable data sources. The highest attention to ethical practices will be essential for anyone in this position.

## WFH Facilitator

The WFH Facilitator must ensure that every remote employee has the technology they need to do their very best work, and should evaluate, budget for and integrate new digital collaboration tools. The WFH facilitator will have a fascination with the application of virtual reality for interaction and collaboration as this is critical to effectively enabling remote work. The WFH Facilitator must ensure that processes and policies are tailored to remote workers, and is responsible for creating a culture that enhances a strong sense of belonging. In one format or another, this job is a reality now.

## Head of Business Behaviour

The Head of Business Behaviour will be a leader on the work force intelligence team, who is responsible for developing data-driven strategies in areas such as employee experience, cross-company collaboration, smart workplace success and employee satisfaction.

## Strategic HR Business Continuity Director

The Strategic HR Business Continuity Director will protect the workforce and ensure its continued productivity and resilience, while being a leader in the development, implementation and maintenance of an HR-specific business continuity programme. They will also, in tandem with business continuity planning leads, establish a strategy that enables employees to continue to function without the risk of endangerment.

## Algorithm Bias Auditor (ABA)

The Head of ABA will lead a team that conducts a methodical and rigorous investigation into every algorithm across every business unit within the organisation. The ABA team will work with development teams (from the technical and business functions) for new AI-based applications and will review existing systems. The Head of ABA will establish an inventory system that logs and tracks each significant algorithm, its objectives, its input and output, related human value judgements, and consequences.

## Second Act Coach

Second Act Coaches support employees who are making career moves, at whatever stage or age (called "second actors"). This may include helping a retiree to start their second act in the gig economy, or a mid-level worker who is determined to pursue their passion.

## Chatbox and Human Facilitator

The Chatbox and Human Facilitator will leverage voice as platform for better digital employment engagement. Accents, reflections, turn-of-phrase, jargon and lingo of current voice-as-a-platform systems should also be optimised by working in concert with voice UX designers to heighten empathetic inputs and create a better working atmosphere.

## Human Bias Officer

The human bias officer will ensure employees are treated fairly, from recruiting to off-boarding, regardless of race, ethnicity, gender, sexual orientation, religion, economic status, background, age or culture. The person in this role will make sure that every person feels empowered to speak up when something may not be right, ask questions when unsure, and live by their values every day, in every interaction.

## Human Machine Team Manager

Human-machine collaboration is the new workforce. This job must help combine the strengths of robots/all software (accuracy, endurance, computation, speed, etc.) with the strengths of humans (cognition, judgement, empathy, versatility, etc.) in a joint environment for common business goals.

The key task for this role is developing an interaction system through which humans and machines mutually communicate their capabilities, goals and intentions, and devising a task planning system for human-machine collaboration. The end goal is to create augmented hybrid teams that generate better business outcomes through human-machine collaboration.

### Chief Climate Response Leader

The Chief Climate Response Leader will build a sustainable strategy and communicate this to prospective candidates, employees and the general public.

### Director of Well-being

The Covid-19 outbreak significantly and immediately increased the requirement for organisations to have a well-being strategy in place. Even before the virus, two-thirds of full time workers experienced burnout on the job, thus the Director of Well-being's primary focus is to design, develop and implement well-being programmes that are aligned with the organisation's culture, mission and values. The vision of the role is a holistic one, with an increasing emphasis on weaving mental, emotional, physical and spiritual well-being into the fabric and culture of the organisation.

### Chief Purpose Planner

This role will be to develop a corporate purpose strategy and narrative, then work as a communication catalyst across the client's company. In addition, it will identify social causes, align stakeholders, negotiate purpose agreements, secure funding and encourage the flow of information, ideas, content and influence with normal and external stakeholders.

### Distraction Prevention Coach

The goal of a Distraction Prevention Coach is to help associates at all levels hone their attention, both inward to align their values and intuitions, and outward to navigate the world around them. Doing so will help them manage their stress and increase their focus, productivity and effectiveness.

The Distraction Prevention Coach will also help associates manage the constant distractions that interrupt and hijack their focus and are the source of related stress. The emphasis should be on instilling self-management practices such as staying calm, impulse control and conflict management.

## HR Capabilities

In light of the new and future challenges facing organisations, workforces and the HR fraternity, a critical analysis of the capabilities that will be required for the HR profession is required.

In this context, capability refers broadly to the ability and the quality or state of being capable. The Business Dictionary defines capability as "a measure of the ability of an entity (department, organisation, person, system) to achieve its objectives, especially in relation to its overall mission".[8] The Association for Talent Development (ATD), meanwhile, defines capabilities as "the set of skills, behaviours and dispositions which allow an individual to apply their knowledge into meaningful action in a range of different settings".[9]

Against this background, a few recent models are discussed below:

## The Association for Talent Development (ATD): Talent Development Model

This model was developed in 2019, and although it was before Covid-19, the researchers point out that the model is future-oriented, reflecting the field of talent development now, but also five years in the future. The model is also flexible and updateable. The ATD model is structured around three domains of practice:

- Capabilities that derive from interpersonal skills.

- Capabilities that come from building professional knowledge related to developing people and helping them learn.

- Capabilities that affect an organisation's ability to drive results and mission success.[10]

This 2019 study found that the knowledge, skills and abilities (KSAs) of effective talent development (TD) professionals at all levels of their career fell into three major domains of practice: capabilities that derive from interpersonal skills, capabilities that come from building professional knowledge related to developing people and helping them learn, and capabilities that impact an entire organisation's ability to drive towards results and mission success. Within those three broad domains of practice, the KSAs are grouped into 23 capabilities (see Figure 14.3).[11]

---

8   Galagan, Hirt & Vital, 2020.
9   Galagan, Hirt & Vital, 2020.
10   Ibid.
11   Ibid.

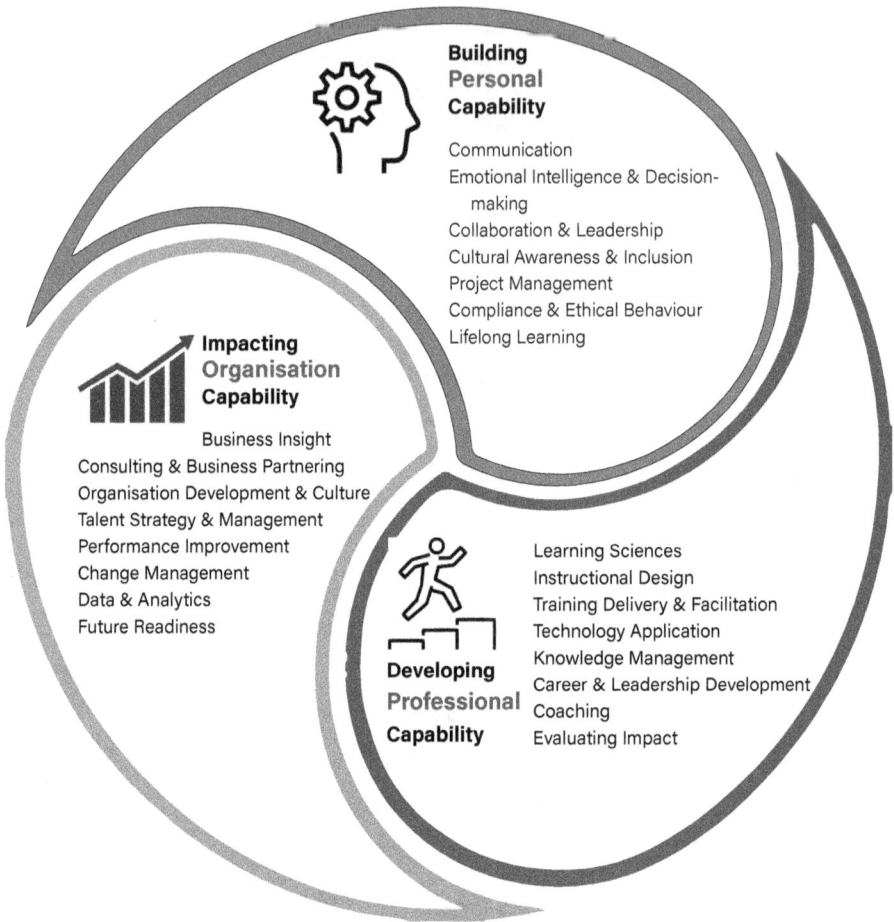

*Figure 14.3: ATD Talent Development Capability Model*

## The WFPMA and BCG Study

The World Federation of People Management Associations (WFPMA) and the Boston Consulting Group (BCG) conducted a worldwide survey on the future of People Management, and in the process the survey indicates that the major priorities can be grouped into Talent Management, Managing Change, HR Technology and Digitisation.[12]

Table 14.1 segments HR topics by current capabilities and future importance, showing that there are 12 capabilities that require fairly urgent attention.[13]

---

12  Galagan, Hirt & Vital, 2020.
13  Ibid.

*Table 14.1: Segmenting HR topics by current capabilities and future importance*

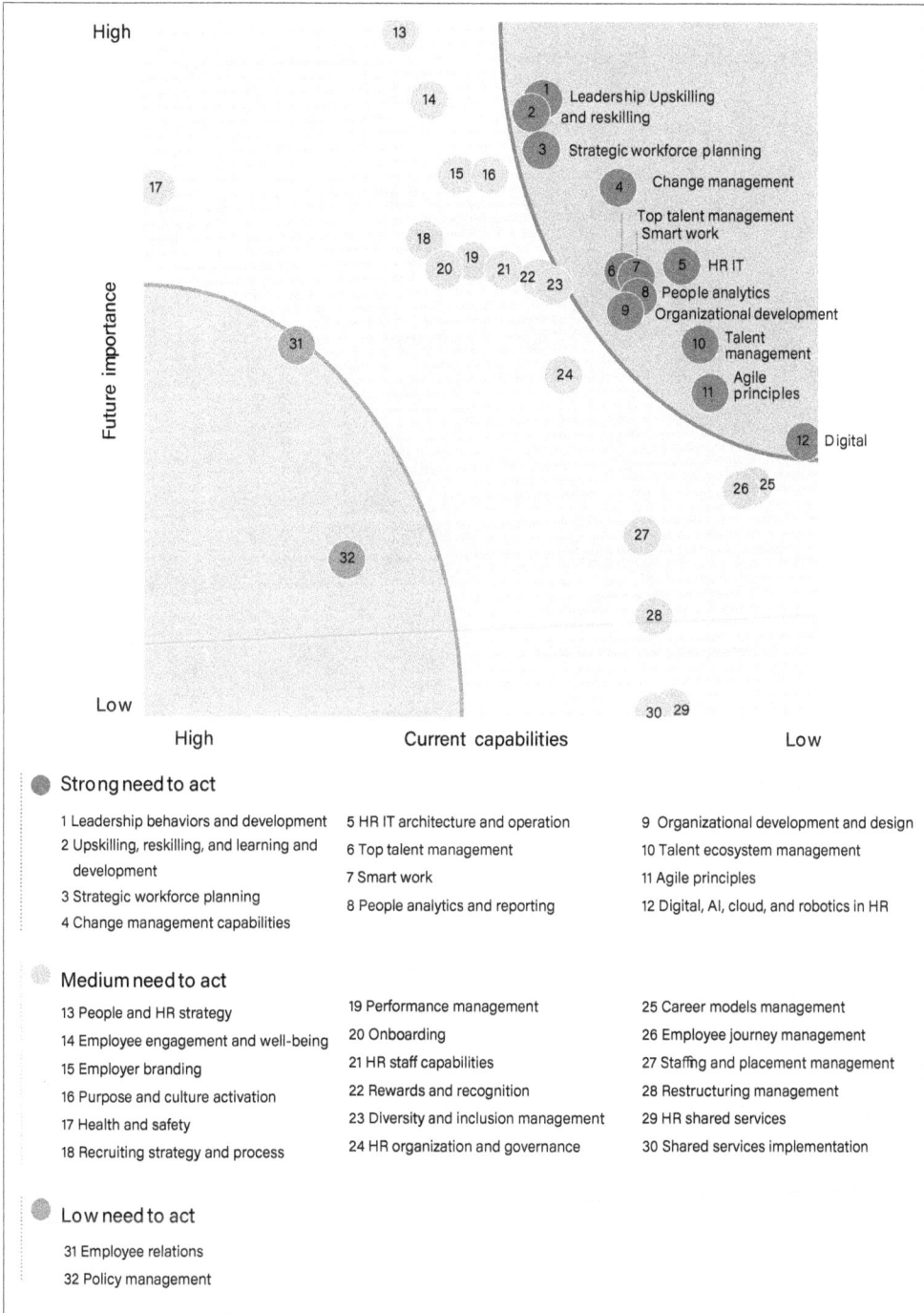

High

13

14

1 Leadership Upskilling and reskilling
2

3 Strategic workforce planning

15  16

4 Change management

17

Top talent management
Smart work

18

20  19  21  22  23

6  7  5 HR IT

8 People analytics

9 Organizational development

10 Talent management

24

11 Agile principles

31

12 Digital

26  25

27

32

28

Low

30  29

High                    Current capabilities                    Low

Future importance

**Strong need to act**

1 Leadership behaviors and development
2 Upskilling, reskilling, and learning and development
3 Strategic workforce planning
4 Change management capabilities

5 HR IT architecture and operation
6 Top talent management
7 Smart work
8 People analytics and reporting

9 Organizational development and design
10 Talent ecosystem management
11 Agile principles
12 Digital, AI, cloud, and robotics in HR

**Medium need to act**

13 People and HR strategy
14 Employee engagement and well-being
15 Employer branding
16 Purpose and culture activation
17 Health and safety
18 Recruiting strategy and process

19 Performance management
20 Onboarding
21 HR staff capabilities
22 Rewards and recognition
23 Diversity and inclusion management
24 HR organization and governance

25 Career models management
26 Employee journey management
27 Staffing and placement management
28 Restructuring management
29 HR shared services
30 Shared services implementation

**Low need to act**

31 Employee relations
32 Policy management

# IOP Capability Model

In a recent major project lead by Theo Veldman to identify the capabilities of future-fit Industrial Organisational Psychologists, the IOP Capability Model was developed.[14]

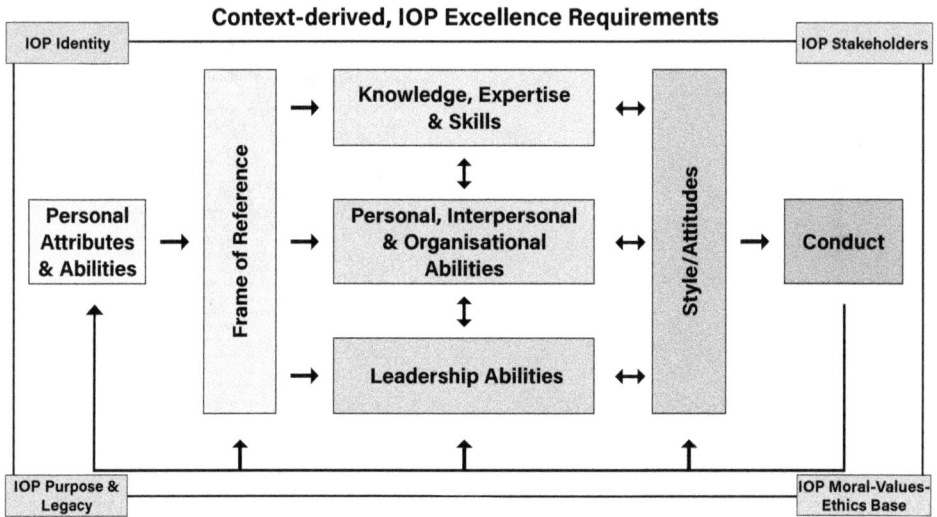

**Context-derived, IOP Excellence Requirements**

*Figure 14.4: IOP Capabilities Framework*

The capabilities domains depicted in Figure 14.4 can be defined as follows:

- Personal attributes and abilities: These refer to who an individual is as a person.

- Frame of reference: The fundamental beliefs, values and norms that a person uses to constitute, make sense of, and give meaning to, reality.

- Knowledge, expertise and skills: What a person knows and does well.

- Personal, interpersonal and organisational abilities: The capabilities needed to form and maintain healthy and productive relationships, while engaging with diverse stakeholders across different contexts.

- Leadership abilities: The mindful, conscious adoption of a role in which a leader intentionally persuades, mobilises and directs others (stakeholders) to pursue a shared, future-centric vision (or dream), in order to actualise a desired future state and outcome (legacy) within a certain context.

- Style/attitude: The general way in which a person engages with contexts, situations and others.

- Conduct: The behaviours a person manifests.

---

14   SIOPSA, 2021.

# HR Capabilities for a Future-Fit HR Practitioner

To develop a reliable and valid capability model for the HR profession will be a major undertaking. Against this context and given the input from the various authors in this book, as well as other recent capability models, the following capabilities are proposed for a future-fit HR professional/practitioner.

An HR Capability Model should have as a foundation and orientation towards Social Citizenship. It is about serving society as a whole.

## Personal capabilities

Covid-19 has put the spotlight on, amongst others, coping mechanisms during and after the pandemic, therefore personal capabilities within this context are very important. These include:

- all the EQ competencies (self-awareness; self regulation; empathy; motivation and social skills);
- a growth mind-set;
- curiosity;
- showing grit;
- having resilience;
- being adaptable;
- showing empathy;
- acknowledging vulnerability;
- being humble;
- having cultural and social intelligence;
- being hopeful;
- having integrity; and
- the kindness.

## Professional capabilities

It goes without saying that HR professionals should be capable in all aspects of the HR Value Chain, within the context of creating a more humane workplace. Having said that, it appears that the following capabilities do and will carry the most weight in the present and the future:

- Talent management, including upskilling and reskilling

- Collaboration and teamwork

- Change management

- Problem solving

- Agile principles

- People analytics

- Hybrid work

- Coaching

- Business acumen

- Communication

## Organisational capabilities

The following capabilities are necessary for the organisation to thrive and grow. HR professionals should be well equipped in establishing and facilitating these capabilities in organisations:

- Organisational purpose

- Organisational resilience

- A culture of belonging which also inspires

- Create meaningful and humane work

- Trust

- Networked teams and collaboration

- Diversity, Equity and Inclusion (DEI)

- Organisational agility

## Digital capabilities

In all the capability models discussed in this chapter, digital literacy and HR tech are included under other headings, i.e., Organisational or Professional Capabilities. However, in the new workplace, ways of work and integration with technology are clearly making digital capabilities much more important than ever before, which is why they now belong in a separate category. The following go beyond just digital literacy:

- AI/Automation
- Algorithms
- Person/Machine interface
- VR/AR
- Person/Chatbox/Robotics/AI Interface
- Collaboration tools and software
- People/Robotics teams
- Data collection and analytics
- General digital literacy

# HR Leadership

In addition to the capabilities discussed above, HR professionals will have to show leadership in order to establish 'humane organisations' and to guide organisations through present and future disruptive times. In Chapter 3, Andrew Millson[15] calls for a "conscious leadership" approach in these times. In brief this is about the following:

## Personal

- Having a deep sense of purpose and self-awareness.
- Speaking with integrity.
- Being authentic and congruent, i.e., practicing what you preach.
- Understanding your strengths and weaknesses.
- Being curious and interested in learning.
- Being in touch with your own emotions and the emotions of others, i.e., the heart is as important as the head.
- Practicing trust more than control.

## Relational

- Listening more than you talk.
- Open to new ideas, even if you've been doing it longer.
- Speaking from a place of fact.
- Living in a state of responsibility and accountability.

---

15   Millson, 2021.

- Not being afraid to speak about your feelings.

- Openly sharing and building.

- Being comfortable having difficult conversations.

- Expressing your feelings about someone to that person from a place of love and support.

# Education and Research for the New HR Agenda

Educational institutions (universities and business schools) will not be isolated from the disruption the world of work is experiencing. Modifications to existing curricula must be made and new programmes will have to be developed, however it takes too long for formal education to develop and introduce such programs and degrees. For that reason, organisations will have to upskill and reskill the HR, Learning and Development related employees. The L and D departments have proven over the last few years that they are perfectly competent to take responsibility for the upskill and reskilling, whether in-house or with other service providers. That trend will continue.

At the same time, the formal education institutions will have to relook their current curricula as a more complex world of work awaits their students. A multi-disciplinary approach to educate students will be required, and education institutions will have to find ways to be more flexible and agile in developing new programmes or modifying existing ones. More importantly, their programs/degrees must pro-actively prepare students for tomorrow's workplace.

This brings us to the research agenda. The theory/practice gaps need to be closed. Researchers should ask themselves, "What can the world of work do with this research?", and "How can this research contribute to solving societal challenges, i.e., inequality, poverty, unemployment, etc.?"

Greater collaboration between specialists and thought leaders in the worlds of work and academia should take place, with the world of work having more input in compiling the research agendas.

Again, we are dealing with complex challenges, for example researching hybrid working arrangements is complicated. A multi-disciplinary approach to address the hybrid work environment could be more appropriate, for instance the following university departments could collaborate: HR/IOP, Psychology, Economics, Anthropology, Social Work, IT, etc. It can also mean that universities collaborate in order to share expertise and resources. Without interfering with the quality of the research output, answers also need to be found to speed up the research process.

# Conclusion

The fact is that the HR profession is at a crossroads. Never before has HR been so blessed with so many wonderful opportunities. It is obvious that the HR profession is facing a new agenda, which has been set by the reality of post Covid-19, 4IR and societal challenges, to name a few. It has become a cliché to refer to HR as ⊠the centre stage". Only history will tell whether HR successfully took on the challenge to create more human-centred workplaces and organisations. It won't be easy and the shift won't happen overnight... this is a journey. Here is where the HR profession will need to have a growth mind-set, show grit to stick it out over the long-term, and at the same time contribute to the overall mission of their organisations.

In essence, HR leaders have to bring hope and I quote Barack Obama:

> *"Hope is not blind optimism. It's not ignoring the enormity of the task ahead or the roadblocks that stand in our path. It's not sitting on the side-lines or shirking from a fight. Hope is that thing inside us that insists, despite all evidence to the contrary, that something better awaits us if we have the courage to reach for it, and to work for it, and to fight for it. Hope is belief that destiny will not be written for us, but by us, by the men and women who are not content to settle for the world as it is, who have the courage to remake the world as it should be."*[16]

---

16  Obama, 2008.

# References

## Chapter 1 References

Deloitte. (2020). *The Adaptable Organisation: Harnessing a networked enterprise of human resilience.* Retrieved from: https://www2.deloitte.com/global/en/pages/human-capital/articles/the-adaptable-organization.html

Deloitte Insights. (2021). *The social enterprise in a world disrupted. Leading the shift from survive to thrive.* Retrieved from: https://www2.deloitte.com/content/dam/insights/us/articles/6935_2021-HC-Trends/di_human-capital-trends.pdf

Nafi, B. (2020). What comes after the Pandemic? Predicting the World to Come. *Al Jazeera.* Retrieved from: https://studies.aljazeera.net/en/policy-briefs/what-comes-after-pandemic-predicting-world-come

PWC Middle East. (2020). *How the new normal is shaping the future of HR.* Retrieved from: https://www.pwc.com/m1/en/publications/how-the-new-normal-shaping-future-hr.html.

Thompson, C. (n.d.). *HR's biggest priorities for post Covid 19 Workplace.* Retrieved from: https://www.rewardgateway.com/blog/top-hr-priorities-for-the-workplace

Volini, E., Schwartz, J., & Roy, I. (2019). *Introduction: Leading the social enterprise - Reinvent with a human focus.* 2019 Global Human Capital Trends, Deloitte Insights. Retrieved from: https://www2.deloitte.com/us/en/insights/focus/human-capital-trends/2019/leading-social-enterprise.html

## Chapter 2 References

Aruda, W. (2021). What the new world of work will actually look like. *Forbes.* Retrieved from: https://www.forbes.com/sites/williamarruda/2021/05/18/what-the-new-world-of-work-will-actually-look-like/?sh=3e91980e231c

Caldwell, J.H., & Krishna, D. (2020). *The Acceleration of Digitization as a Result of COVID-19.* Retrieved from: https://www2.deloitte.com/global/en/blog/responsible-business/blog/2020/acceleration-of-digitisation-as-result-of-covid-19.html

Change Recruitment Group. (2017). *How Will the Fourth Industrial Revolution Impact the Future of Work?* https://www.changerecruitmentgroup.com/knowledge-centre/how-will-the-fourth-industrial-revolution-impact-the-future-of-work

Charlton, E. (2021). *What is the gig economy and what's the deal for gig workers?* Retrieved from: https://www.weforum.org/agenda/2021/05/what-gig-economy-workers/

Chartell Business College. (2019). *What is the new world of work?* Retrieved from: https://chartallcampus.com/what-is-the-new-world-of-work/

Dimock, M. (2019). *Defining generations: Where Millennials end and Generation Z begins.* Retrieved from: https://www.pewresearch.org/fact-tank/2019/01/17/where-millennials-end-and-generation-z-begins/ [Accessed 19 August 2021]

Dwolatzky, B., & Harris, M. (2020). *The World is flat COVID-19 Becomes the Driving Force for 4IR.* Retrieved from: https://www.wits.ac.za/covid19/covid19-news/latest/the-world-is-flat-covid-19-becomes-the-driving-force-for-4ir.html

Francis, T., & Hoefel, F. (2018). *'True Gen': Generation Z and its implications for companies.* Retrieved from: https://www.mckinsey.com/industries/consumer-packaged-goods/our-insights/true-gen-generation-z-and-its-implications-for-companies

Hancock, B., Schaninger, B., & Weddie, B. (2021). *Culture in the hybrid workplace.* Retrieved from: https://www.mckinsey.com/business-functions/organization/our-insights/culture-in-the-hybrid-workplace?cid=other-eml-alt-mip-mck

Jenkins, R. ( 2019). *How Generation Z will transform the Future Workplace.* Retrieved from: https://www.inc.com/ryan-jenkins/the-2019-workplace-7-ways-generation-z-will-shape-it.html

McKinsey & Company. (2021). *Fit for the postpandemic future: Unilever's Leena Nair on reinventing how we work.* Retrieved from: https://www.mckinsey.com/business-functions/people-and-organizational-performance/our-insights/fit-for-the-postpandemic-future-unilevers-leena-nair-on-reinventing-how-we-work

Mckinsey & Company. (2021). *The future of work after Covid-19.* Retrieved from: https://www.mckinsey.com/featured-insights/future-of-work/the-future-of-work-after-covid-19

O.C. Tanner Institute. (2021). *Global Culture Report.* Retrieved from: https://www.octanner.com/global-culture-report.html

Petriglieri, G., Ashford, S.J., & Wrzesniewski, A. (2018). *Thriving in the Gig Economy.* Retrieved from: https://hbr.org/2018/03/thriving-in-the-gig-economy

Chearavanont, S. (2020). *How Digitization and Innovation can Make the Post-COVID World a Better Place.* https://www.weforum.org/agenda/2020/08/how-digitization-and-innovation-can-make-the-post-covid-world-a-better-place/

ThoughtFarmer. (2021). *The Hybrid Workplace: Is this the future of work?* Retrieved from: https://www.thoughtfarmer.com/blog/hybrid-workplace/

Turner, A. (2021). *How Many Smartphones are in the World?* Retrieved from: https://www.bankmycell.com/blog/how-many-phones-are-in-the-world

## Chapter 4 References

World Economic Forum. (2020). *The Future of Jobs Report 2020.* Retrieved from: https://www.weforum.org/reports/the-future-of-jobs-report-2020/in-full

Jesuthasan, R., & Boudreau, J. (2021). Work without Jobs. *MIT Sloan Management Review,* 62(3), 5–8.

Bersin, J. (2021). *HR Predictions for 2021: Transformation at Scale.* Retrieved from: https://joshbersin.com/2021/01/hr-predictions-for-2021-transformation-at-scale/#:~:text=The%20Big%20Reset%20will%20continue,human%2Dcentered%20leadership%20will%20grow.

Barriere, M., Owens, M., & Pobereskin, S. (2018). *Linking Talent to Value.* Retrieved from: https://www.mckinsey.de/~/media/McKinsey/Industries/Technology%20Media%20and%20Telecommunications/High%20Tech/Our%20Insights/Linking%20talent%20to%20value/Linking-talent-to-value.pdf

Charan, R., Barton, D., & Carey D. (2018). *Talent Wins the New Playbook for Putting People First.* Boston, MA: Harvard Business Review Press.

Gartner Research. (2021). *3 Ways to Advance Underrepresented Talent.* Retrieved from: https://www.gartner.com/en/documents/4001786-3-ways-to-advance-underrepresented-talent

Gartner. (2021). *Advancing Underrepresented Talent: 3 Ways You Need to Reset Your Strategy," which equips DEI leaders to reset their strategies and sustainably advance underrepresented talent.* Retrieved from: https://www.gartner.com/en/human-resources/trends/advancing-underrepresented-talent-toolkit

Gartner. (2020a). *What is an Internal Talent Marketplace?* Retrieved from: https://www.
    gartner.com/en/documents/3984933/what-is-an-Internal-talent-marketplace-
Gartner. (2020b). *Succession Management Benchmarking Report.* Retrieved from: https://www.
    gartner.com/en/documents/3981783/2020-succession-management-benchmarking-report
Gartner. (2020c). *Employee-Ownership Strategies to Increase Performance Management's
    Utility.* Retrieved from: https://www.gartner.com/en/documents/3980390/3-employee-
    ownership-strategies-to-increase-performance-
Gartner. (2019). *Performance Management That Delivers.* Retrieved from: https://www.
    gartner.com/en/documents/3969809/performance-management-that-delivers
Gloat. (2021). *Creating an Agile and Inclusive Workforce.* Retrieved from: https://www.gloat.
    com/creating-an-agile-and-inclusive-workforce-download/
Roca, J., & Wilde, S. (2019). *The Connector Manager: Why Some Leaders Build Exceptional
    Talent — and Others Don't.* Retrieved from: https://www.gartner.com/en/human-
    resources/insights/publications/connector-manager

## Chapter 5 References

Accenture. (2018). *Inclusive Future of Work: A Call for Action.* San Francisco: Accenture.
Arora, A. (2020). Prospects and Challenges in building lifelong learning capabilities to grapple
    with 'Future of Work for individuals'. *Economic Challenger: An International Journal,
    22*(87), 49-52.
Baker, M. (2021). *9 Future of Work Trends Post-COVID-19.* Retrieved from: https://www.
    gartner.com/smarterwithgartner/9-future-of-work-trends-post-covid-19
Bennis, W. (1993). *An Invented Life: Reflections on Leadership and Change.* Reading, MA:
    Addison-Wesley.
Browne, R. (2012). *Employee Value Proposition.* Beacon 2012 Management Review, 29-36.
    Retrieved from:  https://www.sibm.edu/assets/pdf/beacon3.pdf
De Smet, A., Lurie, M., & St George, A. (2018). *Leading agile transformation:The new
    capabilities leaders need to build 21st century leaders.* McKinsey and Company. Retrieved
    from: https://www.mckinsey.com/~/media/mckinsey/business%20functions/
    organization/our%20insights/leading%20agile%20transformation%20the%20new%20
    capabilities%20leaders%20need%20to%20build/leading-agile-transformation-the-new-
    capabilities-leaders-need-to-build-21st-century-organizations.pdf
Exxaro. (2020). *Integrated Report.* Johannesburg: Exxaro Resources. Retrieved from: https://
    www.exxaro.com/investors/integrated-reports
Gartner. (2019). *How CHROs Think About the Future of Work.* ID: G00708764. Retrieved from: https://
    www.gartner.com/en/documents/3933997-how-chros-think-about-the-future-of-work
International Labour Organisation. (2020). *Digital skills and the future of work: Challenges
    and opportunities in a post COVID-19 environment.* Geneva: International Labour
    Organisation.
Manyika, J. (2017). *Technology, jobs, and the future of work.* McKinsey Global Institute.
    Retrieved from: https://www.mckinsey.com/featured-insights/employment-and-
    growth/technology-jobs-and-the-future-of-work
Pawar, A. (2016). Employee Value Proposition: A Collaborative Methodology for strengthening
    Employer Brand Strategy. *Journal of Resources Development and Management, 16,* 56-62.
Price Waterhouse Cooper. (2018). *Workforce of the future: the competing forces shaping 2030.*
    Retrieved from: https://www.pwc.com/gx/en/services/people-organisation/workforce-
    of-the-future/workforce-of-the-future-the-competing-forces-shaping-2030-pwc.pdf

Schwartz, J., Hatfield. S., Jones, R., & Anderson, S. (2019). *What is the future of work? rethinking work, workforces and workplaces.* Deloitte Development LLC. Retrieved from: https://www2.deloitte.com/us/en/insights/focus/technology-and-the-future-of-work/redefining-work-workforces-workplaces.html

Senge, P.M. (1990). *The Fifth Discipline: The art and practice of the learning organisation.* London: Century Business.

Serrat, O. (2017). *Knowledge Solutions: Tools, Methods, and Approaches to Drive.* Singapore: Springer Nature.

Torii, K,. & O'Connell, M. (2017). *Preparing young people for the future of work.* Melbourne: Australia: Michell Institute.

World Economic Forum. (2020). *The Future of jobs report 2020.* Geneva: World Economic Forum.

# Chapter 6 References

21st Century. (2021). *RewardOnline.* Rosebank: 21st Century.

Bloomfield, D. (1923). *Financial incentives for employees and executives.* New York: The H.W. Wilson Company.

Foss, N.J. (2020). The impact of the Covid-19 pandemic on firms' organisational designs. *Journal of Management Studies, 58*(1), 270-274.

Goss, P. (2015). *Microsoft CEO: Work is no longer a place you go to.* Retrieved from: https://www.techradar.com/news/world-of-tech/microsoft-ceo-work-is-no-longer-a-place-you-go-to-1308609

Green, T.C., & Zhou, D. (2019). *Pay Inequality, Job Satisfaction, and Firm Performance.* Retrieved from https://ssrn.com/abstract=3415937 or http://dx.doi.org/10.2139/ssrn.3415937

The Dynamic Future of Business. (2015). *The rise of dynamic marketplaces and the access management imperative* [White paper]. Retrieved from: https://www.onelogin.com/resource-center/i/1352683-dynamic-future-of-business-white-paper/0?

Uerbach, A. (2018). '#Bigideas2019: Work is no longer a place you go- it's a thing you *do*'. *LinkedIn.* Retrieved from: https://www.linkedin.com/pulse/bigideas2019-work-longer-place-you-goits-thing-do-anna-auerbach/.

# Chapter 7 References

## Prof Edward Webster's References

Atzeri, M. (2020). Worker Organisation in Precarious times: Abandoning trade union fetishism, Rediscovering Class. *Global Labour Journal, 11*(3), 311-314.

Bernstein, H. (2007). *Capital and labour from centre to margins.* Paper prepared for the Living on the Margins Conference, Stellenbosch, South Africa, 26–28 March.

Castel-Branco, R., Mapukata, S. & Webster, E. (2020). Work from home reserved for the privileged few in South Africa. *Business Day.* Retrieved from: https://www.businesslive.co.za/bd/opinion/2020-09-17-work-from-home-reserved-for-the-privileged-few-in-sa/

Gadgil, M. & Samson, M. (2017). Hybrid Organisations, Complex Politics. When Unions form Cooperatives. In Webster, E., Britwum, A.O. & Bhowmik, S. (eds.). *Crossing the Divide. Precarious Work and the Future of Labour.* Scottsville: UKZ Press, pp. 143-164.

Ludwig, C., Webster, E., Spooner, D., & Masikane, F. (2021). Beyond traditional trade unionism: innovative worker responses in three African cities. *Globalizations, 18*(8), 1-14. 10.1080/14747731.2021.1874253.

Rizzo, M., Kilama, B. & Wuyts, M. (2015). The invisibility of wage employment in statistics on the informal economy in Africa: Causes and consequences. *The Journal of Development Studies, 51*(2), 149–16.

Webster, E., Ludwig, C., Masikane, F. & Spooner, D. 2021. Beyond traditional trade unionism: innovative worker responses in three African cities. Cape Town: *Globalisations, 18*(8), 1363-1376.

**Gideon du Plessis's References**

Benja, A-J. (19 May, 2021). Webinar: *New International and Comparative Labor and Employment Challenges: A Four Country Discussion.* US Labour and Employment Relations Association (US LERA).

BrainyQuotes. (n.d.). *Winston Churchill Quotes.* Retrieved from: https://www.brainyquote. com/quotes/winston_churchill_141781

Crouse, W. (2021). Industrial Relations Conference. *Reviewing the labour market, economy impacting employment and industrial relations.* Johannesburg: KR.

Fisher, R., Ury, W., & Patton, B. (2011). *Getting to Yes: Negotiating Agreement Without Giving In* (3rd ed.). New York: Penguin Books.

Hinxman, L. (2021). *Doing away with 'strike season' could lead to more elegant solutions.* Retrieved from: https://www.businesslive.co.za/bd/opinion/2021-05-13-doing-away-with-strike-season-could-lead-to-more-elegant-solutions/

Hoffmann, R. (2019). *Unions can shape the future of work in the Fourth Industrial Revolution.* Retrieved from: http://www.industriall-union.org/unions-can-shape-the-future-of-work-in-the-fourth-industrial-revolution/

Kahn, N. (2016). *Redesigning conflict resolution to survive the post-consensus society.* Retrieved from: https://www.linkedin.com/pulse/redesigning-conflict-resolution-survive-society-nerine-kahn/

Kochan, T. (19 May, 2021). Webinar: *New International and Comparative Labor and Employment Challenges: A Four Country Discussion.* Labour and Employment Relations Association (LERA).

Mkentane, L. (2021). *Employer body Seifsa expects tough wage talks in steel sector.* Retrieved from: https://www.businesslive.co.za/bd/national/labour/2021-05-23-employer-body-seifsa-expects-tough-wage-talks-in-steel-sector/ Date of Access: 23 May 2021.

Visser, J., Hayter, S., & Gammarano, R. (2017). *Labour Relations and Collective Bargaining: Trends in collective bargaining coverage: Stability, erosion, or decline?* ILO Report. Inclusive Labour Markets, Labour Relations and Working Conditions Branch (INWORK). International Labour Office, Geneva, Switzerland.

**Johan Botes's References**

Babal, S. (2019). *Connect to Life with "The Right to Disconnect".* Retrieved from Connect to life with "The Right to Disconnect" | hrnxt.com *https://hr/the-right-to-disconnect/10501/2019/12/18/*

Bloom, N., Liang, J., Roberts, J., & Ying, Z.J. (2015). *Does Working from Home Work? Evidence from a Chinese Experiment.* Retrieved from: https://nbloom.people.stanford.edu/sites/g/files/sbiybj4746/f/wfh.pdf

Botes, J. (2019). *Harvesting Attention Capital and Reducing the Risks of the Frictionless Workplace*. Retrieved from: https://www.tech4law.co.za/news-in-brief/law/harvesting-attention-capital-and-reducing-the-risks-of-the-frictionless-workplace%EF%BB%BF/

Botes, J. (2019). *The downside of flexible workforces*. Retrieved from: https://chro.co.za/articles/the-downside-of-flexible-workforces/

BusinessTech. (2020). *Report reveals shocking number of job losses in South Africa during lockdown*. Retrieved from: https://businesstech.co.za/news/business/416483/report-reveals-shocking-number-of-job-losses-in-south-africa-during-lockdown/

Carlisi, C., Hemerling, J., Kilmann, J., Meese, D., & Shipman, D. (2017). *Purpose with the Power to Transform Your Organization*. Retrieved from: https://www.bcg.com/publications/2017/transformation-behavior-culture-purpose-power-transform-organization

Cloete, K. (2021). *Labour pains: Trade union membership has declined badly and bosses are calling the shots*. Retrieved from: https://www.dailymaverick.co.za/opinionista/2021-03-02-labour-pains-trade-union-membership-has-declined-badly-and-bosses-are-calling-the-shots/

Employment Relations Exchange (ERX). (2017). *Do trade unions have a future in South Africa?* Retrieved from: https://www.erexchange.co.za/trade-unions-future-south-africa/

Joly, H. (2021). How to Lead in the Stakeholder Era: Focus on purpose and people. The profits will follow. *Harvard Business Review*. Retrieved from: https://hbr.org/2021/05/how-to-lead-in-the-stakeholder-era

Kerrigan, H. (2019). *Strategies to Increase Union Membership That Will Reach Gen Z*. Retrieved from: https://laborandtrust.anthem.com/blog/strategies-to-increase-union-membership-that-will-reach-gen-z/

McLeod, L.E. (2016). Leading with Noble Purpose: How to Create a Tribe of True Believers. Hoboken, NJ: Wiley.

Nathoo, Z. (2020). *How can employees also be social-media activists?* Retrieved from: https://www.bbc.com/worklife/article/20201118-how-can-employees-also-be-social-media-activists

People's World. (2014). *Battle of the overpass: Henry Ford, the UAW, and the power of the press*. Retrieved from: https://www.peoplesworld.org/article/battle-of-the-overpass-henry-ford-the-uaw-and-the-power-of-the-press/

Republic of South Africa Government Gazette. (1987a). Act 66 of 1995 - sections 198A – D. Retrieved from: https://www.gov.za/sites/default/files/gcis_document/201409/a75-97.pdf

Republic of South Africa Government Gazette. (1987b). Act 75 of 1997, section 6(4). Retrieved from: https://www.gov.za/sites/default/files/gcis_document/201409/a75-97.pdf

Smith, C. (2019). *What Are the Top Indicators of Organizational Effectiveness?* Retrieved from: https://change.walkme.com/indicators-of-organizational-effectiveness/

Strack, R., Kovács-Ondrejkovic, O., Baier, J., Antebi, P., Kavanagh, K., & López Gobernado, A. (2021). *Decoding Global Ways of Working*. Retrieved from: https://www.bcg.com/publications/2021/advantages-of-remote-work-flexibility

United Nations. (2021). *COVID's led to 'massive' income and productivity losses, UN labour estimates show*. Retrieved from: https://news.un.org/en/story/2021/01/1082852

Wired. (2019). *The frictionless workforce brings obvious benefits – but at what cost?* Retrieved from: https://www.wired.co.uk/article/bc/wired-consulting-baker-mckenzie-frictionless-workforce.

## Akona Makoboka's References

Anwar, M.A., & Graham, M. (2021). Between a rock and a hard place: Freedom, flexibility, precarity and vulnerability in the gig economy in Africa. *Competition & Change, 25*(2), 237–258.

Botha, M., & Fourie, E, (2019). Decolonising the Labour Law Curriculum in the New World of Work. *Tydskrif vir Hedendaagse Romeins-Hollandse Reg, 82*, 177-192.

Business and Human Rights Resource Centre. (2019). *The Future of Work: Litigating Labour Relationships in the Gig Economy.* Retrieved from: https://media.business-humanrights.org/media/documents/files/documents/CLA_Annual_Briefing-FINAL.pdf

Davidoff, G. (2016). *A Purposive Approach to Labour Law.* Oxford: Oxford University Press.

De Mello, A.M., Marx, R., & Malerno, M.S. (2012). Organizational structures to support innovation: how do companies decide? *Revista de Administração e Inovação, 9*(4), 5 - 20.

De Stefano, V. (2018). *Negotiating the Algorithm: Automation, Artificial Intelligence and Labour Protection.* Geneva: International Labour Organization.

De Vos, M. (2018). Work 4.0 and the Future of Labour Law. *Social Science Research Network*, pp. 1-27. Retrieved from: http://labourlawresearch.net/sites/default/files/papers/MarcDV.pdf

Franca, V., & Doherty, M. (2020). Solving the 'Gig-saw'? *Collective Rights and Platform Work. Industrial Law Journal, 49*(3), 352–376.

Mortensen, M., & Haas, M. (2021). *Making the Hybrid Workplace Fair.* Boston: Harvard Business Review.

Spreitzer, G.M., Cameron, L., & Garrett, L. (2017). Alternative Work Arrangements: Two Images of the New World of Work. *The Annual Review of Organizational Psychology and Organizational Behavior, 4*(1), 473 - 499.

Trebilcock, A. (1998). Labour Relations and Human Resources Management an Overview. In: *ILO Encyclopaedia of Occupational Health and Safety.* Geneva: International Labour Organization.

World Economic Forum. (2020). *The Future of Jobs Report 2020.* Geneva: World Economic Forum.

# Chapter 8 References

April, K., & Blass, E. (2010). Measuring diversity practice and developing inclusion. *Dimensions, 1*(1), 59-66.

April, K., & Forster, D. (2020). Religion and diversity management in the Southern African context. In N. Carrim, & L. Moolman (Eds.), *Diversity management.* Pretoria: Van Schaik Publishers, pp. 123-142.

Basson, A. (February 24, 2020). Dear white people, it is OK to talk about Apartheid and the ANC's failings. *News24*. Retrieved from: https://www.news24.com/news24/columnists/adriaanbasson/adriaan-basson-dear-white-people-it-is-ok-to-talk-about-apartheid-and-the-ancs-failings-20200224-2

Brown, J. (2019). *How to be an inclusive leader: Your role in creating cultures of belonging where everyone can thrive.* Oakland, CA: Berret-Kohler Publishers, Inc.

Brown, S., Gray, D., McHardy, J., & Taylor, K. (2015). Employee trust and workplace performance. *Journal of Economic Behavior & Organizations*, 116, 361-378. https://doi.org/10.1016/j.jebo.2015.05.001

Daya, P., & April, K. (2021). *12 lenses into diversity in South Africa.* Randburg: KR Publishers.

Dressel, P. (2014). Racial equality or racial equity? The difference it makes. *Race Matters Institute*. Retrieved from: https://viablefuturescenter.org/racemattersinstitute/2014/04/02/racial-equality-or-racial-equity-the-difference-it-makes/

Hook, D. (2020). White anxiety in (post-)apartheid South Africa. *Psychoanalysis, Culture & Society, 25*, 612–631 (2020). https://doi.org/10.1057/s41282-020-00178-1

Lewis, C., & Tatli, A. (2020). Leadership and diversity management in a global context. In J. Syed & M. Özbilgin (Eds.). *Managing diversity and inclusion: An international perspective* (2nd ed.). London: SAGE Publications Ltd, pp. 42-80.

Molefi, N. (2017). *A journey of diversity and inclusion in South Africa: Guidelines for leading inclusively*. Randburg: KR Publishers.

Myeza, A., & April, K. (2021). Atypical black leader emergence: South African self-perceptions. *Frontiers in Psychology, 12*(626473), 1-21 https://doi.org/10.3389/fpsyg.2021.626473.

Rotenberg, K.J. (2020). *The psychology of interpersonal trust*. Abingdon, Oxon: Routledge.

Stats SA. (2019). Inequality trends in South Africa: A multidimensional diagnostic of inequality. Report No. 03- 10-19. Retrieved from: http://www.statssa.gov.za/publications/Report-03-10-19/Report-03-10-192017.pdf.

Tapia, A. T., & Polonskaia, A. (2020). *The 5 disciplines of inclusive leaders: Unleashing the power of all of us*. Oakland, CA: Berret-Kohler Publishers, Inc.

Winters, M-F. (2020). *Black fatigue: How racism erodes the mind, body, and spirit*. Oakland, CA: Berret-Kohler Publishers, Inc.

## Chapter 9 References

Cannie, J.K. (1991). *Keeping customers for life.* New York: AMACOM.

Coats, K., & Codrington, G. (2015). *Leading in a Changing World – Lessons for future focused leaders.* Scotts Valley, California: CreateSpace Independent Publishing Platform.

Drucker, P.F. (2006). *The Effective Executive – The Definitive Guide to Getting the Right Things Done.* New York: Harperbusiness.

Gratton, L. (2000). *Living strategy: Putting people at the heart of corporate purpose.* London: Pearson Education.

Tabudi, S.A.T. (2004). *Internal marketing and how it impacts on staff's ability to give good customer service to the paying customer.* Johannesburg: Rand Afrikaans University.

Trooboff, S.K., Schwartz, R., & MacNeill, D.J. (1995). *Travel sales and customer service.* Burr Ridge: Irwin.

Varey, R.J., & Lewis, B.R. (2000). *Internal marketing directions for management.* London: Routledge.

Wikipedia. (2021). *Social Capital.* Retrieved from: https://en.wikipedia.org/wiki/Social_capital

## Chapter 10 References

Afriforte. (n.d.). *The Work Wellbeing Benchmark.* Retrieved from: http://www.afriforte.com/home/work-wellbeing-benchmark/

Ardell, D.B. (1979). High-level wellness at camp. *Elementary School Guidance & Counseling, 14*(2), 168-174.

Bakker, A.B., & Demerouti, E. (2007). The job demands-resources model: State of the art. *Journal of managerial psychology, 22*(3), 309-328.

Camlin, D.A. (2015). 'This is my truth, now tell me yours': emphasizing dialogue within participatory music. *International Journal of Community Music, 8*(3), 233-257.

CIPD. (2021) Health and wellbeing at work survey 2021. London: Chartered Institute of Personnel and Development.

Daniels, K., & Harris, C. (2000). Work, psychological Well-being and performance. *Occupational Medicine, 50*(5), 304-309.

Deci, E. L., & Ryan, R. M. (2008). Hedonia, eudaimonia, and well-being: An introduction. *Journal of happiness studies, 9*(1), 1-11.

Diener, E. (1984). Subjective Well-Being. *Psychological Bulletin, 95*(3), 542-575.

Dunn, H.L. (1959). High-level wellness for man and society. *American journal of public health and the nation's health, 49*(6), 786-792.

Hettler, B. (1976). The six dimensions of wellness. *National Wellness Institute.* Retrieved from: https://nationalwellness.org/resources/six-dimensions-of-wellness/

Martin, J. (2020). *The Five Major Challenges Experienced by Employees During Covid-19.* Retrieved from: https://www.mindsetmanage.com/articles-blog/242-the-five-major-challenges-experienced-by-employees-during-covid-19

Travis, J.W. (1977). *Wellness Workbook for Health Professionals: A Guide to Attaining High Level Wellness.* Boca Raton, FL: Wellness Resource Center.

Veldsman, D., & Van Aarde, N. (2021). The impact of COVID-19 on an employee assistance programme in a multinational insurance organisation: Considerations for the future. *SA Journal of Industrial Psychology/SA Tydskrif vir Bedryfsielkunde, 47*(0), a1863. https://doi.org/10.4102/sajip.v47i0.1863

World Health Organization. (1997). *WHOQOL Measuring Quality of Life.* Geneva: World Health Organisation.

## Chapter 11 References

Anti-slavery. (2021). *Anti-Slavery International: Freedom for everyone, everywhere, always.* Retrieved from: https://www.antislavery.org/

Association of Certified Fraud Examiners. (2020). *Report to the Nations: 2020 Global Study on Occupational Fraud and Abuse.* Retrieved from: https://www.acfe.com/report-to-the-nations/2020/

Business Roundtable. (2019). *Business Roundtable Redefines the Purpose of a Corporation to Promote 'An Economy That Serves All Americans'.* Retrieved from: https://www.businessroundtable.org/business-roundtable-redefines-the-purpose-of-a-corporation-to-promote-an-economy-that-serves-all-americans

Carsten, T. (2017). *A Nobel laureate nudges for ethics.* Retrieved from: https://fcpablog.com/2017/10/17/carsten-tams-a-noble-laureate-nudges-for-ethics/

Curry, O.S., Mullins, D.A., & Whitehouse, H. (2019). Is It Good to Cooperate? Testing the Theory of Morality-as-Cooperation in 60 Societies. *Current Anthropology, 60*(1), 47-69. Retrieved from: https://www.journals.uchicago.edu/doi/full/10.1086/701478

International Labour Organisation. (2018). *Global Wage Report 2018 - 2019: What lies behind gender pay gaps.* Retrieved from: https://www.ilo.org/global/research/global-reports/global-wage-report/2018/lang--en/index.htm

International Labour Organisation. (2019). *Child Labour in Mining and Global supply chains.* Retrieved from: https://www.ilo.org/wcmsp5/groupublic/---asia/---ro-bangkok/---ilo-manila/documents/publication/wcms_720743.pdf

Kahneman D., & Frederick S. (2002). *Representativeness Revisited: Attribute Substitution in Intuitive Judgment* in Gilovich T., Griffin D., and Kahneman D (eds.). *Heuristics and Biases: The Psychology of Intuitive Judgment*. Cambridge: Cambridge University Press, pp. 51–52.

OECD. (2011). *OECD Guidelines for Multinational Enterprises*. Retrieved from: https://www.oecd.org/daf/inv/mne/48004323.pdf

OECD. (n.d.). *OECD Convention on Combating Bribery of Foreign Public Officials in International Business Transactions*. Retrieved from: https://www.oecd.org/corruption/oecdantibriberyconvention.htm

Rock, D. (2009). *Your Brain at Work: Strategies for Overcoming Distraction, Regaining Focus, and Working Smarter All Day Long Hardcover*. New York: Harper Collins.

Thaler, R., & Sunstein, C. (2021). *Nudge: The Final Edition*. New York: Penguin.

The Government Gazette of South Africa. (2017). National Gazette No. 41016: Act No. 5 of 2017 Protected Disclosures Amendment Act., Vol. 626. Retrieved from: https://www.greengazette.co.za/documents/national-gazette-41016-of-02-august-2017-vol-626_20170802-GGN-41016

Transparency International UK. (2012). *Adequate Procedures: Guidance to the UK Bribery Act 2010*. Retrieved from: https://www.transparency.org.uk/publications/adequate-procedures-guidance-uk-bribery-act-2010

Transparency International UK. (2021). *Pandora Papers: 10 Countries That Urgently Need to Act*. Retrieved from: https://www.transparency.org/

United Nations. (2015). *Transforming our World: The 2030 Agenda for Sustainable Development*. Retrieved from: https://sdgs.un.org/sites/default/files/publications/21252030%20Agenda%20for%20Sustainable%20Develop     ment%20 web.pdf

United Nations. (2020). *Take Action for the Sustainable Development Goals*. Retrieved from: http://www.un.org/sustainabledevelopment/sustainable-development-goals/

United Nations Office on Drugs and Crime. (2004). *The United Nations Convention against Corruption*. Retrieved from: https://www.unodc.org/unodc/en/corruption/uncac.html

US Department of Justice Criminal Division. (2020). *Evaluation of Corporate Compliance Programs* Retrieved from: https://www.justice.gov/criminal-fraud/page/file/937501/download

Whoreisky, P., & Siegel, R. (2019). Cocoa's Child Laborers. *The Washington Post*. Retrieved from: https://www.washingtonpost.com/graphics/2019/business/hershey-nestle-mars-chocolate-child-labor-west-africa/

Wingard, J. (2019). Nike Does It: Embracing Controversy and Deepening Customer Relationships. *Forbes*. Retrieved from: https://www.forbes.com/sites/jasonwingard/2019/07/17/nike-does-it-embracing-controversy-and-deepening-customer-relationships/?sh=2401f4925863

World Economic Forum. (2020). *Measuring Stakeholder Capitalism: 'Towards Common Metrics and Consistent Reporting of Sustainable Value Creation'*. White Paper. Retrieved from: https://www.weforum.org/whitepapers/toward-common-metrics-and-consistent-reporting-of-sustainable-value-creation

YPO Global Leadership Survey. (2019). *93% Of CEOs Believe Business Should Create Positive Impact Beyond Profit*. Retrieved from: https://legacy.ypo.org/2019/01/93-of-ceos-believe-business-should-create-positive-impact-beyond-profit/

## Chapter 12 References

Burke, C. S., Stagl, K. C., Salas, E., Pierce, L. & Kendall, D. (2006). Understanding Team Adaptation: A Conceptual Analysis and Model. *Journal of Applied Psychology, 91*(6), 1189-1207.

Edmondson, A. (1999). Psychological safety and learning behavior in work teams. *Administrative Science Quarterly, 44*(2), 34.

Edmondson, A. (2019). *The fearless organization: Creating psychological safety in the workplace for learning, innovation, and growth.* Hoboken, New Jersey: John Wiley & Sons, Inc.

Gordon, S. (2021). *Reimagining magazines.* Retrieved from: https://themediaonline. co.za/2021/06/reimagining-magazines/

Hill, N. (1969). *The law of success in sixteen lessons: teaching, for the first time in the history of the world, the true philosophy upon which all personal success is built* (3rd ed.). Chicago, II: Combined Registry Co.

Hofkes, K., & Busato, V. (2015). *Learning Agility.* Retrieved from: https://www.hfm.nl/ documents/93/Whitepaper-Learning-Agility.pdf

Laczkowski, K., & Mysore, M. (2019). *McKinsey Inside the Strategy Room Podcast: Stronger for longer: How top performers drive through their downturns.* Retrieved from: https:// www.mckinsey.com/~/media/mckinsey/business%20functions/strategy%20and%20 corporate%20finance/our%20insights/stronger%20for%20longer%20how%20top%20 performers%20thrive%20through%20downturns/stronger-for-longer-how-top-performers-thrive-through-downturns-vf.pdf?shouldIndex=false

Pulakos, E.D., Kantrowitz, T., & Schneider, B. (2019). What leads to organizational agility: It's not what you think. *Consulting Psychology Journal: Practice and Research, 71*(4), 305–320.

Senge, P., Kleiner, A., Roberts, C., Ross, R. & Smith, B. (2011). *The Fifth Discipline Fieldbook Strategies and Tools for Building a Learning Organization.* London: Nicholas Brealey Pub.

World Economic Forum (WEF). (2018). *The Future of Jobs Report 2018.* Retrieved from: https:// www.weforum.org/reports/the-future-of-jobs-report-2018

## Chapter 13 References

Bass, D. (2016). Satya Nadella Talks Microsoft at Middle Age. *Bloomberg Businessweek.* Retrieved from: https://www.bloomberg.com/features/2016-satya-nadella-interview-issue/

Business Focus Magazine. (2019). *Microsoft South Africa – Windows of Opportunity.* Retrieved from: https://www.businessfocusmagazine.com/2019/09/20/microsoft-south-africa-windows-of-opportunity/

Day, M. (2015). Nadella promotes Microsoft culture that's unafraid of risks. *Seattle Times.* Retrieved from: https://www.seattletimes.com/business/microsoft/nadella-promotes-microsoft-culture-thats-unafraid-of-risks/

Dweck, C. (2006). *Mindset: The New Psychology of Success.* New York: Ballantine Books.

Eswaran, V. (2019). *The business case for diversity in the workplace is now overwhelming.* World Economic Forum. Retrieved from: https://www.weforum.org/agenda/2019/04/ business-case-for-diversity-in-theworkplace/

Graham, J., Grennan, J., Harvey, C. & Rajgopal, S. (2019). *Corporate Culture: Evidence from the Field.* 27th Annual Conference on Financial Economics and Accounting Paper, Duke I&E Research Paper No. 2016-33.

Graham, J.R., Grennan, J., Harvey, C.R., & Rajgopal, S. (2021). *Corporate Culture: Evidence from the Field*. Columbia Business School Research Paper No. 16-49. Retrieved from: https://papers.ssrn.com/sol3/papers.cfm?abstract_id=2805602

Harter, J., & Mann, A. (2021). The Right Culture: Not Just About Employee Satisfaction. *Gallup*. Retrieved from: https://www.gallup.com/workplace/231602/right-culture-not-employee-satisfaction.aspx

Institute of Information Technology Professionals South Africa (IITPSA). (2019). *2019 JCSE-IITPSA ICT Skills Survey*. Retrieved from: https://www.iitpsa.org.za/wp-content/uploads/2019/09/2019-JCSE-IITPSA-ICT-Skills-Survey-v1.pdf

Lewis, D., & Reynolds, A. (2017). Teams Solve Problems Faster When They're More Cognitively Diverse. *Harvard Business Review*. Retrieved from: https://www.yvettevanaarle.nl/wp-content/uploads/2018/11/Artikel-Cognitive-Diversity-HBR.pdf

Lorenzo, R., & Reeves, M. (2018). How and Where Diversity Drives Financial Performance. *Harvard Business Review*. Retrieved from: https://hbr.org/2018/01/how-and-where-diversity-drives-financial-performance

Microsoft. (2018). *Gaming for Everyone*. Retrieved from: https://news.microsoft.com/stories/xboxadaptive-controller/

Microsoft. (2020a). *Getting the most out of free video conferencing*. Retrieved from: https://www.microsoft.com/en-za/microsoft-365/business-insights-ideas/resources/getting-the-most-out-of-free-video-conferencing

Microsoft. (2020b). *New research reveals future work trends for South African organisations*. Retrieved from: https://news.microsoft.com/en-xm/2020/11/12/new-research-reveals-future-work-trends-for-southafrican-organisations.

Microsoft. (2021a). *Facts About Microsoft*. Retrieved from: https://news.microsoft.com/facts-aboutmicrosoft/#OperationCenters

Microsoft. (2021b). *This is Microsoft Viva*. Retrieved from: https://www.microsoft.com/en-za/microsoftviva

Microsoft. (2021c). *Workplace Analytics*. Retrieved from: https://www.microsoft.com/en-za/microsoft-365/business/workplace-analytics

Strack, R., Kovács-Ondrejkovic, O., Baier, J., Antebi, P., Kavanagh, K., & López Gobernado, A. (2021). *Decoding Global Ways of Working*. 1st ed. [pdf] Boston Consulting Group, pg. 16. Retrieved from: https://webassets.bcg.com/74/33/14077446434fa8685891ba0e2e69/bcg-decoding-global-ways-of-working-mar-2021.pdf

Wharton. (2018). *Microsoft CEO Satya Nadella: How Empathy Sparks Innovation*. Retrieved from: https://knowledge.wharton.upenn.edu/article/microsofts-ceo-on-how-empathy-sparks-innovation/

## Chapter 14 References

April. K. (2022). The New Diversity, Equity and Inclusion (DEI) Realities and Challenges. In P. Norman. (2022). *HR: The New Agenda*. Johannesburg: KR Publishing.

Baier, J., Caye, J-M., Strack, R., Kolo, P., Kumar, A., Ruan, F., Morton, B., Ariganello, A., Jauregui, J., van Wees, L., Burner, T., & Wong, W. (2021). *The Future of People Management Priorities*. Retrieved from: https://web-assets.bcg.com/16/b1/c25cb9e2471c81c355c9dccb8d4f/bcg-creating-people-advantage-2021-jun-2021.pdf

Brown, R.H., Meister, J., Styr, C., & Pring, B. (2020). *21 HR Jobs of the Future: Getting – and Staying – Employed in HR by Helping Employees Find the Future of Work.* Retrieved from: https://www.cognizant.com/us/en/whitepapers/documents/21-hr-jobs-of-the-future-codex5450.pdf

Galagan. P., Hirt. M., & Vital. C. (2020). *Capabilities for Talent Development – Shaping the Future of the Profession.* Alexandria, VA: Association for Talent Development (ATD).

Gartner. (2021). *Top 5 HR Trends and Priorities for 2022.* Retrieved from: https://www.gartner.com/en/human-resources/trends/top-priorities-for-hr-leaders

Ibid.

International Monetary Fund (IMF). (2020). *Six Charts Explains South African Inequality.* Retrieved from: https://www.imf.org/en/News/Articles/2020/01/29/na012820six-charts-on-south-africas-persistent-and-multi-faceted-inequality

Millson, A. Power of Purpose. In P. Norman. (2022). *HR: The New Agenda.* Johannesburg: KR Publishing.

Norman. P. (2022). HR at the Centre. In P. Norman. (2022). *HR: The New Agenda.* Johannesburg: KR Publishing.

Obama, B. (2008). Barack Obama's Caucus Speech. *New York Times.* Retrieved from: https://www.nytimes.com/2008/01/03/us/politics/03obama-transcript.html

Pring, B., & Davis, E. (2021). *The Work Ahead: Digital First (to Last).* Retrieved from: https://www.cognizant.com/us/en/whitepapers/documents/the-work-ahead-digital-first-to-last-codex6154.pdf

SIOPSA. (2021). *Industrial-Organisational Psychologists Engaging with the New World of Work.* Johannesburg: KR Publishing.

SIOPSA. (2021). *Industrial-Organisational Psychologists Engaging with the New World of Work.* Johannesburg: KR Publishing.

# Index

www.ingramcontent.com/pod-product-compliance
Lightning Source LLC
Chambersburg PA
CBHW080524220326

41599CB00032B/6193